SAS/CPE® Software: Reference

The SAS® Business Solution for IT Service Delivery

Version 6
Second Edition

A Division of SAS Institute Inc.

The correct bibliographic citation for this manual is as follows: SAS Institute Inc., *SAS/CPE® Software: Reference, Version 6, Second Edition*, Cary, NC: SAS Institute Inc., 1996. 294 pp.

SAS/CPE® Software: Reference, Version 6, Second Edition

ISBN 1-55544-796-1

SAS Institute Inc., SAS Campus Drive, Cary, North Carolina 27513.

1st printing, June 1996

Contents

Chapter 4 Maintaining the Data Dictionary Using the %CPDDUTL Macro 191

Chapter 1

Overview

Introduction

The *SAS/CPE Software: Reference, Version 6, Second Edition* provides reference documentation for Version 6 of SAS/CPE software for both UNIX and MVS operating systems. This document is a dictionary reference of the macros available for SAS/CPE and is designed to assist you in using SAS/CPE macros in batch mode. The macros are divided into groups, one group in each of the three following chapters, based on the types of tasks the macros perform. Within each chapter, the macros are listed in alphabetcial order.

Chapter 1, Introduction, provides an overview of this book. It will help you

- ☐ understand the conventions used in the other chapters of this book
- ☐ identify which macros you should use to perform specific tasks
- ☐ understand the basic concepts of working with SAS/CPE batch macros, running batch jobs, and handling error conditions.

Chapter 2, SAS/CPE Macros for Building and Managing the Performance Database, describes the macros available to perform tasks such as processing data into the performance database, verifying incoming data, copying the data dictionary and data, purging data from the data dictionary, and deleting data and other components within the data dictionary.

Chapter 3, SAS/CPE Report Macros, describes the macros that you can use to design and run reports on your data. The report types include, but are not limited to,

- ☐ bar and pie charts
- ☐ one and two Y-axis plots
- ☐ 3-D plots
- ☐ spectrum plots
- ☐ tablular reports.

Chapter 4, Maintaining the Data Dictionary Using the %CPDDUTL Macro, describes the %CPDDUTL macro and all associated control statements. It also describes specific syntax guidelines related to this macro and statistical information related to variables and formula variables.

%CPDDUTL is used to manage the data dictionary in batch mode. Using the associated control statements with %CPDDUTL, you can create and modify tables, variables, formula variables, or the entire data dictionary. This chapter also provides concepts about %CPDDUTL, the master data dictionary, performance databases, and how other macros act on tables and the active PDB.

Document Conventions

This macro reference will be available online with a future release of SAS/CPE software and although it could not be provided online for this release, this document was written and designed primarily for use online. You will notice that some macro and parameter names are highlighted in bold and underlined. In the future, these items will serve as online hypertext links, but currently they serve as references to other sections within this document. References to other macros can be located using the book or chapter table of contents. Unless otherwise stated, all references to other parameters are references to parameters for the current macro.

Within this document, all references to how a task is performed in the UNIX environment refer to the SAS/CPE Open Systems product, which runs on UNIX.

Additional information concerning document and syntax conventions is available in **SAS/CPE Macro and Syntax Conventions**.

Additional Documentation

This reference document replaces the SAS/CPE Usage and Reference documents for both MVS and UNIX. Additional information about using SAS/CPE is available in the SAS/CPE online help index available through the interactive interface and in *SAS/CPE Software for MVS: Getting Started* and *SAS/CPE Software for Open Systems: Getting Started.*

Documentation for Other SAS Software Products

The SAS System includes many software products in addition to SAS/CPE software. The following books may be of particular interest to you.

- *Introducing the SAS System, Version 6, First Edition* shows the functional relationship among SAS software features and products.
- *SAS Companion for UNIX Environments: Language, Version 6, First Edition* and the *SAS Companion for the MVS Environment: Language, Version 6, First Edition* provide tutorial and reference information about the SAS System under UNIX and MVS.
- *SAS/GRAPH Software: Graphics Editor, Version 6, First Edition* introduces the interactive graphics editor. This book is useful if you want to tailor the graphics you produce with SAS/CPE.
- *SAS/GRAPH Software: Reference, Version 6, First Edition, Volume 1* and *Volume 2* provide complete reference information about the underlying graphics procedures used to produce graphical reports in SAS/CPE software.
- *SAS Guide to Macro Processing, Version 6, Second Edition* provides complete information about creating and using SAS macros.
- *SAS Guide to TABULATE Processing, Version 6, Second Edition* provides complete information on the TABULATE procedure. This book provides detailed information about the procedure that produces the tabular and exception reports available in SAS/CPE.
- *SAS/INSIGHT User's Guide, Version 6, Second Edition* documents SAS/INSIGHT software. You can access SAS/INSIGHT software for data exploration directly from SAS/CPE software.

- *SAS Language and Procedures: Introduction, Version 6, First Edition* introduces base SAS software and fundamental concepts of the SAS System.

- *SAS Language: Reference Version 6, First Edition* provides reference information about SAS language statements and basic concepts of the SAS System. This book provides useful information on SAS data libraries, SAS data sets, SAS datetime values and formats, and statements that are used extensively in SAS/CPE, such as the WHERE statement.

- *SAS Procedures Guide, Version 6, Third Edition* provides complete information on procedures available with base SAS software. Refer to this book for information on the CORR, CHART, PLOT, and UNIVARIATE procedures.

SAS/CPE Macro and Syntax Conventions

Each SAS/CPE macro description provides the macro name, the purpose or function of the macro, the syntax (or how to call the macro), and the parameters for the macro. When the macro name begins with the letters CP, the macro is usually available on both UNIX and MVS hosts. The letters CS at the front of the macro name indicate that the macro applies only to UNIX hosts, and the letters CM indicate that the macro applies only to MVS hosts.

In a few instances the macro name begins with the letters CP, but the macro is not currently available on both MVS and UNIX, host icons display within the macro description to indicate the hosts on which the macro is available.

When a macro is available on both hosts, some of the parameters may not be available on both hosts, may function differently on each host, or may have host-specific values. In these situations, the host-specific differences are identified with host-specific icons and are described within the parameter definition.

The *Parameter* section of each macro description lists the parameters that can be used with the macro. Macros can use the following types of parameters:

positional parameters
: are not specified using a keyword; the macro understands the purpose of the parameter because it occurs in a specific position in the calling sequence. Positional parameters display in italics. All positional parameters precede keyword parameters and are listed in the order in which they appear in the parameter string.

  You must specify these parameters in the order they appear in the macro and you must separate the parameters with commas. If you want to specify a parameter that is in the second or third position, but do not want to specify the parameter in the first position, you must use a comma as a placeholder for the first parameter. However, if you want to specify positional parameters three and four, but not five, you do not need to place a comma as a placeholder after the fourth parameter and before the first keyword parameter.

  For example, if a macro supports positional parameters A, B, C, D, and E and you want to use parameters B and D, but not A, C, or E, you would list the parameters as `,B,,D,keyword-parm1`. Some positional parameters are required and others are not. Nonrequired positional parameters are enclosed in angle brackets, as shown in the following syntax example.

keyword parameters
: begin with a specific keyword followed by an equal sign and then by a value. You can specify these parameters in any order that you want, but they must be specified after any positional parameters. If a parameter has a default value, this value is identified in the description of the parameter.

  Some keyword parameters are required. Required keyword parameters are listed in alphabetical order just after the positional parameters.

Keyword parameters that are not required are listed in alphabetical order after the required keyword parameters in the syntax section of each macro. They are enclosed in angle brackets, as shown in the syntax example below.

Type styles and some symbols have special meanings when used in the presentation of SAS/CPE software syntax. The following list explains the style conventions used in SAS/CPE syntax.

UPPERCASE ROMAN
: identifies macro names, keyword parameters, and values that are literals.

italics
: identifies positional parameters or values that you supply.

| (vertical bar)
: indicates that you can choose one value from a group. Parameters or values separated by bars are mutually exclusive.

... (ellipsis)
: indicates that the arguments or group of arguments following the ellipsis can be repeated any number of times.

< > (angle brackets)
: identifies optional parameters for the macro. Any parameter not enclosed in angle brackets is required.

Syntax Example

The following example illustrates the syntax conventions. As previously mentioned, you can see that the macro name and the keyword parameters are uppercase and the positional parameters and values that you supply are shown in italics.

```
%MACRO-NAME (positional-parm-1,
             <positional-parm-2>,
             .
             .
             positional-parm-n,
             REQUIRED-KEYWORD-PARM-1=value,
             .
             .
             REQUIRED-KEYWORD-PARM-N=value,
             <NONREQUIRED-KEYWORD-PARM-1=value>,
             .
             .
             <NONREQUIRED-KEYWORD-PARM-N=value>);
```

Note: Separate all parameters with commas. Some keyword parameters permit you to specify multiple values. In this case, use blank spaces to separate the values for a single parameter instead of commas. **Do not use commas to separate values for a single parameter.**

Common Macro Values

The following terms are used in SAS/CPE macro descriptions to indicate parameter values that you supply:

physical-filename
: the physical location and name of a file or library. This includes the complete directory path or high-level-qualifiers and the name of the file or member. For example, in UNIX you would specify the *physical-filename* value in a format such as /sas/apps/cpe/filename and in MVS the format would be SAS.APPS.CPE(MEMBER).

cpe-pdb
: the physical location and name of the PDB. This includes the complete directory path or high-level-qualifiers and the PDB name. It does not include the specific data library name, such as DETAIL, DAY, or WEEK. For example, the PDB=*cpe-pdb* parameter in the %CPSTART macro identifies the active PDB. In UNIX, you would specify the *cpe-pdb* value in a format such as /sas/apps/cpe/dirname and, in MVS you would use a format such as SAS.APPS.CPE.PDBNAME.

cpe-root
: the physical location where SAS/CPE PGMLIB is installed on your host operating system. This includes the directory path or high-level-qualifiers where PGMLIB is installed, but does not include the library name. For example, in the %CPSTART macro, you might specify the *cpe-root* value for the ROOT= parameter as /sas/apps/cpe in UNIX and as SAS.APPS.CPE in MVS.

cpe-sitelib
: the physical location of the SAS/CPE site library on your host operating system. This includes the directory path or high-level-qualifiers and the name of the site library. The site library contains system options and global information for your site. For example, in the %CPSTART macro, you might specify the *cpe-sitelib* value for the SITELIB= parameter as /sas/apps/cpe/sitelibname in UNIX and SAS.APPS.CPE.SITELIB in MVS.

Executing SAS/CPE Macros in Batch

You can submit and run SAS/CPE macros in batch, on both UNIX and MVS platforms. The term batch commonly refers to jobs run in the background, but on some systems, such as UNIX, it can also refer to a collection of jobs that are submitted to run at the same time. In this document, this term is used to refer to jobs that run in the background.

To run SAS/CPE macros in batch, you need to create a batch file that contains calls to one or more SAS/CPE macros. You can then submit the file and the job will be processed in batch on your system. The batch file can be developed and coded by you, independent of the SAS/CPE interactive interface, or you can create it by selecting tasks through the SAS/CPE interactive interface and saving the underlying SAS/CPE macros (SOURCE) in a file. If you create the file by saving options selected through the interactive interface, you may need to edit the file to include additional commands specific to your job and for MVS you should also include the appropriate JCL statements. You can then submit the batch job for background processing.

On UNIX, you can submit the job by issuing the SAS command and within that command, specifying the name of the file you created, such as

```
sas /pathname/cpe1.sas -terminal -batch -dmsbatch -nodms -fsdevice ascii
```

where *cpe1.sas* is the name of your batch file.

For MVS, you would typically submit the batch job, which would include the SAS/CPE macros and the appropriate JCL EXEC statement to invoke SAS.

On both operating systems, the SAS/CPE batch file must include the %CPSTART macro at the beginning of the job, with MODE=BATCH specified and one or more other SAS/CPE macros.

SAS system options shown in the previous UNIX example (*terminal, batch, dmsbatch, nodms, fsdevice, ascii*) are required by SAS/CPE software to enable programs to execute without an associated window. For UNIX, these must be specified on the command line when you submit the job.

For MVS, options such as *memsize=16M, terminal, batch* and *dmsbatch* should be included on the JCL EXEC statement.

If you want to run SAS/CPE programs on a regular basis, you can schedule jobs to execute automatically using operating system utilities, such as a cron job on UNIX or a batch scheduler on MVS.

Refer to the SAS Companion for your operating environment for more information about scheduling and running batch jobs and specifying SAS system options.

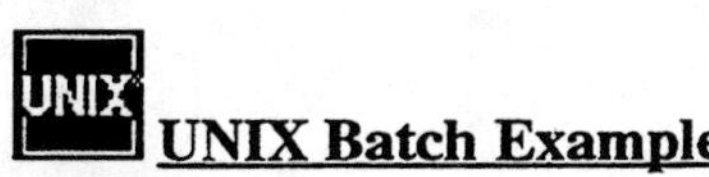

UNIX Batch Example

MVS Batch Example

MVS **MVS Batch Scheduler Example**.

For more information on what to do when batch jobs fail to execute, refer to **Handling Batch Jobs That Fail**.

Example: Creating a Batch File for the UNIX Environment

The program in the following example performs daily processing and reduction on a PDB using data collected with the HP OpenView collector. At any time you can modify a batch file by adding, changing, and deleting statements so that the program performs the tasks that you need.

The comments within the code describe the tasks being performed and areas where you should make changes to customize the code.

For more information, see *SAS/CPE Software for Open Systems: Getting Started.*

```
#!/bin/sh
##############################################################################
# Copyright (C) 1995 by SAS Institute Inc., Cary, NC 27512-8000
# Product: SAS/CPE
# Purpose: Processes HP OpenView raw data into a SAS/CPE PDB
# Input:   HP OpenView raw data
# Output:  Script messages and the SAS log are written to stdout.
#          SAS/CPE PDB is updated with the newly processed raw data.
# Side Effects:
#          Prior to processing, raw data is moved to a new directory
#          using the same name as the source directory with the julian
#          date appended.  These raw data directories are removed
#          after a specfied number of days.
# End
##############################################################################

##############################################################################
# BEGIN USER DEFINITION SECTION
#   This section contains several variables that control the execution
#   of this script.  Users should carefully review each variable and
#   set them as appropriate.
##############################################################################

###  Where to find raw data directories
DATA_PATH='/usr/OV/databases/'

###  Which directory contains the current raw data
DATA_DIR='snmpCollect'

###  %CPSTART 'pdb=' parameter
CPE_PDB='/tmp/pdb-hpov'

###  %CSPROCES tablist (second positional paramter)
CPE_TAB='HN2IFT HN2NIX'

###  %CSPROCES 'rshhost=' parameter
CPE_RSH=''

###  Command to start SAS
SAS_CMD='/usr/local/sas/sas'

###  SAS command line options
SAS_OPT='-terminal -batch -dmsbatch -nodms -fsdevice ascii.vt100'

###  How many days to keep raw data
```

```
KEEP_DAYS=4

### Change to 366 for leap year
DAYS_IN_YEAR=365

##########################################################################
# END OF USER DEFINITION SECTION
##########################################################################

### Trap interrupts
trap 'cleanx' 1 2 3 15

### Define this program name, temporary sas program file and sas log
ProgName=`/bin/basename $0`
PrgFile=/tmp/${ProgName}.prg.$$
LogFile=/tmp/${ProgName}.log.$$

### Define message functions
errmsg () { echo "${ProgName}: ERROR: $*"; }
wrnmsg () { echo "${ProgName}: WARNING: $*"; }
msgmsg () { echo "${ProgName}: $*"; }

### Define clean up and exit function
cleanx () {

    if [ -f $PrgFile ] ; then
        msgmsg "========================================================
        msgmsg "contents of SAS/CPE program follows..."
        msgmsg "========================================================
        cat $PrgFile
        rm $PrgFile
    fi

    if [ -f $LogFile ] ; then
        msgmsg "========================================================
        msgmsg "contents of SAS log follows..."
        msgmsg "========================================================
        cat $LogFile
        rm $LogFile
    fi

    msgmsg "cleaning up and exiting..."
    msgmsg `date`
    exit 1
}

### Print starting time stamp
msgmsg `date`

### Get julian dates.
Today=`date +%j`
RemoveDay=`expr $Today - $KEEP_DAYS`
[ $RemoveDay -lt 1 ] && RemoveDay=`expr $DAYS_IN_YEAR + $RemoveDay`

### Define rawdata destination directory
NewData=${DATA_PATH}${DATA_DIR}.${Today}/

### Define aged data directory that is to be removed
AgedData=${DATA_PATH}${DATA_DIR}.${RemoveDay}/
```

```
### Begin processing...

if [ -d ${NewData} ] ; then
    errmsg "directory ${NewData} already exists"
    cleanx
else
    msgmsg "creating new data directory"
    /bin/mkdir ${NewData} || {
        errmsg "cannot mkdir ${NewData}"
        cleanx
    }

    msgmsg "copying ! files"
    find ${DATA_PATH}${DATA_DIR}/ -type f -name \*! -exec cp -p {} $NewDat
        errmsg "cannot cp ! files"
        cleanx
    }

    msgmsg "moving data files"
    find ${DATA_PATH}${DATA_DIR}/ -type f -name \*[!!] -exec mv {} $NewDat
        errmsg "cannot mv data files"
        cleanx
    }

    if [ -d ${AgedData} ] ; then
        msgmsg "removing aged data"
        /bin/rm -r ${AgedData} || wrnmsg "could not rm ${AgedData}"
    fi

    msgmsg "running SAS/CPE program"

cat < $PrgFile
%CPSTART( pdb=${CPE_PDB}, access=write, mode=batch);
%CSPROCES(${NewData}, ${CPE_TAB}, collectr=HP-OV, rshhost=${CPE_RSH});
%CPREDUCE();
EOF

    `$SAS_CMD $PrgFile $SAS_OPT -log $LogFile`

    cleanx
fi
```

MVS Example: Creating a Batch File for the MVS Environment

The program in the following example performs daily processing and reduction on a PDB. At any time you can modify a batch file by adding, changing, and deleting macros so that the program performs the tasks you want. Items in the code that are discussed later in this document are indicated in bold.

Note: For similar machine-readable models of this job, see the CMJCLLD member in the PDS set up at installation time with the name *cpe-root*.CPE.CPMISC. For the full name of this file at your site, see your SAS/CPE administrator or your SAS Software Representative. The *cpe-root* refers to the high-level qualifiers where the data set is located on your host operating system.

```
//DAILY   JOB (accounting info),'CPE daily job',
//        MSGLEVEL=(1,1),TIME=20,REGION=32M,NOTIFY=
//*********************************************************************
//*                                                                   *
//* This job is a SAS/CPE for MVS example daily run that processes   *
//* new data from SMF log file(s) and adds it to the DETAIL level    *
//* of the PDB. Then reduces the data in the detail level into       *
//* the DAY, WEEK, MONTH, and YEAR reduction levels.                 *
//*                                                                   *
//* This job now also includes a step to back up your PDB by using   *
//* IBM's DFDSS program. You can use the DFDSS DUMP command to back  *
//* up volumes and data sets, and you can then use the RESTORE       *
//* command to recover them. You can also make incremental backups   *
//* of your data sets by doing a data set DUMP with RESET specified  *
//* and filtering on the data-set-changed flag.                      *
//* For more information on this facility reference the IBM manual:  *
//* Data Facility Data Set Services: Reference V2R5 (SC26-4389-03).  *
//* You may want to update that step with the backup procedure       *
//* commonly used at your site instead.                              *
//*                                                                   *
//*==================================================================*
//*                                                                   *
//* NOTE:   This job requires that the PDB already exist.            *
//*         If you need to allocate a PDB first,                     *
//*         see the member CMPDBALC in this CPMISC pds.              *
//*                                                                   *
//* This job requires the following customization:                   *
//*                                                                   *
//*  1) Change the JOB card to a valid job card for your system.     *
//*                                                                   *
//*  2) Do a global change of YOUR.SMF.DATA to the dataset           *
//*     name of your SMF data sets.                                  *
//*                                                                   *
//*  3) Do a global change of MXG.USERID.SOURCLIB to the name        *
//*     of your customized MXG source library.                       *
//*                                                                   *
//*  4) Do a global change of MXG.MXG.SOURCLIB to the name of the    *
//*     PDS containing the original MXG source library.              *
//*                                                                   *
//*  5) Do a global change of MXG.MXG.FORMATS to the name            *
//*     of your MXG format library.                                  *
//*                                                                   *
//*  6) Do a global change of YOUR.SASCPE to the high-level          *
//*     qualifiers of SAS/CPE for MVS on your system. In particular  *
//*     make sure this qualifier has been set correctly for the      *
```

```
//*      CONFIG parameter.                                             *
//*                                                                    *
//*   7) Do a global change of YOUR.CPE.PDB to the high-level          *
//*      qualifier for your PDB. This PDB should have one or more      *
//*      tables already in it.                                         *
//*                                                                    *
//* Plus, especially in the BACKUP step using IBM's ADRDSSU program: *
//*                                                                    *
//*   8) Modify characteristics on the DD named TAPE allocation        *
//*      and/or on the DUMP command according to your needs or         *
//*      site-specific rules. For instance, you may want to create     *
//*      and use GDGs for the backup tape datasets.                    *
//*                                                                    *
//**********************************************************************
//BACKUP   EXEC PGM=ADRDSSU
//TAPE       DD DSN=your.cpe.pdb,DISP=(OLD,KEEP),
//              UNIT=cart,RETPD=30
//SYSPRINT DD SYSOUT=A
//SYSIN    DD *
  DUMP DATASET(INCLUDE(your.cpe.pdb.*)) OUTDD(TAPE) -
       SHARE COMPRESS
//*
//LOAD    EXEC SAS,WORK='10500,2000',
//        CONFIG='your.sascpe.CPMISC(CMCONFIG)'
//SMF      DD DSN=your.smf.data,DISP=SHR
//SYSIN    DD DATA,DLM='$$'

  *-------------------------------------------------------------*
  * SAS/CPE will not run unless %CPSTART has been executed.     *
  * %CPSTART allocates the SAS/CPE software and the PDB.        *
  * The MXGLIB= and MXGSRC= parameters are required for the     *
  * MXG software tool used  within %CMPROCES below.             *
  * The ROOTSERV= and SHARE= parameters should only be used if *
  * SAS/SHARE is being used with SAS/CPE.                       *
  * If the _RC= parameter is nonzero from %CPSTART,             *
  * check the explanatory message in the SAS log.               *
  *-------------------------------------------------------------* ;

  %LET cpstrc=.;

  /* verify root= pdb= mxglib= mxgsrc= in the following macro */
  %CPSTART(MODE=BATCH,
           SYSTEM=MVS,
           ROOT='your.sascpe.',
           ROOTSERV=,
           PDB='your.cpe.pdb.',
           DISP=OLD,
           SHARE=N/A ,
           MXGLIB=mxg.mxg.formats,
           MXGSRC=('mxg.userid.sourclib' 'mxg.mxg.sourclib'),
           _RC=cpstrc
          );

  %PUT CPSTART return code is &cpstrc;


  *-------------------------------------------------------------*
  * The %CMPROCES macro processes data into the PDB that was    *
  * established by the %CPSTART macro above.                    *
  * As no table list is specified as the second parameter all   *
```

```
   * the tables in the PDB for this collector with a table kept *
   * indicator of YES will be processed.                        *
   * TOOLNM=SMF and COLLECTR=MXG parameters must be specified.  *
   * If the _RC= parameter is nonzero from %CMPROCES,           *
   * check the explanatory message in the SAS log.              *
   *------------------------------------------------------------* ;

   %LET cmprrc=.;

   %CMPROCES(,
             COLLECTR=SMF,
             TOOLNM=MXG,
             _RC=cmprrc
            );

   %PUT CMPROCES return code is &cmprrc;


   *------------------------------------------------------------*
   * The %CPREDUCE macro reduces data in the current PDB detail *
   * level into the day, week, month and year reduction levels. *
   * The variables and statistics kept are defined in the data  *
   * dictionary.                                                *
   * As no table list is specified as the first parameter,      *
   * reduction will be performed on all the tables in the PDB.  *
   * If the _RC= parameter is nonzero from %CPREDUCE            *
   * check the explanatory message in the SAS log.              *
   *------------------------------------------------------------* ;

   %LET cpredrc=.;

   %CPREDUCE(,_RC=cpredrc);

   %PUT CPREDUCE return code is &cpredrc;

$$
//
```

Notes

1. Before you submit the job for the first time, you must perform the following steps, typically from the SAS/CPE interactive interface:

   - ☐ Estimate space requirements for your PDB and allocate space. This can be done by following this path in the SAS/CPE interactive interface:

     PDB Admin -> Manage/Switch PBD -> Actions -> Estimate Space

   - ☐ Add table definitions to the PDB, as required. If the table definitions that are explicitly specified by a table list in the %CMPROCES macro are not in the PDB, the %CMPROCES macro automatically adds those table definitions to the PDB by copying them from the master data dictionary.

   - ☐ Edit the table definitions to adjust durations for retention of DETAIL, DAY, WEEK, MONTH, and YEAR data, as required.

- ☐ Add, update, or delete variables in the tables, as required.

- ☐ Edit the variable statistics to adjust which statistics are requested for DAY, WEEK, MONTH, and YEAR levels, as required.

- ☐ Verify that all tables and variables that you want to use are marked KEPT=YES.

2. The %CPSTART() macro invokes SAS/CPE software and allocates the PDB.

The MODE= parameter must be set to *batch* and the SYSTEM= parameter must be set to *MVS.*

The ROOT= parameter specifies the high-level qualifiers in the data set names for SAS/CPE software. For example, if SAS/CPE is located in a SAS library that is installed at your site with the name *your.sascpe.pgmlib*, use *your.sascpe* as the value for the ROOT= parameter. Similarly, the PDB= parameter specifies the high-level qualifers in the data set names for the SAS data libraries in the PDB. For example, if the PDB is in libraries that are all named *your.sascpe.pdbname*, where *pdbname* varies depending on the library name, (such as DETAIL, DAY, WEEK, MONTH, and YEAR), then use *your.sascpe* as the value for the PDB= parameter.

The MXGLIB= parameter specifies the fully- qualified name of the SAS library that contains the SAS formats provided by MXG. The MXGSRC= parameter specifies fully qualified names of one or more PDSs that contain MXG SOURCLIB source entries and user overrides to these source entries. List the PDSs in search order. If the same member name exists in more than one of the PDSs, the member used is the first one encountered. Thus, typically, list the PDS that has your source entries in front of the PDS with the MXG source entries.

3. If the batch job contains the %CMPROCES macro, you must specify the name of the data set that contains the logged SMF-style data in one of the following ways:

- ☐ with a DD statement

- ☐ with a FILENAME statement as follows:

  ```
  filename smf SMF_style_log_name;
  ```

  If you use the FILENAME statement, place it before the %CMPROCES macro invocation.

- ☐ as the first positional parameter in the %CMPROCES macro

4. The %CMPROCES macro reads logged SMF data from the log file and processes it into the detail level of the PDB for the specified tables. Specifying a list of table names is optional. If no names are specified, the macro processes all tables in your PDB with KEPT=YES.

The COLLECTR= parameter in the %CMPROCES macro can be set to SMF or SASDS.

The PDB into which the data are processed is the one specified in the %CPSTART macro by the PDB= parameter. This is referred to as the active PDB.

The TOOLNM= parameter in the %CMPROCES macro can be set to MXG or GENERIC. SAS/CPE uses the SAS library and the PDSs that are specified in the %CPSTART macro by the MXGLIB= and MXGSRC= parameters.

5. The %CPREDUCE macro reduces the data in the DETAIL level of the current PDB into the DAY, WEEK, MONTH, and YEAR reduction levels. Specifying a table name is optional. If no table name is specified, the macro reduces all tables in your PDB that have KEPT=YES and AGELIMIT > 0 in at least one of the DAY, WEEK, MONTH, YEAR, levels. The *level* must also have at least one variable with a selected statistic and KEPT=YES.

MVS Example: Using the SAS/CPE MVS Batch Scheduler

If you are using SAS/CPE on an MVS system you can use the Batch Utility in the interactive interface to save and schedule jobs to be processed. You can then create a file that calls the %CPBATCH macro to submit the job to run in batch mode. For example, if you run the job on a Tuesday, the Batch Utility runs all the tasks with a schedule of Daily, all the tasks with a schedule of Weekday, and all the tasks with a schedule of Tuesday. The order in which it runs the tasks is determined by the priorities set in the Batch Utility. For more information about the MVS batch scheduling subsystem refer to the documentation for your operating system.

The following job submits the tasks set up using the Batch Utility. The comments within the program describe areas of the code that you should change to customize the code.

Note: For a similar machine-readable model for this job, see the CMJCLSCD member in the PDS, *cpe-root*.CPE.CPMISC that is set up at installation time at your site. For the full name of this PDS at your site, see your SAS/CPE administrator or your SAS Software Representative. The *cpe-root* refers to the high-level-qualifiers where CPE is installed at your site.

```
//SCHEDUL JOB (accounting info),'CPE schedule job',
//        MSGLEVEL=(1,1),TIME=20,REGION=32M,NOTIFY=
//*******************************************************************
//*                                                                 *
//* This job is a SAS/CPE for MVS example daily schedule run.      *
//* It runs the list of SAS/CPE tasks that have previously been    *
//* set up by the SAS/CPE site administrator.                      *
//* To set up the schedule the Batch Utility path                  *
//* on the interactive SAS/CPE interface must be used.             *
//* Schedule the job to run after the nightly SMF dump.            *
//*                                                                 *
//*=================================================================*
//*                                                                 *
//* NOTE:  This job requires that the PDB already exist.           *
//*        If you need to allocate a PDB first,                    *
//*        see the member CMPDBALC in this CPMISC pds.             *
//*                                                                 *
//* This job requires the following customization:                 *
//*                                                                 *
//*  1) Change the JOB card to a valid job card for your system.   *
//*                                                                 *
//*  2) Do a global change of YOUR.SMF.DATA to the dataset         *
//*     name of your SMF data sets.                                *
//*                                                                 *
//*  5) Do a global change of MXG.USERID.SOURCLIB to the name      *
//*     of your customized MXG source library.                     *
//*                                                                 *
//*  6) Do a global change of MXG.MXG.SOURCLIB to the name of the  *
//*     PDS containing the original MXG source library.            *
//*                                                                 *
//*  7) Do a global change of MXG.MXG.FORMATS to the name          *
//*     of your MXG format library.                                *
//*                                                                 *
//*  8) Do a global change of YOUR.SASCPE to the high-level        *
//*     qualifiers of SAS/CPE for MVS on your system. In particular *
//*     make sure this qualifier has been set correctly for the    *
//*     CONFIG parameter AND for the SITELIB data library,         *
//*     which contains your site specific settings for SAS/CPE.    *
```

```
//*                                                                  *
//*  7) Do a change of YOUR.CPE.PDB to the high-level                *
//*     qualifier for your PDB. This PDB should have one or more     *
//*     tables already in it if your SAS/CPE site administrator      *
//*     has included inquire task(s) to the batch utility.           *
//*                                                                  *
//********************************************************************
//SASCPE EXEC SAS,WORK='10500,2000',
//        CONFIG='your.saspe.CPMISC(CMCONFIG)'
//SMF      DD DSN=your.smf.data,DISP=SHR
//SYSIN    DD DATA,DLM='$$'

   *-------------------------------------------------------------*
   * SAS/CPE will not run unless %CPSTART has been executed.     *
   * %CPSTART allocates the SAS/CPE software and the PDB.        *
   * The MXGLIB= and MXGSRC= parameters are required for the     *
   * MXG software tool used  within %CMPROCES below.             *
   * The SITELIB= parameter must be specified.                   *
   * The SITEACC= parameter must be set to OLD disposition.      *
   * The ROOTSERV=, SHARE=, and SITESHR= parameters should only *
   * be used if SAS/SHARE is being used with SAS/CPE.            *
   * If the _RC= parameter is nonzero from %CPSTART,             *
   * check the explanatory message in the SAS log.               *
   *-------------------------------------------------------------* ;

   %LET cpstrc=.;

   /* verify root= pdb= sitelib= mxglib= mxgsrc= in the following */
   %CPSTART(MODE=BATCH,
            SYSTEM=MVS,
            ROOT='your.sascpe.',
            ROOTSERV=,
            PDB='your.cpe.pdb.',
            DISP=OLD,
            SHARE=N/A,
            SITELIB='your.sascpe.SITELIB',
            SITEACC=OLD,
            SITESHR=,
            MXGLIB=mxg.mxg.formats,
            MXGSRC=('mxg.userid.sourclib' 'mxg.mxg.sourclib'),
            _RC=cpstrc
           );

   %PUT CPSTART return code is &cpstrc;


   *-------------------------------------------------------------*
   * The following %CPBATCH macro runs the list of scheduled     *
   * tasks that have been set up by your SAS/CPE administrator. *
   * You must code the ENV= parameter and capitalize it's value.*
   *-------------------------------------------------------------* ;
   %CPBATCH(ENV=BACK);

$$
//
```

Notes

1. Before you submit the job for the first time, you must perform the following steps, typically

from the SAS/CPE interactive interface:

- □ Estimate space requirements for your PDB and allocate space. This can be done by following this path in the SAS/CPE interactive interface:

  PDB Admin -> Manage/Switch PBD -> Actions -> Estimate Space

- □ Add table definitions to the PDB, as required.
- □ Edit the table definitions to adjust durations for retention of DETAIL, DAY, WEEK, MONTH, and YEAR data, as required.
- □ Add, update, or delete variables in the tables, as required.
- □ Edit the variable statistics to adjust which statistics are requested for DAY, WEEK, MONTH, and YEAR levels, as required.
- □ Verify that all tables and variables that you want to use are marked KEPT=YES.

2. The %CPSTART macro invokes SAS/CPE software and allocates the PDB.

The MODE= parameter must be set to *batch* and the SYSTEM= parameter defaults to *MVS*.

The ROOT= parameter specifies the high-level qualifiers in the data set names for SAS/CPE software. For example, if the SAS/CPE PGMLIB is located in a SAS library that is installed at your site with the name *your.sascpe.pgmlib*, use *your.sascpe* as the value for the ROOT= parameter. Similarly, the PDB= parameter specifies the high-level qualifers in the data set names for the SAS data libraries in the PDB. For example, if the PDB is in libraries that are all named *your.sascpe.pdbname*, where *pdbname* varies depending on the library name, (such as DETAIL, DAY, WEEK, MONTH, and YEAR), then use *your.sascpe* as the value for the PDB= parameter.

The MXGLIB= parameter specifies the fully- qualified name of the SAS library that contains the SAS formats provided by MXG. The MXGSRC= parameter specifies fully-qualified names of one or more PDSs that contain MXG SOURCLIB source entries and user overrides to these original entries. List the PDSs in search order. If the same member name exists in more than one of the PDSs, the member used is the first one encountered. Thus, typically, list the PDS that has your modified source entries in front of the PDS with the MXG source code.

3. The %CPBATCH macro runs the tasks that have been set up using the *Batch Utility* item on the main menu of the interactive interface to run on days that match the day of this run.

Handling Batch Jobs That Fail

The following guidelines will assist you in locating and solving problems when running batch jobs. In the event that your batch job fails, it will be important to have access to backups of your PDB. It is a good idea to backup your PDB daily and to retain several days' worth of backups. You should also always check the results of your batch job in order to recognize any problems.

If a batch job fails, the first thing you should do is check the SAS log for information about the reason for failure. You should then fix that problem before rerunning the job. Some common failure errors are outlined below. Follow these guidelines to recover the PDB:

- **If a batch job fails while running the %CPSTART macro,** correct the error as directed by the error message and rerun %CPSTART. You should also verify that the specified name and location of the *cpe-pdb* is correct. The *cpe-pdb* includes the directory path or high-level qualifiers that identify the location of the PDB on your operating system. You should also verify that quotes and commas are specified correctly.

- **If a batch job fails while running the %CSPROCES macro (on OpenSystems) or %CMPROCES macro (on MVS),** fix the problem and resubmit the job, preceded by a %CPSTART macro.

  If you are running the %CMPROCES or %CSPROCES macro and a batch job fails due to insufficient space, restore yesterday's backup of the PDB, check the disk volume or file system that the PDB resides on to assure that it has sufficient free space and rerun the job. It is unlikely that the process task will have added any new data to the detail level. If it has, the duplicate data are automatically discarded by the resubmitted %CSPROCES macro. By default, %CMPROCES allows duplicate data to be processed into the PDB. However, you can change this by specifying the appropriate parameters on %CMPROCES.

- **If a batch job fails while running the %CPREDUCE macro,** fix the problem and resubmit the %CPREDUCE macro step, preceded by a %CPSTART macro. You do not need to specify the CKPTINIT= parameter on the %CPREDUCE macro because its default value is NO, which is the correct setting at this point. %CPREDUCE restarts from the last checkpoint and, if successful, performs the following tasks:

  1. reduces the table in which the error occurred (even if the table is not indicated by the resubmitted %CPREDUCE table list)

  2. updates the checkpoint records for the table

  3. reduces the other tables in the (resubmitted) table list if you provide a list. If you do not provide a list, the macro checks the tables that have KEPT=YES in the active PDB in the data dictionary and reduces data that were processed after the last reduction on the tables.

  If a %CPREDUCE job fails due to insufficient space, check the disk volume or file system that the PDB resides on to assure that it has insufficient space, and rerun.

When you resubmit the %CPREDUCE macro, the time required to rerun is primarily the time required for the remainder of the job to complete.

If you resubmit the %CPREDUCE macro and it fails again use one of the following methods to fix the problem so that you can continue. If you choose method 2 or 3, you can still perform method #1 later.

- ☐ **Method #1.** Restore the PDB from your backup, fix the problem with the table, and submit a job to process and reduce the files of logged data that were collected since the time of the backup.

- ☐ **Method #2.** For the table in which the error occurred, set the value of the KEPT= parameter to NO in the data dictionary. The table will not be available to process or reduce new data to the DAY, WEEK, MONTH, and YEAR levels. However, you can use it to run reports based on the existing data in all of the levels.

  Resubmit the %CPREDUCE macro (preceded by the %CPSTART macro) and set CKPTINIT=YES on the %CPREDUCE macro.

- ☐ **Method #3.** Do not use this method on a production PDB or important table. Use this method only on a practice PDB or unimportant table. Resubmit the %CPREDUCE macro (preceded by the %CPSTART macro) and have the CKPTINIT= parameter set to YES. By doing so, there is a high probability you will lose statistics that were being calculated for the day, week, month, or year level when the error occurred.

Caution: Using the **CKPTINIT=YES** option can lead to loss of data for the table and time period being reduced. You will not receive a warning message when this occurs. Do not use this option unless you can accept losing data for the table and time period being reduced when the previous failure occurred, or unless instructed to do so by SAS/CPE Technical Support. For more information on this parameter, see the **%CPREDUCE** macro.

If the **%CPREDUCE** macro fails and you have not finished fixing the problem, wait to run the **%CSPROCES** or **%CMPROCES** macro (on OpenSystems or MVS respectively) or **%CPBATCH** macro until the problem is fixed. The process task would not fail, but it would complicate the recovery procedures.

- ☐ **If a batch job fails while running a report macro,** fix the problem and resubmit the report macro. Do not reload the data from backup.

- ☐ **If a batch job fails while running the %CPDBCOPY macro,** fix the problem, recreate the empty PDB, and rerun the macro.

- ☐ **If a batch job fails while running the %CPDBKILL macro,** check to see that you have specified ACCESS=WRITE (UNIX) or DISP=OLD (MVS) on the %CPSTART macro and resubmit the %CPDBKILL macro.

- ☐ **If a batch job fails while running the %CPDBPURG macro,** check to see that you have specified ACCESS=WRITE (UNIX) or DISP=OLD (MVS) on the %CPSTART macro and resubmit the %CPDBPURG macro.

- ☐ **If a batch job fails while running the %CPDDUTL macro,** check the SAS log for the nature of the failure and follow these guidelines:

- □ If the failure is due to a syntax error, correct the error and resubmit the job.
- □ If a failure occurs because the disk is full the data dictionary may be damaged. Repair the dictionary and resubmit the job to repair the data dictionary. Run the SAS DATASETS procedure with a REPAIR statement that points to the data set, or start the SAS/CPE interactive interface and answer Y when prompted to repair the requested data set.
- □ Otherwise, restore the PDB from your most recent backup, fix the problem, and resubmit.

MVS In addition to these general guidelines for recovery after a batch job has failed, the following supplemental guidelines apply specifically to batch jobs running on MVS platforms.

It is a good idea to do preventive maintenance on the space allocations for the SAS libraries in the PDB. Check ISPF/PDF 3.2 periodically for the current allocations and usage.

- □ If the percent used in DICTLIB is greater than 50%, reallocate.
- □ At the DETAIL level, if after processing the first weekday's data, the percent used multiplied by the retention period of data at the detail level is greater than 90%, reallocate. Also, if the percent used is greater than 90% when the detail level contains as many days' data as the number of days in the retention period for detail-level data, you should reallocate.
- □ If the percent used is greater than 80% for the DAY, WEEK, and MONTH libraries you should reallocate.
- □ If the percent used is greater than 90% for the YEAR library, you should reallocate. Be especially careful to check the size of the YEAR library after you run the reduce task for the first time in January.
- □ If the percent used is greater than 80% for ADMIN, you should reallocate.
- □ Check COLLECT after you process the number of days specified in IMACSPIN and if the percent used is greater than 50% you should reallocate.
- □ For PDBWORK, submit these statements from the PROGRAM EDITOR to check the size of the largest data set at the detail level:

```
libname detail 'high-level-qualifiers.detail' disp=shr;
proc contents data=detail._all_; run;
```

  The size of the data sets is listed under Engine/Host Dependent Information as *Total Blocks Used.* Allocate PDBWORK to be two to five times as large as the largest data set.

  Follow these guidelines to reallocate:

  1. Rename the too-small library.

2. Allocate a larger version of the library with the same blocking size.

3. Copy the contents of the smaller library to the larger library by using the SAS DATASETS procedure. For more about PROC DATASETS, see the *SAS Procedures Guide, Version 6, Third Edition.*

- **If a batch job fails while running the %CPBATCH macro,** first check the SAS log to see what task was running. Then, follow the previously outlined procedures for a failure during the process, reduce, or report tasks and then resubmit the %CPBATCH macro.

Macros for Building and Managing the PDB

The SAS/CPE menu interface accomplishes most of its actual data manipulation by invoking underlying SAS macros. Many of these macros also are useful to programmers who may want to invoke them outside of the menu, for example, in batch mode or as a background process.

The following table lists common tasks for building and managing the Performance Database (PDB) and shows which macros to use to perform those tasks.

Note: Keep in mind that you must use the **%CPSTART** macro at the beginning of each session or batch script to initiate the SAS/CPE system before using any of these macros.

If you want to...	use these macros...
Load data into a PDB, reduce the data into day-through-year levels	**%CSPROCES** to process data into the PDB (UNIX). **%CMPROCES** to process data into the PDB (MVS). **%CPREDUCE** to reduce the data. **%CSCSIFMT** to identify the names of hosts on your system. (This macro must preceed the %CSPROCES macro and is only for use with Cabletron Spectrum data on UNIX.)
Control processing of duplicate data into the PDB, using input filtering macros	**%CPDUPCHK** verifies the datetime information for incoming data. **%CPDUPUPD** updates the input filtering information for incoming data. **%CPDUPFMT** recovers input filtering formats. **%CPDUPINT** loads macro definitions for use by input filtering macros. **%CPDUPDSN** generates the name of the input filtering data set. **%CPDUPMXG** modifies MXG source to support input data filtering. *The input filtering macros are currently only available on MVS.*
Copy the structure of an existing PDB	**%CPDBCOPY** to copy the data dictionary information and data.
Delete a PDB	**%CPDBPURG** to delete the data from all tables in a PDB and leave the data dictionary intact. **%CPDBKILL** to delete the tables, data, and contents of the data dictionary, but retain the libraries and structure of the data dictionary.

Manage the data dictionary	**%CPDDUTL** to create, modify or print tables, variables, formula variables, or the entire data dictionary. **%CPCAT** to copy %CPDDUTL Control Statements to and from SAS catalog source entries.
List records from raw data	**%CSRAWLST** to produce a list of records from a raw data file (UNIX only).
Convert UNIX DATETIME to SAS DATETIME	**%CSUT2ST** converts a UNIX DATETIME value to a SAS DATETIME value for use with a generic collector (UNIX only).
Run scheduled jobs using the SAS/CPE batch scheduler	**%CPBATCH** to run SAS/CPE jobs that have been scheduled through the batch utility on SAS/CPE for MVS. (MVS only)

Using SAS/CPE Macros to Generate Reports

The report-generating macros in SAS/CPE software produce graphics and text reports based on data in a performance database (PDB). All of the capabilities available with the Design Reports facility on the Reports menu of the SAS/CPE interactive interface are also available in batch mode through the SAS/CPE macros. The %CPSRCRPT macro also provides the additional capability of running user-written SAS programs if they are stored as SOURCE catalog entries.

For more information on recovery procedures to use if a batch job fails while running a report macro, refer to **Handling Batch Jobs that Fail**.

The following table describes the types of reports that you can produce and lists the macros that you would use to produce specific types of reports.

The parameters for many of the report macros are similiar. Each report section lists the syntax for the report macro and describes the parameters that can be used with the macro. The parameter descriptions define the parameter and identify any differences in how the parameter works for specific macros.

Note: Keep in mind that you must use the **%CPSTART** macro to invoke SAS/CPE before using any of these macros. Also, these reports are affected by the settings of global macro variables. Refer to **Global and Local Report Macro Variables** for more information.

If you want to. . .	use this macro . . .
chart multiple variables in one report (category bar chart)	**%CPCCHRT**
chart values of a single variable (bar or pie chart)	**%CPCHART**
combine multiple reports into a one- two-, three-, or four-part template (graph template)	**%CPGTPLT**
produce three-dimensional plots (3-D Plot)	**%CPG3D**
plot one or more Y variables against an X variable, using one Y axis (one Y-axis plot)	**%CPPLOT1**
plot two Y variables against time, using two Y axes (two Y-axis plot)	**%CPPLOT2**
generate a 3-dimensional report with color as the third dimension	**%CPSPEC**

(spectrum plot)	
run existing SAS source code and provide access to the global macro variables	%CPSRCRPT
generate statistics on performance data in a tabular format (tabular report)	%CPTABRPT
create an exception report in tabular format (exception report)	%CPXTAB

Viewing Examples of Report Macros

Through the interactive interface you can look at examples of how to use most of these report macros. Start the interactive interface if it is not already active, and then activate a demonstration PDB by following this path from the main SAS/CPE window:

PDB Admin -> **Manage PDBs/Switch PDB** -> *select a demonstration PDB*

Then follow this path:

Item Actions -> **Activate** -> *select* **READ Access**

Then follow this path:

OK -> **File** -> **End**

To see a list of reports, follow this path from the main window of the SAS/CPE interactive interface:

Reports -> **SuppliedRpts**

From the list of supplied reports, look in the `RptType` column for a report of the type you want to see. The report type matches the macro name. Select the report you want to view, and then follow this path:

ItemActions -> **Preview Source** to see the source for the report
or
ItemActions -> **Explanation** for sample source code and comments
or
ItemActions -> **Example Output** to see sample output from the report

UNIX For UNIX platforms, only the HP-OV sample reports currently include explanation and example output, though other supplied reports will run on their corresponding demo PDB. See *What's New* in the online help index of the SAS/CPE interactive interface for updates to the list of reports with extended information.

Chapter 2

SAS/CPE® Macros for Building and Managing the Performance Database

%CMPROCES

Process Data into the Active PDB on MVS

Purpose

The %CMPROCES macro reads, validates, and transforms performance data into the DETAIL level of the active performance database (PDB) from the files containing the logged data. In addition, %CMPROCES updates data dictionary entries that describe the amount of data in the PDB and the most recent date and time of processing data into the detail level of the tables. The %CMPROCES macro runs the process task.

To use this macro during recovery from an error condition refer to the guidelines for **Handling Batch Jobs that Fail.**

Syntax

```
%CMPROCES(<rawdata>,
         <tablist>,
          COLLECTR=collector-name,
          TOOLNM=tool,
         <DUPMODE=INACTIVE | FORCE | DISCARD | TERMINATE>,
         <EXITSRC=exit-source>,
         <GENLIB=libref>,
         <JES=JES2 | JES3>,
         <_RC=varname>,
         <UNIT=DISK|TAPE|CART|etc.>,
         <VOLSER=volser> );
```

%CMPROCES Parameters

rawdata

is the name of the data set that contains the logged data to be processed. **This positional parameter is not required**, but if specified, it must be first. If you omit this parameter, you must use a comma as a placeholder. You must specify this parameter if the value of COLLECTR=SMF and the value of TOOLNM=MXG. The data set can be any of the following:

- a Generation Data Group (GDG), in which case the generation number is 0 for current, -1 for previous, -2 for one before that, and so on.
- any other collection of SMF-style data.

You can omit this parameter under the following circumstances:

- if the data set is defined with a *DD* statement or a SAS FILENAME statement.
- if you are processing data using a generic collector, in which case you would specify the GENLIB= parameter instead of *rawdata.*

tablist

lists the tables into which the logged data should be processed. **This positional parameter is not required**, but if specified it must be in the second position. If you do not specify this parameter, use a comma as a placeholder. Use blanks to separate the tables in the list. If you omit this parameter, SAS/CPE software reads the active PDB and processes those tables for which the KEPT= parameter is set to YES.

If a table in the list is not found in the active PDB, the default table is copied into the active PDB from the master data dictionary.

COLLECTR=*collector-name*

specifies the name of the SAS/CPE supported collector that created the logged data. The current valid values are SMF or GENERIC. If you are using a user-defined collector or a third-party collector instead of a SAS/CPE supported collector, use the value GENERIC. **This parameter is required.**

Additional information on using each collector is available in the online Help Index in the SAS/CPE interactive interface.

TOOLNM=*tool*

specifies the name of the software that %CMPROCES will use to transform the logged data and stage the data into SAS data sets or views. The %CMPROCES macro then processes the SAS data sets into the PDB libraries. **This parameter is required.**

Valid values are MXG, which means data are transformed by MXG software, and SASDS, which means data are transformed by user-provided software for use by the GENERIC collector.

Optional Keyword Parameters

DUPMODE=INACTIVE I FORCE I DISCARD I TERMINATE

specifies whether or not to allow duplicate data to be processed into the active PDB and automatically invokes the input data filtering routines. Filtering the data involves comparing the timestamp information for incoming data to the timestamp information for existing data, and recording the timestamp information for new (nonduplicate) data. **The default value is INACTIVE.** Valid Values are:

INACTIVE

does not review the incoming data and therefore, allows duplicate data to be processed into the active PDB.

FORCE

reviews the incoming data and records information on the duplicate data, but still allows (forces) duplicate data to be processed into the active PDB.

DISCARD

reviews the incoming data and rejects (discards) duplicate data, but allows processing to continue.

TERMINATE

reviews the incoming data and terminates the macro if duplicate data are found.

Notes: If you are running %CMPROCES to collect SMF data and you want to enable input filtering, you must set the DUPMODE= parameter on the %CMPROCES macro. %CMPROCES will automatically submit the **%CPDUPCHK** and **%CPDUPUPD** input filtering macros for you. However, if you are running %CMPROCES to collect data using a generic collector and you want to enable input filtering, you must set the DUPMODE= parameter on %CMPROCES and you must include %CPDUPCHK in your code that reads the raw data.

Specifying TERM=YES or FORCE=YES on the %CPDUPCHK macro overrides the values of the DUPMODE= parameter on the %CMPROCES macro.

Before you can enable input filtering via the %CMPROCES or %CPDUPCHK macros, you must create the appropriate input filtering files as described in the *Input Data Filtering* document that is available through the online Help Index in the SAS/CPE interactive interface or through the DUPCHECK member in CPMISC.

For more information, see also the **%CPDUPCHK** macro.

EXITSRC=*exit-source*

specifies the location where SAS/CPE exit source programs are stored. The value of this parameter can be the name of a SAS catalog specified in the form of *libref.catname* or the fully-qualified name of a partitioned data set.

If you specify a SAS catalog name, use a SAS LIBNAME statement to associate the *libref* with the SAS library that contains the catalog.

If you want to process your data without exits, do not specify this parameter.

For more information on SAS/CPE exit processing, see the *Process Exits Overview* document available in the online Help Index in the SAS/CPE interactive interface.

GENLIB=*libref*

specifies the *libref* for the SAS library that contains the staged data created by user-provided software, which are to be processed into a PDB using the GENERIC collector. The staged data may be a SAS data set, a SAS DATA step view, a SAS SQL view, or a SAS/ACCESS view. Use this parameter to specify the input data set for the process macro (%CSPROCES on UNIX or %CMPROCES on MVS), only if you specify COLLECTR=GENERIC and TOOLNM=SASDS. If you specify this parameter do not specify the *rawdata* parameter.

JES=JES2 | JES3

specifies the job entry subsystem running at the site at which SMF data are being collected. **The default value is JES2**, therefore, you only need to specify this parameter if your data are being collected at a JES3 site. JES2 indicates that TYPE26J2 data are collected and JES3 indicates that TYPE26J3 data are collected.

_RC=*varname*

identifies a macro variable that will contain the return code from this macro. For example, you might specify the variable name `retcode` to show the return code values from this macro. Values that may be returned are 0 and nonzero. A value of 0 indicates that the macro was successful. A nonzero value indicates that the macro failed. Check the explanatory message in the SAS log.

The macro variable value that is set by this parameter should only be used in batch.

UNIT= DISK | TAPE | CART|*etc.*

is the standard IBM unit specification. It specifies the type of unit on which the SMF-style log is stored. The UNIT= parameter is used only if the *rawdata* parameter is specified. **The default is TAPE.**

VOLSER=*volserno*
specifies the volume serial number of the unit on which the *rawdata* file is stored. Use this parameter only if you specify the *rawdata* parameter.

Example: %CMPROCES

This example processes SMF data in the current generation of the SMF log into the XTY70, XTY71, and XTY72 tables. In this example, the logged SMF-style data are stored as part of a generation data group (GDG):

```
%let retcode=.;
%cmproces( smf-gdg-name(0),
         xty70 xty71 xty72,
         collectr=smf,
         toolnm=mxg,
         _rc=retcode);
%put CMPROCES return code is &retcode;
```

This example processes non-SMF data into the PDB from the SAS data library named `your.SAS.data`:

```
libname input 'your.SAS.data' disp=shr;
%let retcode=.;
%cmproces(,
         collectr=generic,
         toolnm=sasds,
         genlib=input
         _rc=retcode) ;
%put CMPROCES return code is &retcode;
```

Notes

Before you run %CMPROCES for the first time you should review the help file available by following this path from the main menu in the interactive interface:

`Help -> To Use MXG`

SAS/CPE uses a SAS format to determine the necessary MXG macros to run for each table selected in the PDB. The source for this format is stored in PGMLIB.CPEMAIN.CMMXGLX.SOURCE. If the correct MXG macro is not found when the data are processed into the PDB, there may be a problem with the SAS/CPE format for the MXG macro. If you experience this problem, contact your SAS/CPE Technical Support Representative.

It is not necessary to select the component tables from which the tables XJOBS, XPRINT, XSTEPS, and XRMFINT tables are created, unless you want to keep the data from the component tables in your PDB. SAS/CPE will determine that these tables are needed during the process phase and will build them in data sets in the WORK library and will then delete them at the end of the process step. Furthermore, since SAS/CPE creates temporary data sets in the WORK library during the process step, you should verify that the IMAC members in your MXG exit library (such as `mxg.userid.sourcelib`) specify that data sets should be created in the WORK library.

A member named CMQSTART has been added to the CPMISC PDS that is built during SAS/CPE installation. This file contains a sample batch job that allocates a PDB, runs the process and reduce tasks on a set of tables, and runs reports at the end. This sample can be used as a quick start after you have installed SAS/CPE.

%CPBATCH

Run Scheduled Work

Purpose

%CPBATCH runs all tasks that have been scheduled using the Batch Utility item on the primary menu of the SAS/CPE interactive interface. If you want to use the SAS/CPE batch scheduler, you must submit a batch job that contains at least the %CPSTART macro and this macro. This job should run after the nightly SMF dump (or the equivalent if you are using non-SMF style records) and is normally part of an MVS scheduling system.

You may want to use %CPBATCH to run the process task, the reduce task, and any reporting tasks or you could process and reduce your data and then run your reports at a later time using %CPBATCH. The SAS log and output from any of these tasks can be distributed to individual users if you specify this option under the Batch Utility item on the main menu of the SAS/CPE interactive interface.

If you use the %CPBATCH macro, the SITELIB= parameter must be specified on the %CPSTART macro because SITELIB is where task scheduling information is stored.

Syntax

```
%CPBATCH(ENV=BACK) ;
```

%CPBATCH Parameters

ENV=BACK
: specifies whether the macro should run in background. The only value and the default for this parameter is BACK.

Example: %CPBATCH on MVS

This example runs tasks that have been scheduled through the SAS/CPE Batch Utility.

```
%cpstart(mode=batch,
         system=mvs,
         root= cpe-root,
         pdb= cpe-pdb,
         disp=old,
         sitelib= cpe-sitelib,
         siteacc=old,
         mxglib= mxg.mxg.formats,
         mxgsrc=('mxg.userid.sourcelib' 'mxg.mxg.sourcelib'),
         _rc=retcode
         );

%cpbatch(env=BACK);
```

%CPCAT

Copies control statements to and from SAS catalog source entries

Purpose

%CPCAT is used to copy control statements to or from a SAS catalog source entry. You can copy control statements from a SAS catalog source entry only if you are copying them to a SAS data set or to the SAS log. This statement is useful when used in conjunction with the %CPDDUTL macro because after copying instream statements into a SOURCE catalog the SOURCE can be used as input to %CPDDUTL.

Syntax

```
%CPCAT (<CAT=SAS-source-catalog-entry>,
       <ODS=output-SAS-data-set | LOG> ) ;
```

%CPCAT Parameters

CAT=*SAS-source-catalog-entry*

is the name of the input or output SAS source catalog entry, depending on whether ODS= is specified.

CAT= is used to specify the output SAS source catalog entry when you want to copy instream code to a SOURCE catalog entry as shown in this example:

```
%CPCAT ; CARDS4 ;
   ... any lines of code, except no ;;;; in columns 1 through 4...
;;;;
%CPCAT (CAT=output-SAS-source-catalog-entry);
```

In the previous example, the CAT= parameter is used to specify the output source catalog and in this case, you cannot use the ODS= parameter

The CARDS4 statement indicates that data lines containing semicolons follow the statement. After the last data line, a line consisting of four semicolons in columns 1 through 4 signals the end of the data. SAS/CPE reads the data lines, including the internal semicolons, until it encounters the line of four semicolons.

CAT= is used to specify the input SAS source catalog entry when you are copying *from* a SOURCE catalog entry *to* a SAS data set or the SAS log such as:

```
%CPCAT (CAT=input-SAS-source-catalog-entry ,
        ODS=output-SAS-data-set | LOG);
```

In this example, the value of CAT= is used to specify the input SOURCE catalog and ODS= should be used to specify the output location. If ODS= is not specified, the code specified in the prior %CPCAT; CARDS4; statements are written to the SOURCE catalog entry specified in the CAT= parameter.

ODS=*output-SAS-data-set* | LOG

Specifies the destination for the statements being copied. It can be either a SAS data set or the SAS log. You should specify this parameter if you are copying a SOURCE catalog entry to a SAS data set or the SAS log. String variables in the output data set have a maximum length of 200 characters.

Examples: %CPCAT

The following example copies %CPDDUTL ADD TABLE control statements to a SAS catalog member SAS-CATALOG-SOURCE and then invokes %CPDDUTL to execute the statements. When using the CARDS4 statement, the four ;;;; must appear alone on a line.

```
%cpcat; cards4 ;
  add table name=tab01 ;
  add table name=tab02 ;
;;;;
%cpcat(cat=sas-catalog-source) ;
%cpddutl(entrynam=sas-catalog-source,list=Y) ;
```

The following example copies a source catalog entry to an output data set and prints the data set.

```
%cpcat(cat=sasuser-test-source, ods=work-temp) ;
proc print data=work-temp noobs uniform ;
  var card ;
run ;
```

The following example copies a source catalog entry to the SAS log.

```
%cpcat(cat=sasuser-test-source, ods=LOG) ;
```

Note

When using %CPCAT to copy instream data to a SAS source catalog entry you must invoke %CPCAT twice. The first invocation specifies the instream data, and the second invocation specifies the name of the output SAS source catalog entry, as shown in the following example.

```
%CPCAT ; CARDS4 ;
  any lines of code, except no ;;;; in columns 1 through 4
;;;;
%CPCAT (CAT=output-SAS-source-catalog-entry);
```

%CPDBCOPY

Copy PDB Data Dictionary and Data

Purpose

The %CPDBCOPY macro copies the data dictionary and data from one PDB to another PDB.

Caution: *%CPDBCOPY erases the data dictionary and data in the destination PDB before it begins the copy.*

Syntax

```
%CPDBCOPY(pdbfrom,
          pdbto,
          <_RC=varname>);
```

%CPDBCOPY Parameters

pdbfrom
: is the name of the source PDB. The name includes the complete directory path or high-level-qualifiers and pdb name, but it does not include the lowest libraries such as ADMIN, DAY, or any others.

pdbto
: is the name of the target PDB. This includes the complete directory path or high-level-qualifiers and the PDB name, but it does not include the lowest libraries such as ADMIN, DAY, or any others.

UNIX On UNIX, the directory structure for this PDB must exist before you run %CPDBCOPY. To create the directory structure, use the interactive interface or use the `mkdir` command.

MVS On MVS, the *pdbto* PDB must be created before you run %CDBCOPY. To create it, use the interactive interface or use the CMBPDALC member in the *install-prefix*.CPE.MISC PDS, which is set up at installation time. For the complete physical location of this PDS at your site, see your SAS/CPE administrator or your SAS Software Representative.

Optional Keyword Parameters

_RC=*varname*
: identifies a macro variable that contains the return code from %CPDBCOPY. The values that can occur in this variable are 0 and nonzero. A value of zero (0) means %CPDBCOPY was successful and a nonzero value indicates a failure. You should check the explanatory message in the SAS log.

Example: %CPDBCOPY

This example copies all of the data dictionary information and data in PDB1 to PDB2.

```
%cpdbcopy(physical-filename-pdb1, physical-filename-pdb2);
```

Note

The *pdbfrom* can be the active PDB, which is the current PDB specified in the PDB= parameter in the %CPSTART macro. The *pdbto* cannot be the active PDB.

%CPDBKILL

Deletes the Data Dictionary, Tables, and Data from a PDB

Purpose

The %CPDBKILL macro deletes tables, data, and the contents of the data dictionary from the specified PDB, but keeps the structure of the data dictionary (directories and libraries) in the PDB.

Syntax

```
%CPDBKILL(cpe-pdb);
```

%CPDBKILL Parameters

cpe-pdb
: is the name of the PDB from which the tables and data are to be deleted. The name includes the complete directory path or high-level-qualifiers and the PDB name, but does not include the lowest libraries such as DETAIL, DAY, or any of the other libraries within the PDB.

Example: %CPDBKILL

This example deletes all of the tables and data in the PDB *physical-filename-pdb*, but keeps the structure of the data dictionary in the PDB.

```
%cpdbkill(physical-filename-pdb);
```

Notes

If you only want to delete the data from all tables in a PDB, you can use the **%CPDBPURG** macro. If you only want to purge data from a specific table in the PDB, use the **%CPDDUTL** control statement **PURGE TABLE**. If you want to delete both the data in a specific table as well as the table's definition, use the %CPDDUTL control statement **DELETE TABLE**.

%CPDBPURG

Purge Data from a PDB

Purpose

The %CPDBPURG macro deletes the data from all levels of all tables in a PDB, leaving the PDB otherwise intact. You can use the KEEP= parameter to keep the detail-level data sets when you delete the data from the other levels.

Syntax

```
%CPDBPURG(cpe-pdb,
        <DELETE=DETAIL | ALL>,
        <KEEP=DETAIL | NONE> ) ;
```

%CPDBPURG Parameters

cpe-pdb
: is the name of the PDB that contains the data to be deleted. This includes the complete directory path or high-level-qualifiers, but does not include the lowest directory levels, such as DETAIL, DAY, or any of the other libraries within the PDB.

Optional Keyword Parameters

DELETE=DETAIL | ALL
: specifies whether %CPDBPURG is to delete only the data in the DETAIL library. If you specify DELETE=DETAIL, %CPDBPURG deletes all data at the DETAIL-level, but keeps the performance data at the other levels in the PDB. If you specify DELETE=ALL, %CPDBURG deletes the data from all levels of the active PDB. **The default is DELETE=ALL**. You can specify this parameter or the KEEP= parameter, but not both.

KEEP=DETAIL | NONE
: specifies whether %CPDBPURG is to delete all data in the DETAIL= level library. If you specify KEEP=DETAIL, %CPDBURG keeps all the detail-level data when it purges the rest of the performance data. If you specify KEEP=NONE, %CPDBPURG deletes the detail-level data as-well-as the data from the other levels. **The default is KEEP=NONE**. You can specify this parameter or the DELETE= parameter, but not both.

Example: %CPDBPURG

This example deletes the data at all levels in all tables in the PDB *physical-filename-pdb*.

```
%cpdbpurg(physical-filename-pdb);
```

Notes

If you want to delete the tables, data, and contents of the data dictionary, but keep the structure of the PDB, such as the libraries and directories, you can use the **%CPDBKILL** macro. If you only want to purge data from a specific table in the PDB, use the **%CPDDUTL** control statement **PURGE TABLE**. If you want to delete both the data in a specific table as well as the table's definition, use the %CPDDUTL control statement **DELETE TABLE**.

%CPDUPCHK

 *Checks for duplicate data by examining timestamps on data being processed into the PDB*

Complete information for this macro was not available at the time this document was printed. For more information about this macro, see the CPDUPCHK and CPDUP Input Filtering Routines *entries in the online help index of the SAS/CPE interactive interface or the* CPDUPCHK *member in CPMISC.*

Purpose

The %CPDUPCHK macro filters your incoming data and checks for duplicates. It allows or prevents duplicate data from being processed into the active PDB based on the data's timestamp (when the input data was created by the collector). The timestamp information is saved in a SAS data set.

To enable input filtering, you must set the DUPMODE= parameter to DISCARD or TERMINATE on the **%CMPROCES** macro. If you are processing SMF data, setting the DUPMODE= parameter automatically invokes this and other input filtering macros for you. However, if you are using a generic collector and you want to enable input filtering, you must set the DUPMODE= parameter on %CMPROCES and also invoke %CPDUPCHK in your code that stages the raw data to be processed by %CMPROCES.

If you do not want duplicate data to be processed into the PDB, %CPDUPCHK will read the timestamp of the incoming data and then reject the data if the timestamp for the data falls within an existing datetime range in the datetime data set.

If you want duplicate data to be processed into the active PDB, %CPDUPCHK will read the timestamp of the incoming data, but even if the timestamp falls within an existing datetime range, the data will still be processed into the active PDB.

Notes

Currently, this and other SAS/CPE input filtering macros are only available for use on MVS when you are using SMF or the generic collector.

Before you can enable input filtering via the %CMPROCES or %CPDUPCHK macros, you must create the appropriate input filtering files as described in the CPDUPCHK member in CPMISC. See also the **%CPDUPUPD**, **%CPDUPINT**, **%CPDUPDSN**, **%CPDUPFMT**, and **%CPDUPMXG** macros and the DUPMODE= parameter on the **%CMPROCES** macro.

%CPDUPDSN

MVS *Generates the name of the data set to contain datetime ranges for the data being processed into the active PDB*

Complete information about this macro was not available at the time this document was printed. For more information about this macro, see the CPDUPDSN and CPDUP Input Filtering Routines *entries in the online help index of the SAS/CPE interactive interface or the* CPDUPCHK *member in CPMISC.*

Purpose

The %CPDUPDSN macro creates the name of the SAS data set that will contain the datetime information for data being processed into the active PDB. When you process data and are using input filtering, the datetime information for the data is saved in the data set created by %CPDUPDSN and can be used by other input filtering macros, such as %CPDUPCHK.

If you are using SMF, this macro is automatically submitted for you when you turn on input filtering using the DUPMODE= parameter on **%CMPROCES**. If you are using the SAS/CPE generic collector, you must enable input filtering using the DUPMODE= parameter, but must also run this macro as described in the *CPDUP Input Filtering Routines* document available in the online help index of the SAS/CPE interactive interface.

Notes

Currently, the SAS/CPE input filtering macros are only available for use on MVS when you are using the generic collector or SMF data.

For more information, see the **%CPDUPCHK**, **%CPDUPINT**, **%CPDUPUPD**, **%CPDUPFMT**, and **%CPDUPMXG** macros and the DUPMODE= parameter on the **%CMPROCES** macro.

%CPDUPFMT

Recovers formats to be used with input filtering macros

Complete information for this macro was not available at the time this document was printed. For more information about this macro, see the CPDUPFMT and CPDUP Input Filtering Routines *entries in the online help index of the SAS/CPE interactive interface or the* CPDUPCHK *member in CPMISC.*

Purpose

The %CPDUPFMT macro re-creates SAS formats used with the SAS/CPE input data filtering macros. For example, if you accidently delete the format file or catalog on your system and you run the %CMPROCES macro with input filtering enabled, you will receive an error stating that your formats are missing. Run this macro to re-create the formats.

Notes

Currently, this and other SAS/CPE input filtering macros are only available for use on MVS when you are using SMF or the generic collector.

For additional information on input filtering, see the **%CPDUPUPD**, **%CPDUPINT**, **%CPDUPDSN**, **%CPDUPCHK**, and **%CPDUPMXG** macros and the DUPMODE= parameter on the **%CMPROCES** macro.

%CPDUPINT

Loads macro definitions that are used by other input filtering macros

Complete information for this macro was not available at the time this document was printed. For more information about this macro, see the CPDUPINT and CPDUP Input Filtering Routines *entries in the online help index of the SAS/CPE interactive interface or the* CPDUPCHK *member in CPMISC.* see the %CPDUPINT and Input Filtering entries in the online help index of the SAS/CPE interactive interface.

Purpose

%CPDUPINT loads macro definitions that are required in order to filter data that was collected using a generic collector. If you are using the SMF collector with SAS/CPE, the necessary macros are set up and enabled for you and you do not need to run this macro. However, if you are using a generic collector you need to run the %CPDUPINT macro as described in the *CPDUP Input Filtering Routines* entry in the online help index of the SAS/CPE interactive interface.

Notes

Currently, this and other SAS/CPE input filtering macros are only available for use on MVS when you are using SMF or the generic collector.

For more information on input filtering, see the **%CPDUPUPD**, **%CPDUPCHK**, **%CPDUPDSN**, **%CPDUPFMT**, and **%CPDUPMXG** macros and the DUPMODE= parameter on the **%CMPROCES** macro.

%CPDUPMXG

Modifies MXG source to support input data filtering

Complete information for this macro was not available at the time this document was printed. For more information about this macro, see the CPDUPMXG and CPDUP Input Filtering Routines *entries in the online help index of the SAS/CPE interactive interface or the* CPDUPCHK *member in CPMISC.*

Purpose

The %CPDUPMXG macro modifies MXG source code to support the input data filtering routines, when you are using MXG code to stage non-SMF data into SAS data sets for processing by the SAS/CPE generic collector. When you use the input filtering macros the input filtering macros must be called or executed at a specific place within your code. Because SAS/CPE understand the format of MXG data sets, %CPDUPMXG can modify your MXG source code for you, placing calls to the following macros in the appropriate places: %CPDUPINT, %CPDUPDSN, and %CPDUPCHK.

You should only run this macro when you are using MXG to stage non-SMF data into SAS data sets for processing by the SAS/CPE generic collector. If you are using the generic collector with any other type of data, SAS/CPE does not automatically know the format of the data source and you must manually insert in your source code, calls to the input filtering macros. For more information on inserting the macros in your source code, refer to the CPDUPCHK member in CPMISC.

If you are using SMF it is not necessary to run %CPDUPMXG because SAS/CPE knows that MXG has staged the SMF data and therefore, the input filtering macros are automatically invoked when you set the DUPMODE= parameter on **%CMPROCES**.

After you run %CPDUPMXG, you should review the contents of the $$GENxxx member, where xxx is the value of the SOURCE= parameter on %CPDUPMXG. For more information on this and other parameters for this macro, refer to the previously referenced online help files.

Notes

Currently, this and other SAS/CPE input data filtering macros are only available for use on MVS when you are using SMF or the generic collector.

For additional information, see the **%CPDUPUPD**, **%CPDUPINT**, **%CPDUPDSN**, **%CPDUPFMT**, and **%CPDUPCHK** macros and the DUPMODE= parameter on the **%CMPROCES** macro.

%CPDUPUPD

Updates the input filtering datetime information

Complete information about this macro was not available at the time this document was printed. For more information about this macro, see the CPDUPUPD and CPDUP Input Filtering Routines *entries in the online help index of the SAS/CPE interactive interface or the* CPDUPCHK *member in CPMISC.*

Purpose

The %CPDUPUPD macro works with the %CPDUPCHK macro to allow or prevent duplicate data from being processed into the active PDB. After the data are filtered by %CPDUPCHK, the %CPDUPUPD macro groups the incoming data into separate SAS data sets based on the collector used to gather the data. The macro then merges the new datetime information with the existing datetime information in the input filtering data sets.

Notes

Currently, the SAS/CPE input data filtering macros are only available for use on MVS when you are using SMF or the generic collector.

The %CPDUPUPD macro must be submitted by the **%CMPROCES** macro. It is automatically submitted when you set DUPMODE=DISCARD, FORCE, or TERMINATE on %CMPROCES.

For more information on input filtering, see also the **%CPDUPCHK**, **%CPDUPINT**, **%CPDUPDSN**, **%CPDUPFMT**, and **%CPDUPMXG** macros and the DUPMODE= parameter on the **%CMPROCES** macro.

%CPREDUCE

Reduce Data

Purpose

The %CPREDUCE macro summarizes data in the DETAIL level of the PDB into the DAY, WEEK, MONTH, and YEAR levels of the PDB. This summary takes place for the specified tables (or all tables if none are specified) that meet the following criteria:

- the KEPT= parameter is set to YES
- the value of the AGELIMIT= parameter is greater than zero in at least one of the DAY, WEEK, MONTH, or YEAR levels
- the table has at least one variable with a selected statistic that has KEPT=YES

The %CPREDUCE macro also removes data and statistics that have exceeded the age limit for these levels: DAY, WEEK, MONTH, and YEAR. %CPREDUCE only removes data from the DETAIL level if the DETAIL level age limit is zero for a specific table. The %CSPROCES macro on UNIX or the %CMPROCES macro, on MVS normally removes old data in the DETAIL level.

If a system failure or some other problem interrupts the reduction process before it completes, you can restart the %CPREDUCE macro and it continues processing where it stopped. Additional information on using this macro during recovery from an error condition is available in the guidelines for **Handling Batch Jobs That Fail**.

Syntax

```
%CPREDUCE(tablist,
          <CKPTINIT=NO|YES>,
          <_RC> ) ;
```

%CPREDUCE Parameters

tablist

specifies which tables to reduce. Separate the table names with blanks. **This is a required positional parameter.** The tables in the list will be reduced if they meet the following reduce criteria:

- the KEPT= parameter is set to YES
- the value of the AGELIMIT= parameter is greater than zero in at least one of the DAY, WEEK, MONTH, or YEAR levels
- the table has at least one variable with a selected statistic that has KEPT=YES

If you omit the list, the macro reduces all tables in your PDB that meet the previously specified criteria.

Optional Keyword Parameters

CKPTINIT=NO|YES

indicates whether to delete all checkpoint records. When %CPREDUCE runs, flags are placed in the checkpoint data set (DICTLIB.CKPTINFO) to indicate the completion status of reduction steps. **CKPTINIT=NO is the default.**

If a %CPREDUCE failure occurs, the checkpoint data set will contain information on the failure so that the next %CPREDUCE can automatically recover from the failure. Intermediate data sets that are used for reduction processing also remain in the SAS data library PDBWORK, so that data is not lost when the automatic %CPREDUCE recovery procedure takes place.

CKPTINIT=NO means keep the checkpoint file intact and do not delete the data sets in PDBWORK.

CKPTINIT=YES means clear the checkpoint file and delete the data sets in PDBWORK.

Additional information on using this macro in recovery from an error condition is available in **Handling Batch Jobs That Fail**.

Caution: The use of the CKPTINIT=YES option can lead to a loss of data for the table and time period being reduced with no further warning. Do not use this option unless you can accept losing data for the table and time period being reduced when the previous failure took place, or unless instructed to do so by SAS Institute's Technical Support.

Note: If AGELIMIT=0 at the DETAIL level, your data is stored in DETAIL until the next reduce or process runs. Therefore, if reduce runs immediately after the process step, the data is processed, reduced into the non-DETAIL levels, and then removed from DETAIL. However, if the process step runs again before the data has been reduced, the existing data in DETAIL is deleted before it can be reduced into the non-DETAIL levels.

This means that if %CPREDUCE fails for tables with an AGELIMIT=0 at the DETAIL level, you should fix the cause of the failure and re-run %CPREDUCE before the next process task runs.

Using AGELIMIT=0 at the DETAIL level is useful if you are collecting and processing large amounts of data on a daily basis, but, to avoid losing data at the non-DETAIL levels, you should always reduce the data immediately after it is processed.

_RC=*varname*

identifies a macro variable that will contain the return code from this macro. For example, you might specify the variable name `retcode` to show the return code values from this macro. Values that may be returned are 0 and nonzero. A value of 0 indicates that the macro was successful. A nonzero value indicates that the macro failed. Check the explanatory message in the SAS log.

The macro variable value that is set by this parameter should only be used in batch.

Examples: %CPREDUCE

Example 1

This example reduces the data in the DETAIL level of all tables that meet the reduction criteria to the non-DETAIL levels specified in the data dictionary for the PDB.

```
   /* reduce all tables in the active PDB */
%cpreduce();
```

Example 2

This example reduces data in tables TABLE3 and TABLE8 and keeps the checkpoint data set. If an error occurred in a previous reduction task, %CPREDUCE starts where it stopped and, if the error has been fixed it continues.

```
   /* reduce two tables in the active PDB */
%cpreduce(table3 table8);
```

Example 3

Use this method only if this is a practice PDB, if you can accept possible data loss, or if instructed to do so by SAS Institute Technical Support.

This example turns off the error flag in the checkpoint data set (DICTLIB.CKPTINFO), deletes the data sets in the PDBWORK library, and reduces the data in all of the tables in the PDB. Some data may be lost from the DAY, WEEK, MONTH, or YEAR levels. The data that may be lost are updates to statistics that were being calculated for a level of the table when the error occurred.

```
   /* may lose data from a previous interrupted reduction job */
%cpreduce(,ckptinit=yes);
```

Note

If you want all of your data to be reduced, you must run the reduce step at least as often as the shortest detail-level age limit of your tables. For example, if your shortest detail-level age limit is 0, you must run the reduce task before the next process task runs. Otherwise, the process step will age out the data before the reduce step has an opportunity to see it.

%CPSTART

Start SAS/CPE Software

Purpose

The %CPSTART macro allocates PDB libraries, establishes system options and global values for SAS/CPE software, defines the active PDB and, optionally, starts the SAS/CPE interactive interface. The %CPSTART macro establishes your environment before you begin using any other SAS/CPE macros.

You must run this macro to start SAS/CPE in batch. You can start SAS/CPE from the SAS display manager by submitting this macro from the program editor window, or from the command line in the program editor window, you can submit the command that invokes SAS/CPE and automatically submits this macro. That command is `cpe` on UNIX and `cmcpe` on MVS.

If you execute the %CPSTART macro without specifying the PDB= parameter, it uses the PDB that you last accessed. The only exception to this is for MVS batch jobs where there is no default PDB.

The active PDB is the PDB that you have most recently selected to use or act upon, and on which most subsequent SAS/CPE operations operate. For example, all of the reporting macros will report on data contained in the active PDB. There are exceptions, for example, the **%CPDBCOPY** macro cannot use the active PDB as the target PDB. You can set a different PDB to be the active PDB at any time, using the %CPSTART macro.

Syntax

```
%CPSTART (<ACCESS=READONLY | WRITE>,
          <DISP=OLD | SHR | NEW>,
          <MODE=MENU | NOMENU | BATCH>,
          <MXGLIB=data-set-name>,
          <MXGSRC=('mxg-userid-sourcelib' 'mxg-mxg-sourcelib')>,
          <PDB=cpe-pdb>,
          <PROMPT=>,
          <_RC=varname>,
          <ROOT=cpe-root>,
          <SHARE=pdb-server>,
          <SITEACC=sitelib-access>,
          <SITELIB=cpe-sitelib>,
          <SITESHR=sitelib-server>,
          <SYSTEM=MVS | OSYS> ) ;
```

%CPSTART Parameters

 ACCESS=READONLY | WRITE

specifies the level of access to the performance database. You must specify ACCESS=WRITE if you are processing or reducing data.

If you create a new PDB, your access level is WRITE by default. If you are accessing an an existing PDB and you do not specify the ACCESS= parameter, your level of access is

the same level you had for this PDB the last time you accessed it. If you are accessing an existing PDB that you have not used before, your default level of access is READONLY.

This parameter is only used on UNIX.

DISP=OLD | SHR | NEW

is the standard IBM disposition value. It applies to the access level of the PDB. **The default setting is DISP=SHR, which indicates that you and others have read access to the PDB so that multiple users can read the PDB at the same time.**

If you specify DISP=OLD, you have write access to the PDB and therefore, have exclusive control. If you specify DISP=NEW a new PDB is built using default space allocations.

This parameter is only used on MVS.

MODE=MENU | NOMENU | BATCH

specifies the interface to use when you start SAS/CPE. This value determines how missing values for the location of ROOT and PDB are handled, as described below. **The default value is MODE=MENU.**

MODE=BATCH

must be used in batch jobs. It invokes SAS/CPE software, but does not start the SAS/CPE interactive interface. If the location of ROOT (as specified in the ROOT= parameter) is not found, this mode terminates the %CPSTART macro. The location includes the complete directory path or high-level-qualifier for the ROOT and PDB libraries.

On UNIX, if the location of the PDB cannot be found and ACCESS=WRITE, this mode creates an empty PDB; otherwise, the macro fails. On MVS, if the location of the PDB cannot be located, the macro fails and you will receive an error message.

MODE=MENU

may be specified only when this macro is used in a SAS interactive session. This value invokes SAS/CPE software and starts the SAS/CPE interactive interface. If you specify MODE=MENU and the location of ROOT or PDB are not found, you are prompted for the correct location (for ROOT) or you are asked to confirm the creation of a new PDB. The location includes the complete directory path or high-level-qualifiers for the ROOT and PDB libraries.

MODE=NOMENU

may be specified only when this macro is used in a SAS interactive sesstion. For example, you can use

```
%cpstart(mode=nomenu);
```

This invokes SAS/CPE software, but does not start the SAS/CPE interactive interface. If the location of the PDB is not found, MODE=NOMENU gives you an error. If the location of ROOT is not found, you are prompted for the correct location. The location includes the complete directory path or high-level-qualifiers for the ROOT and PDB libraries.

MXGLIB=*data-set-name*

specifies the physical location and name of the SAS library containing the MXG formats to be used with MXG variables. The MXG documentation refers to this library as MXG.MXG.FORMATS.

For UNIX systems, use this parameter only if you created a PDB on MVS and ported it to UNIX.

 MXGSRC=*('mxg-userid-sourcelib' 'mxg-mxg-sourcelib')*

specifies the high-level-qualifiers and name of one or more partitioned data sets (PDS) that contain your MXG source and the MXG source library. List the PDSs in search order. If the same member name exists in more than one of the PDSs, the first member encountered is the one that is used. Thus, you generally list the PDS containing your source code before the PDS containing the MXG source code.

This parameter is only used on MVS.

PDB=*cpe-pdb*

specifies the name of the active PDB. This includes the complete directory path or high-level-qualifier and the PDB name, but does not include the lowest directory levels such as ADMIN, DAY, or any of the other libraries within the PDB. **If you omit this argument, the system uses the PDB that you last accessed. If the physical location is not valid, or if you have not previously used a PDB, the system may prompt you to supply a location.** Refer to the MODE= argument for more details.

You can switch the active PDB in the middle of a batch job by using the %CPSTART macro with a new name as the value of the PDB= parameter.

All information below this point applies only to SAS/CPE for Open Systems.

Though SAS/CPE performance databases must be protected from concurrent update access by multiple users (by using careful coding practices or adding restrictive ACLs), you can provide multi-read/single-write access to a PDB using the *-filelocks none* option on the SAS command.

If you start SAS with -filelocks none, you can do ad hoc reporting on the PDB concurrently with processing and reducing data. You will sometimes get 'data set not found' messages or incomplete graphs (if the date range in the data dictionary doesn't match the date range in the data itself because an update is in progress). In that case, wait briefly and request the report again.

Also, if you start SAS with -filelocks fail, you can do ad hoc reporting on the PDB concurrently with processing and reducing data. You will sometimes get 'lock fail' messages. In that case, wait briefly and request the report again. In either case, you would not be required to run SAS/SHARE.

Caution: The *-filelocks none* option allows concurrent updates from multiple SAS sessions and this could cause files to become corrupt. However, using the *-filelocks fail* option DOES

NOT protect against corruption of a PDB because a PDB is multiple SAS data sets (multiple UNIX files) and the data sets can get out of sync if multiple SAS sessions attempt to update them concurrently. You *must* ensure that only one process attempts to update a PDB at a time.

PROMPT=
: for internal use only.

_RC=*varname*
: identifies a macro variable that will contain the return code from this macro. For example, you might specify the variable name `retcode` to show the return code values from this macro. Values that may be returned are 0 and nonzero. A value of 0 indicates that the macro was successful. A nonzero value indicates that the macro failed. Check the explanatory message in the SAS log.

  The macro variable value that is set by this parameter should only be used in batch.

ROOT=*cpe-root*
: is the physical location where the SAS/CPE software is installed on your system. This includes the complete directory path or high-level-qualifiers where PGMLIB is installed. **On MVS, this parameter has no default and is required. On Open Systems, ROOT= defaults to *!sasroot/saspgm/cpe*, where *!sasroot* is the directory in which SAS is installed at your site.**

  Check with your SAS CPE Site Administrator or your SAS Software Representative for the correct location at your site.

SHARE=*pdb-server*
: names the SAS/SHARE server that is used with the active PDB. Use this paramater only if you are using SAS/SHARE software with the SAS/CPE PDB at your site. A SAS/SHARE server allows multiple users to have update access to SAS data libraries. It should only be used if multiple users need concurrent update access to a PDB. For the SHARE= value to use at your site, check with your SAS administrator or your SAS/CPE Software Representative.

  This parameter is only used on MVS.

  For more information about SAS/SHARE software, refer to *SAS/SHARE Software: Usage and Reference, Version 6, First Edition.*

SITEACC=*sitelib-access*
: specifies the level of access to the site library.

  Valid options for UNIX are READONLY or WRITE. For MVS, valid options are SHR and OLD. Do not place quotes around the value of this parameter.

  SHR (MVS) or READONLY (Open Systems) specifies that you and others have concurrent read access to the SAS/CPE SITELIB. OLD (MVS) or WRITE (Open Systems) specifies that you have exclusive control and write access to the SAS/CPE SITELIB.

  If you specify the SITELIB= parameter, but do not specify the SITEACC= parameter, the system provides WRITE (Open Systems) or OLD (MVS) access to the specified SITELIB library. If you do not specify the SITELIB= or the SITEACC= parameters, the system provides READONLY (Open Systems) or SHR (MVS) access to the default SITELIB library.

SITELIB=*cpe-sitelib*
is the physical location and name of your SITELIB library. This includes the complete directory path or high-level-qualifiers of the site library and the library name. The SITELIB library contains system options and global information for your site. This library must exist before you start SAS/CPE software. If it is a new empty library, SAS/CPE will initialize it the first time it is specified on %CPSTART. **The default value for the SITELIB parameter is set when SAS/CPE is installed.**

If you specify the SITELIB parameter, but do not specify the SITEACC parameter, the system provides WRITE (Open Systems) or OLD (MVS) access to the specified SITELIB library. If you do not specify the SITELIB or the SITEACC parameters, the system provides READONLY (Open Systems) or SHR (MVS) access to the default SITELIB library.

UNIX For SAS/CPE on UNIX, see the installation instructions for more information on changing the default SITELIB library location.

SITESHR=*sitelib-server*
names the SAS/SHARE server that is used with SAS/CPE for controlling access to SITELIB. This parameter is optional. Use this paramater only if you are using SAS/SHARE software with SAS/CPE at your site. A SAS/SHARE server allows multiple users to have updated access to SAS data libraries. It should only be used if multiple users need concurrent update access to SITELIB. For the value to use at your site, check with your SAS/CPE administrator or your SAS Software Representative.

This parameter is not used on Open Systems.

For more information about SAS/SHARE software, refer to *SAS/SHARE Software: Usage and Reference, Version 6, First Edition.*

SYSTEM=MVS | OSYS
specifies the system on which you are running SAS/CPE. Valid values are MVS, if your host system is MVS, or OSYS, if your host system is UNIX. You can only specify the option that is valid for your system, and if you do not specify an option **the parameter defaults to the appropriate value for your system.**

Examples: %CPSTART

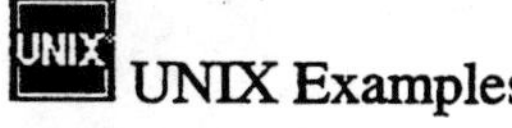

UNIX Examples

Example 1

To start SAS/CPE software in a batch job and specify the active PDB pathname, use the following statements. These examples use *pathname*/pdbxxx to indicate the name of a PDB.

```
%let retcode=.;
%cpstart(mode=batch,
```

```
        pdb=pathname/pdbxxx,
        access=write,
        _rc=retcode);
%put cpstart retcode=&retcode;
```

Note: Use the ACCESS=WRITE parameter only when you need to update the PDB.

Example 2

To start the SAS/CPE interactive interface when do you do not need update access to a PDB, but you want to access the same PDB you used the last time you ran SAS/CPE software, use this statement or type `cpe` on the SAS command line:

```
%cpstart();
```

MVS Example

To start SAS/CPE software in a batch job and specify exclusive access to the active PDB, use the following statements.

```
%let retcode=.;
%cpstart(mode=batch,
        system=mvs,
        root= high-level-qualifiers-for-cpe,
        pdb= high-level-qualifiers-for-pdb,
        disp=old,
        sitelib= fully-qualified-library-name,
        siteacc=old,
        share= pdb-server,
        mxglib= mxg-mxg-formats,
        mxgsrc=('mxg-userid-source' 'mxg-mxg-source'),
        _rc=retcode
        );
%put CPSTART return code is &retcode;
```

By specifying SITEACC=OLD, you have the option of using the %CPBATCH macro later in the SAS/CPE session, because you must have write access to SITELIB in order to perform some tasks, such as invoking the %CPBATCH macro.

%CSCSIFMT

Build Site-Specific Formats for Cabletron SPECTRUM Data on UNIX

Purpose

The %CSCSIFMT macro creates SAS formats that associate the Cabletron SPECTRUM model handles (the host ID used by SAS/CPE) with the model name of the host. These formats are used to identify the data when you run **%CSPROCES** to process the data.

The host names used by SPECTRUM Data Gateway software are stored in the model data set. This data set, which SPECTRUM names model by default, is read by CSCSIFMT using the MODELDS= parameter. SAS/CPE then creates the formats based on the model data set and stores them in your SITELIB directory. Therefore, you must have write access to your site's SITELIB directory to run this macro.

The first time you process SPECTRUM data and any time you change a host name in your network, you must follow these steps:

1. Re-build the model handle data set by running SPECTRUM Data Gateway software.

2. Run %CSCSIFMT to create the necessary SAS formats in SITELIB.

Perform these steps before running %CSPROCES on the data set that includes the new model handles.

Syntax

```
%CSCSIFMT(<MODELDS=sas-dataset-name>,
          <_RC=varname> );
```

%CSCSIFMT Parameters

MODELDS=*SAS-data-set*

specifies the name of the Spectrum model SAS data set that was created by the Spectrum Data Gateway software. The name includes the complete directory path and filename. The value for this parameter is usually *libref*.MODEL. Use a SAS LIBNAME statement to associate the *libref* with the SPECTRUM Data Gateway SAS data library, as illustrated here:

```
libname specgway 'pathname/gateway';
```

_RC=*varname*

identifies a macro variable that contains the return code from %CSCSIFMT. The values that can occur in this variable are 0, 4, and 8. The value 0 means %CSCSIFMT was successful. The value 4 means the model type handle is unknown. Use only model type handles supplied by SAS/CPE, or create your own table for the model type. A value of 8 means no input was specified. For more information on creating your own table, see the online help entry Processing Data with Cabletron Spectrum, which is available through the SAS/CPE interactive interface.

Example: %CSCSIFMT

This example updates your SITELIB library with the formats for network host names and model types and then processes SPECTRUM data.

```
%cpstart(mode=batch,
         pdb= pathname/pdbxxx,
         access=write,
         sitelib= sitelib-to-update ,
         _rc=retcode);
%put cpstart retcode=&retcode;

   /* assign libref for SPECTRUM data */
libname specgway 'pathname/gateway';

   /* create SAS formats in SITELIB library */
%cscsifmt(modelds=specgway.model);
%put cpstart retcode=&retcode;


   /* process SPECTRUM data  */
%csproces(specgway.stat,
          cciifp cxytse csibce csil23 csihi2 csipng cciigs,
          collectr=spectrum,
          _rc=retcode);
%put csproces return code is &retcode;
```

Note

Format definitions are stored in memory. When you create a format definition in batch with %CSCSIFMT, you can use the format immediately. However, when you use %CSCSIFMT to redefine a format definition while the SAS/CPE interactive interface is running, you must restart the SAS/CPE interactive interface before using the updated format definition.

%CSPROCES

Processes Data into the Detail Levels of the active PDB on UNIX

Purpose

The %CSPROCES macro runs the process task, which includes reading and validating performance data and transforming the performance data from its original logged files into the detail level SAS libraries of the active performance database (PDB). In addition, %CSPROCES updates data dictionary entries that describe the amount of data in the PDB and the most recent date and time of processing data into the detail level of the tables.

To use this macro during recovery from an error condition, refer to **Handling Batch Jobs that Fail.**

Syntax

```
%CSPROCES(<rawdata>,
            tablist,
            COLLECTR=collector-name,
            TOOLNM=tool,
          <AGELIMIT=number>,
          <COLDUMP=command>,
          <COLLVER=version-number>,
          <EXITSRC=exit-source>,
          <GENLIB=libref>,
          <GROUP=group-file>,
          <OPTIMIZE=TIME | DISK>,
          <PASSWD=password-file>,
          <_RC=varname>,
          <RSHHOST=remote-command>,
          <SUBSET=expression> ) ;
```

%CSPROCES Parameters

rawdata

specifies the name of the raw data file. The name includes the complete directory path and name of the raw data file to be processed by this %CSPROCES run. This positional parameter is not required, but if specified, it must be first. If you omit this parameter you must use a comma as a placeholder. The name can be any of the following:

- the name of the raw file containing data from your data collector (e.g. HP Network Node Manager or IBM NetView). The name of the file can be enclosed in quotation marks, but quotes are not required.
- a PIPE command that sends the raw file records to standard output.
- a SAS data set containing SPECTRUM data, as created by the Spectrum Gateway for SAS. This data set is typically the "stat" data set created by the gateway. Specify this name in the form

```
<libref.>dataset
```

You can omit the *libref* if the data set is in WORK.

You can omit the *rawdata* parameter under the following circumstances:

- you want to process existing data in the DETAIL level using the AGELIMIT= or SUBSET= parameters.
- you are processing data using a generic collector, in which case you would specify the GENLIB= parameter instead of *rawdata.*

When processing UNIX accounting data (collected by the **accton** command), you must edit the data file and add a line at the beginning of the file that contains the host name:

```
machine= hostname
```

where *hostname* is the machine that created the data. or, you can also use a **pipe** command to prefix the host name to the dat file. SAS/CPE software uses this information to set the MACHINE variable in the PDB data libraries. See the Accton example for an illustration of using the PIPE command as described here.

tablist

lists the tables into which the logged data should be processed. **This positional parameter is required** and must be specified in the second position. Use blanks to separate the tables in the list.

For HP MeasureWare input files, you can specify an asterisk (*) to process data from the rawdata file into the appropriate SAS/CPE tables.

COLLECTR=*collector-name*

specifies the name of the SAS/CPE supported collector that created the log file data, for example if you are using SUNETMGR:

```
collector=sunetmgr
```

This parameter is required. The current valid values are:

- ACCTON
- HP-PCS
- HP-OV
- HP-OV-C
- PROBEX
- SPECTRUM
- SUNETMGR
- TRAKKER
- GENERIC

If you are using a user-defined collector or a third-party collector instead of a SAS/CPE supported collector, use the value GENERIC.

If you specify COLLECTR=SPECTRUM you must run the **%CSCSIFMT** macro before you process your data for the first time or the %CSPROCES macro will fail.

The ACCTON, PROBENET, SUNETMGR, TRAKKER, or HP-PCS collectors present time information in Greenwich Mean Time (GMT). Therefore, if you specify one of these collectors, you must specify the distance (in time zones) of your site from Greenwich, England before you process your data. This can be done through the SAS/CPE interactive interface by selecting *PDB Admin* and *Set Active PDB Options*.

Additional information on using each of these collectors with SAS/CPE is available in the online Help Index in the SAS/CPE interactive interface.

TOOLNM=*tool*

specifies the name of the software that %CSPROCES will use to transform the logged data and stage the data into SAS data sets or data views. The %CSPROCES macro then processes the SAS data sets into the PDB libraries. **This parameter should be specified only if COLLECTOR=GENERIC, in which case the value should be SASDS.**

Optional Keyword Parameters

AGELIMIT=*number*

is the number of days worth of data to keep in the DETAIL level records of the PDB. **The default is the value defined in the Data Dictionary for each table**. Use this parameter to override on a single run, the age limit specified in the data dictionary for a table in the PDB. When you specify this parameter, it does not reset the dictionary value.

If you do not specify an input data set using the *rawdata* parameter or the GENLIB= parameter, the %CSPROCES macro reprocesses any existing data in DETAIL (and possibly ages out old data) based on the values of the AGELIMIT= and SUBSET= parameters.

Note: If AGELIMIT=0 at the DETAIL level in the data dictionary, your data is stored in DETAIL until the next reduce or process task runs. Therefore, if the reduce task runs immediately after the process task, the data is processed, reduced into the DETAIL levels, and then removed from DETAIL. However, if the process task runs again before the data have been reduced, the existing data in DETAIL is deleted before it is reduced to the non-DETAIL levels.

Using AGELIMIT=0 is useful if you are collecting and processing large amounts of data on a daily basis, but, to avoid losing data, you should always reduce the data immediately after they are processed.

COLDUMP=*command*

specifies the name of the snmpColDump command to be used to dump HP-OV data at your site. **The default is /usr/OV/bin/snmpColDump**.

COLLVER=*version-number*

specifies the version number of the SunNetManager collector from which you are processing data. This parameter is used to process data from older versions of the collector. Specify this parameter only if the data was collected using SunNet Manager Version 1, and in this case use the value COLLVER=1. Otherwise, do not specify this parameter.

EXITSRC=*exit-source*

specifies the location where SAS/CPE exit source programs are stored. The value of this parameter can be the name of a SAS catalog specified in the form of *libref.catname* or the complete pathname of a directory.

If you specify a SAS catalog name, use a SAS LIBNAME statement to associate the *libref* with the SAS library that contains the catalog.

If you want to process your data without exits, do not specify this parameter.

For more information on SAS/CPE exit processing, see the *Process Exits Overview* document available in the online Help Index in the SAS/CPE interactive interface.

GENLIB=*libref*
: specifies the *libref* for the SAS library that contains the staged data created by user-provided software, which are to be processed into a PDB using the GENERIC collector. The staged data may be a SAS data set, a SAS DATA step view, a SAS SQL view, or a SAS/ACCESS view. Use this parameter to specify the input data set for the process macro (%CSPROCES on UNIX or %CMPROCES on MVS), only if you specify COLLECTR=GENERIC and TOOLNM=SASDS. If you specify this parameter do not specify the *rawdata* parameter.

GROUP=*group-file*
: specifies the /etc/group file that can be used to translate **accton** process data group IDs from numbers to text strings. You must specify the group file from the host that collected the accounting data. **The default value is /etc/group.**

OPTIMIZE=TIME | DISK
: specifies whether you prefer to optimize the processing speed or the disk space while you are processing data into a PDB. When you process data into a PDB, SAS/CPE makes a copy of the PDB to prevent destroying the PDB if problems occur during processing. When you specify OPTIMIZE=TIME or omit this parameter, the extra copy of the PDB is made on the same disk that the original PDB is stored on. However, if you have limited disk space on the disk that contains the PDB's DETAIL data sets, you can specify OPTIMIZE=DISK, and the second copy of the PDB will be placed on another disk drive. **The default is OPTIMIZE=TIME**.

Note: When you specify OPTIMIZE=DISK, the second copy of the PDB is actually stored in your SAS WORK library. To specify where the work library is located, use the `-work` option on the SAS command. Be sure that both the PDB directory and the WORK directory that you specify are on disks that have sufficient space to store the largest DETAIL table that you will process.

PASSWD=*password-file*
: specifies the /etc/passwd file that can be used to translate **accton** process data userids from numbers to text strings. You must specify the password file from the host system that collected the accounting data. **The default value is /etc/passwd**.

_RC=*varname*
: identifies a macro variable that will contain the return code from this macro. For example, you might specify the variable name `retcode` to show the return code values from this macro. Values that may be returned are 0 and nonzero. A value of 0 indicates that the macro was successful. A nonzero value indicates that the macro failed. Check the explanatory message in the SAS log.

The macro variable value that is set by this parameter should only be used in batch.

RSHHOST=*remote-command*
: specifies the command and host to use in submitting other commands for remote execution, if you are using the HP-OV collector. For example, you might specify `rshhost=remsh netmon1`, where `remsh` is the UNIX command for executing remote commands and `netmon1` is the remote host on which to execute the commands. The value of RSHHOST= is used as the prefix for the value of the COLDUMP= parameter.

SUBSET=*expression*
: specifies a data subsetting expression or filtering criteria for new data that is being processed and stored in the detail-level library and for existing data already stored in the detail-level. If the expression is true, the observation is stored in the detail-level library. If the expression is false, the observation is not stored in or is deleted from (for currently stored data) the detail-level. If you do not specify the *rawdata* parameter, SUBSET= only affects the data currently stored at the DETAIL level of the PDB.

The format of the value *expression* follows the rules for IF expressions. Refer to *SAS Language: Reference, Version 6, First Edition* for details on specifying expressions.

Note: %CSPROCES does not verify the syntax of the subsetting expression before it attempts to run the expression. If you specify an invalid expression, the macro invocation fails.

Examples: %CSPROCES

1. SPECTRUM Data Gateway
2. SunNet Manager
3. HP Measure Ware
4. HP Network Node Manager
5. TRAKKER
6. UNIX Accounting Data
7. PROBE Agent Data
8. Example Subsetting Holiday Data
9. Example Using Multiple Time Zones

Note

If you have made dictionary updates that require table views to be rebuilt, such as adding variables or formula variables, the views will be rebuilt automatically when %CSPROCES runs. For more information on updating tables in batch, see %CPDDUTL.

If you are using the HP-OV collector and are planning to use the UNIX command REMSH to execute commands on remote hosts, you must have write access to the *rawdata* file specified on %CSPROCES.

Example: %CSPROCES for SPECTRUM Data Gateway

This example processes selected tables from a SPECTRUM Data Gateway data set. See the %CSCSIFMT macro for additional information on processing SPECTRUM data.

```
/*assign libref for SPECTRUM data */
libname specgway 'pathname/specgway';

/*create SAS formats in sitelib library */
%CSCSIFMT (modelds=specgway.model);

/*process SPECTRUM data */
%csproces(specgway.stat,
          cciifp cxytse csibce csil23 csihi2 csipng cciigs,
          collectr=spectrum,
          _rc=retcode);
%put csproces return code is &retcode;
```

Example: %CPROCES for SunNet Manager

This example processes a compressed SunNet Manager raw file. It pipes the output of the **uncompress** command to the %CSPROCES macro. The example keeps data for only host1 through host5:

```
%csproces(pipe 'uncompress -c /usr/snm/rawdata/log.15jan93.Z',
          snmhpf snmioc snmiod snmltp snmlup snmpgs snmrnc snmrns,
          collectr=sunetmgr,
          subset=machine in ('host1','host2','host3','host4','host5'),
          _rc=retcode);
%put csproces return code is &retcode;
```

Example: %CSPROCES for HP-PCS

This example processes one day of global records from the HP PCS raw files from host1 and host2 using the **pcsextract** shell script. It routes the *stderr* file to *extract.msgs*.

```
x '/bin/rm ~/extract.msgs';
%csproces(pipe "cspcsext -xp d-1 -g host1 host2 2>> ~/extract.msgs",
          *,
          collectr=hp-pcs,
          _rc=retcode);
%put csproces retcode=&retcode;

   /* list extract messages in case an error occurred */ -->
filename extrmsgs '~/extract.msgs';
data _null_;
   infile extrmsgs;
   input;
   put _infile_;
   run;
```

Note: The **pcsextract** shell script uses the PCS extract command to write PCS performance data to stdout. The script uses standard PCS options followed by a list of host names. Look for an example of the extract shell script in *sasroot*/misc/cpe/cspcsext. This file must be tailored for use at your site.

Example: %CSPROCES for HP Network Node Manager or IBM NetView for AIX

These examples process HP OpenView data. HP OpenView is used by both HP Network Node Manager and IBM NetView for AIX to collect MIB data.

Example 1

This example assumes that HP-OV is installed on the same machine on which you are running %CSPROCES.

```
%CSPROCES( '/usr/OV/databases/snmpCollect',
           hn2nix,
           collectr=HP-OV );
```

Example 2

This example uses the RSHHOST= parameter to specify that HP-OV is installed on a different machine from the one on which you are running %CSPROCES. It specifies that the HP-OV machine is named 'netmon1' and the command used to execute commands on the HP-OV machine is 'remsh'. The rawdata input directory used by %CSPROCES must be writable from both systems (for example, via nfs):

```
%CSPROCES( /nfs/mo/usr/OV/databases/snmpCollect,
           hn2nix hn2ift,
           rshhost=remsh netmon1,
           collectr=HP-OV );
```

Example 3

This example assumes that you have created a sequential file of HP-OV data using, for example, the script in `!sasroot/misc/cpe/cpecoldm`. When you use %CSPROCES in this manner it is generally less convenient than if you read the directory of files of raw HP-OV data directly, but it may be necessary if it is difficult for you to obtain the required mount authorities to volumes on the HP-OV host at your site.

```
%CSPROCES( /usr/tmp/snmpCollect.01Jan96,
           hn2nix hn2ift,
           collectr=HP-OV );
```

Example: %CSPROCES for TRAKKER

This example processes TRAKKER data. Note that the name of the raw data file in the %CSPROCES macro is enclosed in quotation marks, but the quotes are not required.

```
%csproces('/disk1/tkr/rawdata/concord.9302.rawdata',
          tkrpcl tkrsts tkrip_ tkrdll,
          collectr=trakker,
          _rc=retcode);
%put csproces retcode=&retcode;
```

Example: %CSPROCES for UNIX Accounting Data

This example processes UNIX accounting data for an HP/UX system and uses a **pipe** command to prefix the machine name to the raw file:

```
%csproces(pipe 'echo "machine=cpu1";cat /usr/pacct',
          acchp7,
          passwd=/nfs/disk1/etc/passwd, group=/nfs/disk1/etc/group,
          collectr=accton,
          _rc=retcode);
%put csproces retcode=&retcode;
```

Example: %CSPROCES for PROBE Agent Data

Example 1

This example processes PROBE Agent data. Note that in Example 1 and Example 2, the name of the raw data file in the %CSPROCES step is enclosed in quotation marks, but the quotes are not required.

```
%csproces('/probex/logfile',
          prxbuf prxcld,
          collectr=probex,
          _rc=retcode);
%put csproces retcode=&retcode;
```

Example 2

In this example the data collected by SunNet Manager and PROBE Agent are identical.

```
%csproces('/snm/logfile',
          spxbuf spxcld,
          collectr=sunetmgr,
          _rc=retcode);
%put csproces retcode=&retcode;
```

Example: %CSPROCES for Subsetting Holiday Data

This example processes data only for nonholidays. In this example, the shift CODE for holidays is 0, which is also the SAS/CPE default holiday shift CODE.

```
%csproces('/raw/file',
          snmhpf snmiod,
          collectr=sunetmgr,
          subset=shift^="0",
          _rc=retcode);
%put csproces retcode=&retcode;
```

Example: %CSPROCES for Using Multiple Timezones

This example processes data from one file using the default time zone for the PDB (the Eastern time zone of the United States) and then resets the time zone macro variable to process data from a different time zone. These values can be set via the *PDB Admin, Set Active PDB Options* menu selections in the SAS/CPE interactive interface, or using the `cpgmtdev` global macro variable as demonstrated in this example.

```
%csproces('/snm/cary/logfile', /* this processes the local data */
          snmhpf,
          collectr=sunetmgr,
          _rc=retcode);
%put return code from Cary csproces is &retcode;
  /* this sets up to process data from a different time zone*/
%let olddst=&cpdstime;   /* save previous Daylight Savings Time */
%let olddev=&cpgmtdev;   /* save previous time zone */
%let cpdstime=;          /* no Daylight Savings Time */
%let cpgmtdev=-1;        /* specifies a city one hour east of Greenwich */
    /* process the new daylight savings time data */
%CSPROCES('/snm/cityname/logfile',
          snmhpf,
          collectr=sunetmgr,
          _rc=retcode);
%put Return code from CSPROCES is &retcode;

%let cpdstime=&olddst;   /* restore previous Daylight Savings Time */
%let cpgmtdev=&olddev;   /* restore previous time zone */
```

%CSRAWLST

Produces a list of records from a raw data file on UNIX

Purpose

The %CSRAWLST macro provides a list ouptut from your raw data file. This macro must run after the %CSPROCES macro because %CSPROCES provides the name of the *rawdata* file. The %CSRAWLST macro is useful in debugging or diagnosing problems with logged data. When you run this macro, the first 10 lines of raw data are listed by default, or you can specify the number of lines to display.

Syntax

```
%CSRAWLST(<NLINES=>);
```

%CSRAWLST Parameters

NLINES=*number-of-lines*
: is the number of lines to list from the raw data file. **The default number of lines is 10.**

%CSUT2ST

Convert UNIX Datetime to SAS Datetime

Purpose

The %CSUT2ST macro converts a UNIX datetime value, which is the number of seconds since January 1, 1970, in Greenwich Mean Time, to a SAS datetime value, which is the number of seconds since January 1, 1960. It is useful when writing a SAS data step to read data from a collector that is not supported by SAS/CPE, into a SAS data set. The data can then be passed into SAS/CPE using a Generic Collector (see the **%CSPROCES** macro).

You can also use %CSUT2ST to set the SHIFT and HOUR variables based on the datetime stamp because these variables are commonly used to classify data in a SAS/CPE performance database. You must run this macro before you run the %CSPROCES macro to process the data with the new datetime formats.

Syntax

```
%CSUT2ST(<GMTDEV=hours-difference>,
         <DSTEXPR=date-range>,
         <HOLIDAY=YES | NO>,
         <_RC=varname>,
         <SASDATM=sas-datetime-variable>,
         <SHIFT=shift-variable>,
         <SHIFTS=shift-description>,
         <UNIXDATM=unix-datetime-variable>) ;
```

%CSUT2ST Parameters

GMTDEV=*hours-difference*

specifies the number of hours difference in the local time zone from Greenwich Mean Time. **This value is required**. For example, the value for the eastern coast of the United States is 5 and the value for Heidleburg, Germany is -1. The value of GMTDEV= is used with the UNIXDATM= parameter to create the value that is assigned to the variable named in the SASDATM= parameter.

DSTEXPR=*date-range*

specifies the range of dates when Daylight Savings Time is in effect. This value is required if your site uses Daylight Savings Time. If this value is not defined, **the default value is used, which is set when SAS/CPE is installed at your site**. The default value is based on the U.S. standard Daylight Savings Time for the current year when SAS/CPE is installed or updated. If Daylight Savings Time is not used in your time zone, set DSTEXPR= to a blank. The following example sets the Daylight Savings Time for 1995 and 1996:

```
dstexpr="03APR96:3:0"dt<datetime<"30OCT96:2:0"dt |
        "04APR95:3:0"dt<datetime<"31OCT95:2:0"dt
```

HOLIDAY=YES | NO

indicates whether the shift for holidays is defined in the CPHDAY format in the interactive interface. If you specify NO, the system treats holidays as the standard day of the week on which the holiday falls. **The default is HOLIDAY=NO**. If HOLIDAY=YES, you must supply a format called CPHDAY that specifies what shift value to use for holidays. This can be done by following this path from the interactive interface:

PDB Admin -> Define Work Shifts

To use this format, specify HOLIDAY=YES and add the SAS/CPE format catalog CPFMTS to the standard format search path as shown here:

```
libname f "sasroot/saspgm/cpe/pgmlib";
options fmtsearch=(f.cpfmts);
```

To use the holidays established for your site, add your site's format catalog to the standard format search path as shown here:

```
libname f "/your/sitelib";
options fmtsearch=(f.cpfmts);
```

_RC=*varname*

identifies the name of a macro variable that will contain the return code from %CSUT2ST. The values that can occur in this variable are 0 and nonzero. The value 0 indicates that this macro was successful. A nonzero value indicates a failure. Check the explanatory message in the SAS log.

SASDATM=*SAS-datetime-variable*

is the name of the variable where the reformatted SAS datetime value is stored. **The default variable is DATETIME**.

SHIFT=*shift-variable*

is the name of the variable to contain the shift code. *shift-variable* must be a single-character shift code. **The default variable name is SHIFT**. If you specify this parameter, you must also specify the SHIFTS= parameter.

SAS/CPE software sets the value of the SHIFT= variable by using the SHIFTS= value and the value of the SASDATM= variable to determine the shift for the data. However, if HOLIDAY=YES and the observation falls on a site holiday, the holiday code is used instead of the value from the SHIFTS= parameter.

SHIFTS=*shift-descriptions*

lists which shift is in effect for each of the 168 hours in a week. **By default, 8 a.m. to 5 p.m., Monday through Friday is the first shift; all other times are second shift**. You set these values by creating a grid of time and specifying the shift for each hour in the week. The values for this parameter are based on this grid:

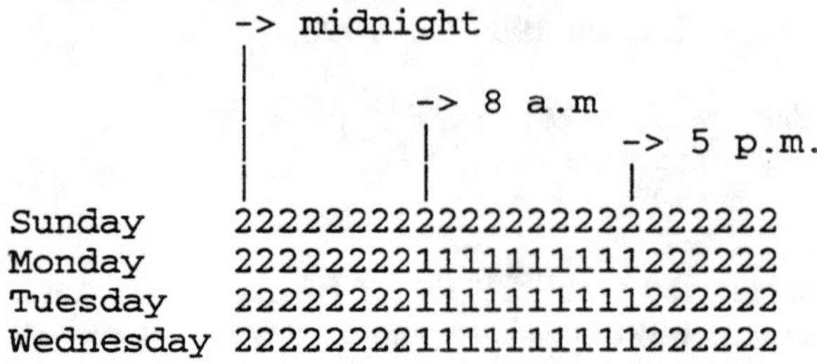

```
          -> midnight
          |
          |       -> 8 a.m
          |       |         -> 5 p.m.
          |       |         |
Sunday    222222222222222222222222
Monday    222222221111111112222222
Tuesday   222222221111111112222222
Wednesday 222222221111111112222222
```

```
Thursday  222222221111111111222222
Friday    222222221111111111222222
Saturday  222222222222222222222222
```

This example illustrates how to specify 8 a.m. through 4 p.m., Monday through Friday, as shift 1 and all other times as shift 2.

```
shifts="222222222222222222222222" ||
       "222222221111111122222222" ||
       "222222221111111122222222" ||
       "222222221111111122222222" ||
       "222222221111111122222222" ||
       "222222221111111122222222" ||
       "222222222222222222222222"
```

UNIXDATM=*UNIX-datetime-variable*

specifies the name of the variable which contains the UNIX datetime value in your data. **The default variable name is UNIXDATM**. The value of GMTDEV= is used with the UNIXDATM= parameter to create the value that is assigned to the variable named in the SASDATM= parameter.

Chapter 3

SAS/CPE® Report Macros

%CPCCHRT

Multiple Variable Category Charts

Purpose

The %CPCCHRT macro plots statistics for as many as 15 analysis variables in one chart. Each analysis variable represents a category or group of data and each analysis variable is represented by a separate bar, block, star, or pie slice. You can select any of the following types of charts:

- horizontal bar chart
- vertical bar chart
- pie chart
- block chart
- star chart.

If the chart TYPE=HBAR, the analysis variables and labels display on the left (Y) axis. If the chart TYPE=VBAR, the analysis variables and labels display on the X axis. The other chart types do use X and Y axes to display the analysis variables.

This type of report is useful when you have multiple analysis variables and each variable represents a category or group of data. For example, if you are analyzing packet rates, your data might be displayed in groups, such as incoming packets, local packets, and outgoing packets, which would be your analysis variables. All variables for the chart should have the same unit of measurement. By default, the mean value of each variable is charted. Use the STAT= parameter to change the statistic that is plotted.

For more information on the underlying procedure, refer to "The GCHART Procedure in Chapter 23 of *SAS/GRAPH Software: Reference, Version 6, First Edition, Volume 2*.

Syntax

```
%CPCCHRT(dataset,
          var1,lab1 ... var15, lab15,
          REDLVL=reduction-level,
         <ACROSS=number>,
         <AXIS=value-list>,
         <BEGIN=SAS-datetime-value>,
         <BY=BY-variable-list>,
         <DOWN=number>,
         <END=SAS-datetime-value>,
         <GROUP=grouping-variable>,
         <GRP_LAB=label>,
         <OUTDESC=text>,
         <OUTLOC=output-location>,
         <OUTMODE=output-format>,
         <OUTNAME=physical-filename|entry-name>,
         <PERIOD=time-interval>,
         <SGRP_LAB=label>,
         <STAT=statistic>,
         <STACKVAR=variable>,
         <SUBGROUP=variable>,
```

```
<TABTYPE=INTERVAL|EVENT>,
<TYPE=chart-type>,
<WHERE=where-expression>,
<YVAL=number> ) ;
```

%CPCCHRT Parameters

dataset

specifies the table name from which to generate the report. **This positional parameter is required** and it can be specified in one of three ways.

If the data are in the DETAIL, DAY, WEEK, MONTH, or YEAR levels of the active PDB:

- ☐ Specify a tablename via the *dataset* parameter and a level via the **REDLVL=** parameter. If the REDLVL= parameter is not specified for the table name, REDLVL=DETAIL.

- ☐ Specify the name in the format of *REDLVL.TABLE*, in which case the REDLVL= parameter is not required.

If the data are in a SAS library that is not in the DETAIL, DAY, WEEK, MONTH, or YEAR level of the active PDB:

- ☐ Specify a two-level name in the format *libref.data-set-name* and specify REDLVL=OTHER.

Note: When specifying the data set name using the *libref* format, you must assign a *libref* before this macro is invoked. For more information see the LIBNAME statement in Chapter 9 of *SAS Language: Reference, Version 6, First Edition.*

var1,lab1 . . . var15,lab15

specifies a paired list of analysis variable names and labels (up to 16 characters) for the analysis axis. The maximum number of pairs you can specify is 15. **This positional parameter is required.** You must specify at least one variable and one label.

The analysis variable typically displays on the left (Y) axis. However, certain combinations of parameters may affect the axis on which the analysis variable is displayed or the number of variables that can be specified for a specific report. For a detailed explanation of the variables displayed on each axis and the maximum number of variables that can be specified for the report, refer to the *Purpose* section of the macro description.

If you specify multiple analysis variables, the unit of measure for all of the variables should be the same and the range of values should be similar. You may use blank characters in the label and you may enclose the label in single quotes, but the quotes are not required.

Caution: *Do not include commas, equal signs, parentheses, or ampersands in the labels.*

REDLVL=*reduction-level*

specifies which level of the table you are reporting on: DETAIL, DAY, WEEK, MONTH, YEAR, or OTHER. **The default is DETAIL**. The value of this parameter is used as a libref. You should specify REDLVL=OTHER if you want to select a SAS data set. The SAS data set should contain a variable named DATETIME, which represents the datetime stamp for each observation.

Note: When specifying the data set name using the *libref* format, you must assign a *libref* before this macro is invoked. For more information see the LIBNAME statement in Chapter 9 of *SAS Language: Reference, Version 6, First Edition.*

Optional Keyword Parameters

ACROSS=*number*

specifies the number of star or pie charts to place across a single graph page. **The default is one.**

AXIS=*value-list*

specifies the value for the major tick marks on the analysis axis (the X axis for horizontal bar charts and the Y axis for vertical bar charts). These examples illustrate ways you can specify the *value-list*:

```
n n . . . n
n TO n <BY increment>
n n . . . n TO n <BY increment> <n . . . n>
```

For more information about the *value-list*, see the ORDER= parameter in Chapter 9, "The AXIS Statement," of *SAS/GRAPH Software: Reference, Version 6, First Edition, Volume 1.*

Note: The values for AXIS= must be specified as actual values, not formatted values. Thus, the tick marks for time values must be either a count of seconds or a SAS time constant, such as '12:20:01.8't. You must specify percentages as decimal values, such as .10 to .80 for 10% to 80%.

BEGIN=*SAS-datetime-value*

represents the first date and time for data to include in the report. The *sas-datetime-value* must be in the DATETIME13. SAS format. For example, BEGIN=01jul96:08:45. Use this parameter in combination with **END=** to define the range for subsetting data for the report. You can also use the TODAY[-*nnnn*]@*hh:mm* format, which uses the current date value minus *nnnn* days at the specified hour. This format supports the symbol or the word (@ or at) for the "at" instruction. For example, the following combination of values reports on the last three days of data, beginning at 8:00 a.m. three days ago and ending today at 5:00 p.m.

```
begin=today-3@08:00, end=todayat17:00
```

If you omit the time, the default time for the BEGIN= parameter is 00:00 on the specified date and the default time for the END= parameter is 23:59 on the specified date.

This example illustrates specific dates:

```
begin=01jul96:08:00, end=31jul96:17:00
```

If you omit the BEGIN= and END= parameters, the macro uses the information stored with the table definition (in the data dictionary) for the earliest and most recent datetime values at the specified level. The values stored with the table definition are based on the data currently in that level of the table. Exception: If the level is set to OTHER, the macro reads the data to determine the earliest and most recent datetime values (because there is not a table definition).

If you use only one parameter, BEGIN= or END=, that datetime is restricted and the other value is based on the data.

BY=*BY-variable-list*

lists the variables by which your data is sorted in the PDB. Use blanks to separate the variables in the list. A separate graph is produced for each value of the BY variable or for each combination of BY variable values, if you have multiple BY variables. For example, if you have four *diskids* on three machines, the following setting for the BY= parameter produces twelve reports, one for each of the twelve unique combinations of machine and *diskid* values.

```
by=machine diskid
```

For an alternate method of handling unique values of variables, refer to the description of class variables in the report you are producing.

If there is no BY= parameter, observations are sorted in the order that the variables are listed in the BY variable list or class variable list in the PDB. To check the order, follow this path from the main menu of the SAS/CPE interactive interface:

PDB Admin -> **Config Active PDB Dictionary** -> *select table*
-> **ItemActions** -> **Browse Definition**

or submit a batch job in which the **%CPDDUTL** macro runs a LIST TABLE control statement.

If you want to change the BY variables or their order for a one-time job, the fastest way to do so is to run a SAS program that contains the following statements:

```
proc sort data=level.table out=sasuser.table;
   by one-time-BY-variables-list;
```

where *level* is the reduction level on which to base the report, *table* is the table that you want to base the report on, *cpe-pdb* is the complete directory path or high-level-qualifiers and the name of the PDB you want to base your report on, and *one-time-BY-variables-list* is a list of the BY variables you want to use in the report. Order the variables from major to minor and separate the variables by blanks. After you run this program, run the report definition on the data in SASUSER.*table*.

Before changing the BY-variables or their order in the data dictionary you should be aware of the following:

- Changes to the BY-variables will not take effect in the data until the next process or reduce task runs or you execute the %CPDDUTL macro with the BUILD VIEWS control statement.
- The BY-variables list specified on any reports must match the current BY-variables list in the PDB. Therefore, if you have updated the BY-variables for a table in the PDB, you should examine all report definitions that use this table to see if the

definition should be changed to match the new BY-variables list.

- When the BY-variables list is updated (via the process or reduce task or the BUILD VIEWS statement), the data in the PDB is physically sorted. Depending on the number of observations in the tables being sorted, this can take a considerable amount of time.
- It is not good practice to change the BY-variables list frequently. If you are changing the BY-variables list regularly in order to produce reports, you either have not chosen a good set of BY-variables or you have an incomplete understanding of how to create the report you want.

To change the BY variables list using the interactive interface, invoke SAS/CPE with update access to the PDB and then follow this path from the primary menu:

PDB Admin -> Config Active PDB Dictionary -> ***select table***
-> ItemActions -> Edit Definition

You can also use the **UPDATE TABLE** statement in the %CPDDUTL macro to change the BY variables list in batch mode.

DOWN=*number*

specifies the number of star or pie charts to place vertically on a single graph page. **The default is 1.**

END=*SAS-datetime-value*

represents the last date and time for data to include in the report. The *sas-datetime-value* must be in the DATETIME13. SAS format or in the today[-*nnnn*]@*hh:mm* format. For example, END=01jul96:17:00 or END=today-1@17:00.

Use this parameter in combination with BEGIN= to define the range for subsetting data for the report. Refer to **BEGIN=** for more information on using these parameters.

GROUP=*grouping-variable*

is the name of a variable that subsets the observations. The analysis variables are represented by bars and display in groups, with one group for each value of the group variable. If the TYPE= parameter for this macro is BAR or BLOCK, the groups of bars display in the form of a chart, with all groups on one chart. If TYPE= STAR or PIE, the analysis variables are represented by stars or pieces of pie and a separate chart displays for each unique value of the group variable. You may use the GROUP= parameter with either the STACKVAR= parameter or the SUBGROUP= parameter, but not both.

GRP_LAB=*label*

is the label (as many as 16 characters) for the variable specified by the GROUP= parameter. You may use blank characters. You may enclose the label in single quotes, but the quotes are not required.

Caution: *Do not include commas, equal signs, parentheses, or ampersands in the label.*

OUTDESC=*text*

is a description (as many as 40 characters) of the output.

If OUTMODE=CATALOG, the description is stored with the entry in the SAS catalog

specified in the OUTLOC= parameter. Otherwise, the description is ignored.

OUTLOC=*output-location*

is the physical location of a graphics stream file, a SAS catalog name, or the physical location of the file or catalog member (for text reports only). The value of the OUTNAME= parameter is appended to the value of this parameter to specify the complete output location. Specify this parameter if you specify the OUTMODE= parameter.

OUTMODE=*output-format*

specifies the format for the output. **The default value is GWINDOW for all reports except %CPTABRPT. The default for %CPTABRPT is the output window.**

Valid values for this parameter are:

LP

stores the output as a text file. If you specify OUTMODE=LP, you should also specify the OUTLOC and OUTNAME parameters for the text report. If you do not specify the output location (OUTLOC=), the output is sent to the output window or standard SASLIST file. **This value is not valid for the %CPSPEC, %CPG3D, or %CPGTPLT macros.**

GSF

stores the output as a graphics stream file. If you specify OUTMODE=GSF, you must also specify the OUTLOC and OUTNAME parameters. **This value is not valid for the %CPXTAB and %CPTABRPT macros.**

CATALOG

stores the output as a GRSEG entry in a SAS catalog. If you are producing a graph report and you specify OUTMODE=CATALOG, you should also specify the OUTLOC, OUTNAME, and OUTDESC parameters. **This value is not valid for the %CPXTAB and %CPTABRPT macros.**

The following table summarizes which parameters should be specified in addition to OUTMODE=, based on the report type and the value of the OUTMODE= parameter.

When OUTMODE=	Specify these additional parameters			Not valid for these macros
LP	-	OUTLOC	OUTNAME	%CPSPEC, %CPG3D %CPGTPLT
GSF	-	OUTLOC	OUTNAME	%CPXTAB, %CPTABRPT
CATALOG	OUTDESC	OUTLOC	OUTNAME	%CPXTAB, %CPTABRPT

For more information on using OUTMODE= with OUTNAME= and OUTLOC=, see **Examples of the OUTMODE= Parameter**.

Caution: *OUTMODE=LP is the only valid option for reports that produce text output, for example those that use procedures such as TABULATE, REPORT, or PRINT. If you specify*

OUTMODE=CATALOG for a text report, the OUTLOC= and OUTNAME= parameters are ignored.

The OUTNAME and OUTLOC parameters execute PROC PRINTTO in the background to set the output filename and location. When PROC PRINTTO is set, it stays in effect for subsequent text reports for the current SAS session until it is reset by another PROC PRINTTO. Therefore, after you set the OUTNAME and OUTLOC parameters and run your report, you must reset these values if you want the output from future reports to go to another location.

Furthermore, unless you have experience using PROC PRINTTO, you should not use the OUTNAME and OUTLOC parameters when PROC PRINTTO is executed because the commands may override each other and send your output to a location other than the one you expected. PROC PRINTTO does not produce a data set or printed output. It is useful when you want to route output from different steps in a SAS job to different files.

For more information on using PROC PRINTTO, refer to Chapter 28 of the *SAS Procedures Guide, Version 6, Third Edition.*

Note: The SAS/CPE interactive interface handles report output different from the OUTMODE=, OUTLOC=, and OUTNAME= batch parameters. In the interactive interface, use the value GWINDOW to display the report output in a GRAPH window, and use the value LP to display the report output in an OUTPUT window. In both cases, omit the OUTDESC=, OUTLOC=, and OUTNAME= parameters. Specify these parameters only if you use OUTMODE=GSF or CATALOG.

If you are running SAS/CPE in batch mode (i.e., you have executed it from within a cron job or from the MVS batch scheduler) and are running a graph report, you should specify an output location other than the graph window.

OUTNAME=*physical-filename* | *entry-name*

is the name of the external file or the entry-name in the SAS catalog where you want to store output results. Catalog entries are stored as GRSEG type entries. The value of this parameter is appended to the value of the OUTLOC= parameter to specify the complete output location.

Specify this parameter whenever you specify the OUTMODE= parameter, except when you specify OUTMODE=CATALOG.

PERIOD=*time-interval*

is the summarization period for the report. **The default is ASIS**. For values other than ASIS, the values for the time period within a class or category are combined to form a single point on a plot, a bar on a chart, or a row or column in a table.

Notes: For the %CPCHART and %CPXTAB macros, PERIOD= is only valid if the class variable is DATETIME. For the %CPCCHRT macro, PERIOD= is only valid if the DATETIME variable is selected in any category.

```
Period     Effect                     Example
```

ASIS	leaves datetime in its present form.	09Jun94:14:37:25
15MIN	transforms the time to the first minute of the 15-minute period in the hour and retains the date.	09Jun94:14:30
HOUR	transforms the time to the first minute of the hour and retains the date.	09Jun94:14:00
24HOUR	transforms the time to its hour component and omits the date. Range: 0-23.	14
DATE	omits the time and retains the date.	09Jun94
WHOLEDAY	same as DATE.	
WEEKDAY	transforms the day to the day of the week (where 1=Sunday, 2=Monday, and so on) and omits the month, year, and time. Range: 1-7, which displays as Sunday-Saturday.	Thursday
MONTHDAY	omits everything but the day of the month. Range: 1-31.	9
YEARDAY	transforms the day to the day of the year and omits the month, year, and time. Range: 1-366.	160
WEEK	transforms the date to first date in the week (where the week begins on the day on which January 1 falls in the year) and omits the time.	04Jun94
MONTH	omits the day and the time	Jun94
YEARMONTH	omits everything but the month of the year. Range: 1-12.	6
QTR	transforms the month to the first month of the quarter and omits the day and time.	Apr94

SGRP_LAB=*label*

is the label (as many as 16 characters) for the variable specified by the SUBGROUP=

parameter for this macro. You may use blank characters. You may enclose the label in single quotes, but the quotes are not required.

Caution: *Do not include commas, equal signs, parentheses, or ampersands in the label.*

STAT=*statistic*

specifies what statistic to use to summarize data that span the time interval specified by **PERIOD=**. The selected statistic is used for all variables in the report. **The default statistic is MEAN**. The STAT= parameter is not valid if PERIOD=ASIS. Valid values for STAT= are:

CSS

is the sum of squares corrected for the mean.

CV

is the coefficient of variation. It is calculated as the standard deviation divided by the mean and multiplied by 100.

MAX

is the maximum value for all observations.

MEAN

is the arithmetic average. Mean is one measure used to describe the center of a distribution of values.

MIN

is the minimum value for all observations.

N

or COUNT, is the number of observations with nonmissing values for the variables being summarized.

NMISS

the number of observations with missing values for the variable being summarized.

RANGE

is the maximum of the difference between the maximum and minimum values for the variables, RANGE=MAX-MIN.

STD

is the standard deviation or square root of variance. Like the variance, it is a measure of the dispersion about the mean, but in the same unit of measure as the data.

STDERR

is the positive square root of the variance of a statistic.

SUM

is the sum of values for all observations.

USS

is the uncorrected sum of squares.

VAR

is a measure of the dispersion or variability of the data about the mean. When values are close to the mean, the variance is small. When values are scattered widely about the mean, the variance is large.

Note: If you specify the **BY=** parameter, the statistics are calculated separately for each value of the BY variable or for each combination of the BY variable values, if you specified multiple BY variables.

STACKVAR=*variable*

is the name of a variable by which your data is subdivided. A separate bar or block is produced for each value of the STACKVAR variable. Each bar is divided into sections, one for each analysis variable. The variable contains the same information as the SUBGROUP= parameter, but the presentation is different. Do not use the STACKVAR= parameter if you use the SUBGROUP= parameter.

SUBGROUP=*variable*

is the name of a variable. This variable subdivides the groups that are specified by the value of the GROUP= parameter. Each subdivision becomes a section of a bar. The variable contains the same information as the STACKVAR= parameter, but the presentation is different. You cannot specify a subgroup variable if the TYPE= parameter value is PIE or STAR.

TABTYPE=INTERVAL | EVENT

specifies whether the data cover a specified interval of time or whether they are logged in response to an event that occurs, such as when a job begins or ends. **INTERVAL is the default value.**

INTERVAL

each observation represents an interval of time.

EVENT

each observation represents an event.

TYPE=*chart-type*

is the type of chart to produce. **The default type is HBAR.** Valid values are:

BLOCK

creates a three-dimensional block chart in which the height of each block represents the statistic for the variable being charted.

HBAR

creates a horizontal bar chart in which the length of each bar represents the statistic for the variable being charted.

PIE

creates a circular pie chart in which the size of each piece represents the statistic for the variable being charted.

STAR

creates a star chart in which the size of each piece represents the statistic for the variable being charted.

VBAR

creates a vertical bar chart in which the height of each bar represents the statistic for the variable being charted.

WHERE=*where-expression*

specifies an expression that subsets the data to be reported on. Valid operators include, but are not limited to, BETWEEN AND, CONTAINS, LIKE, IN, IS NULL or IS MISSING. For example, the following statement limits the included observations to only those where the value of machine is 'host1' or 'host2':

```
where=machine in ('host1','host2')
```

For more information on these and other where operators, see the WHERE statement in Chapter 9 of *SAS Language: Reference, Version 6, First Edition.*

YVAL=*number*

is the number of Y values to print on one page of the graph. For example, if the graph TYPE= BLOCK, HBAR or PIE for this macro, this parameter specifies the number of block, bar, or pie charts to print on one page. **The default number is based on the output device type**. If the number of specified variables, groups, sub-groups, or stack variables is greater than the value of YVAL=, the chart is broken into multiple pages. For example, if you specfied a group variable that had nine instances, such as nine different machines, and you set YVAL=6, your graph would print on two pages. The first page would contain a graph with the first six bars or slices of pie and the second page would contain a graph with the last three bars or slices of pie.

Example: %CPCCHRT

This example generates a report with horizontal bars, one bar for each value (0-9) of the performance group variable. Each bar is subdivided into segments, one segment for each value of the shift variable. The length of each bar and each subdivision of a bar is based on the number of active frames that are in the observations with the specified performance group variable and the specified shift variable. The report's destination is an entry in a SAS catalog named SASUSER.CPUPGMS.CHCCHRT.GRSEG. You should specify a catalog or filename appropriate for your host operating system.

```
options pagesize=60 linesize=132;

goptions reset=title reset=footnote colors=(w r b g);
%cpcchrt(tababc,acfrmtn,Active frame
         ,group=perfgrp
         ,outmode=catalog
         ,subgroup=shift
         ,type=hbar
         ,weight=duration
         ,yval=16
         ,redlvl=detail
         ,where=perfgrp<=9
         ,outloc=sasuser.cpupgms
         ,outname=cpcchrt);
```

Note

If you want to use a single analysis variable, you may use the GROUP=, STACKVAR=, or SUBGROUP= parameter to group or subdivide the data on the report. If you want to use a primary and a secondary analysis variable, you may use either the GROUP= parameter and the STACKVAR= parameter, or the GROUP= parameter and the SUBGROUP= parameter. The STACKVAR= and SUBGROUP= parameters both subdivide the data and cannot be used at the same time. The difference between them is how the subdivisions are presented. The STACKVAR= parameter uses separate bars for the subdivisions. The SUBGROUP= parameter uses separate sections of the bar for subdivisions.

%CPCHART

Single Variable Charts

Purpose

The %CPCHART macro charts the values of a single analysis variable (*var1*) categorized by the values of a single class variable (*classname*). This macro can produce any of these types of charts:

- horizontal bar chart
- vertical bar chart
- pie chart
- block chart
- star chart.

Each bar, pie slice, block, or star peak represents a value of the analysis variable for each discrete value of the classification variable. A separate bar or pie slice is produced for each value of the class variable. Use the STAT= parameter to define the type of statistic calculated for the analysis variable.

For more information on the underlying procedure, refer to "The GCHART Procedure," in Chapter 23 of *SAS/GRAPH Software: Reference, Version 6, First Edition, Volume 2*.

Syntax

```
%CPCHART(dataset,
         classname,
        <classlabel>,
         var1,lab1,
         REDLVL=reduction-level,
        <ACROSS=number>,
        <AXIS=value-list>,
        <BEGIN=SAS-datetime-value>,
        <BY=BY-variable-list>,
        <DOWN=number>,
        <END=SAS-datetime-value>,
        <GROUP=grouping-variable>,
        <GRP_LAB=label>,
        <ORDER=DESCENDING|ASCENDING|MIDPOINT>,
        <OUTDESC=text>,
        <OUTLOC=output-location>,
        <OUTMODE=output-format>,
        <OUTNAME=physical-filename|entry-name>,
        <PERIOD=time-interval>,
        <SGRP_LAB=label>,
        <STAT=statistic>,
        <SUBGROUP=variable>,
        <TABTYPE=INTERVAL|EVENT>,
        <TOPN=number>,
        <TYPE=chart-type>,
        <WHERE=where-expression>,
        <YVAL=number> ) ;
```

%CPCHART Parameters

dataset

specifies the table name from which to generate the report. **This positional parameter is required** and it can be specified in one of three ways.

If the data are in the DETAIL, DAY, WEEK, MONTH, or YEAR levels of the active PDB:

- ☐ Specify a tablename via the *dataset* parameter and a level via the **REDLVL=** parameter. If the REDLVL= parameter is not specified for the table name, REDLVL=DETAIL.

- ☐ Specify the name in the format of *REDLVL.TABLE*, in which case the REDLVL= parameter is not required.

If the data are in a SAS library that is not in the DETAIL, DAY, WEEK, MONTH, or YEAR level of the active PDB:

- ☐ Specify a two-level name in the format *libref.data-set-name* and specify REDLVL=OTHER.

Note: When specifying the data set name using the *libref* format, you must assign a *libref* before this macro is invoked. For more information see the LIBNAME statement in Chapter 9 of *SAS Language: Reference, Version 6, First Edition.*

classname

specifies the name of the class variable for the report. For each unique value of the class variable the macro creates a separate portion of the chart, for example a piece of pie on a pie chart, but all values of the class variable are included in a single chart. This is different from the **BY=** parameter, which creates separate charts for each unique value of the BY= parameter. **This positional parameter is required.**

classlabel

is the label for the class variable. The label can be a maximum of 16 characters in length and you may use blank characters. You may enclose the label in single quotes, but the quotes are not required. **This positional parameter is not required**, however if you do not specify this parameter you must specify a comma as a placeholder.

Caution: *Do not include commas, equal signs, parentheses, or ampersands in the label.*

var1,lab1

specifies the analysis variable name and label (up to 16 characters). **This positional parameter is required**. You may use blank characters and you may enclose the label in single quotes, but the quotes are not required.

Caution: *Do not include commas, equal signs, parenthesis, or ampersands in the labels.*

REDLVL=*reduction-level*

specifies which level of the table you are reporting on: DETAIL, DAY, WEEK, MONTH, YEAR, or OTHER. **The default is DETAIL**. The value of this parameter is used as a libref. You should specify REDLVL=OTHER if you want to select a SAS data set. The SAS data set should contain a variable named DATETIME, which represents the datetime stamp for each observation.

Note: When specifying the data set name using the *libref* format, you must assign a *libref* before this macro is invoked. For more information see the LIBNAME statement in Chapter 9 of *SAS Language: Reference, Version 6, First Edition.*

Optional Keyword Parameters

ACROSS=*number*

specifies the number of star or pie charts to place across a single graph page. **The default is one.**

AXIS=*value-list*

specifies the value for the major tick marks on the analysis axis (the X axis for horizontal bar charts and the Y axis for vertical bar charts). These examples illustrate ways you can specify the *value-list*:

```
n n . . . n
n TO n <BY increment>
n n . . . n TO n <BY increment> <n . . . n>
```

For more information about the *value-list*, see the ORDER= parameter in Chapter 9, "The AXIS Statement," of *SAS/GRAPH Software: Reference, Version 6, First Edition, Volume 1.*

Note: The values for AXIS= must be specified as actual values, not formatted values. Thus, the tick marks for time values must be either a count of seconds or a SAS time constant, such as '12:20:01.8't. You must specify percentages as decimal values, such as .10 to .80 for 10% to 80%.

BEGIN=*SAS-datetime-value*

represents the first date and time for data to include in the report. The *sas-datetime-value* must be in the DATETIME13. SAS format. For example, BEGIN=01jul96:08:45. Use this parameter in combination with <u>END=</u> to define the range for subsetting data for the report. You can also use the TODAY[*-nnnn*]@*hh:mm* format, which uses the current date value minus *nnnn* days at the specified hour. This format supports the symbol or the word (@ or at) for the "at" instruction. For example, the following combination of values reports on the last three days of data, beginning at 8:00 a.m. three days ago and ending today at 5:00 p.m.

```
begin=today-3@08:00, end=todayat17:00
```

If you omit the time, the default time for the BEGIN= parameter is 00:00 on the specified date and the default time for the END= parameter is 23:59 on the specified date.

This example illustrates specific dates:

```
begin=01jul96:08:00, end=31jul96:17:00
```

If you omit the BEGIN= and END= parameters, the macro uses the information stored with the table definition (in the data dictionary) for the earliest and most recent datetime values at the specified level. The values stored with the table definition are based on the data currently in that level of the table. Exception: If the level is set to OTHER, the macro reads the data to determine the earliest and most recent datetime values (because there is not a table definition).

If you use only one parameter, BEGIN= or END=, that datetime is restricted and the other value is based on the data.

BY=*BY-variable-list*

lists the variables by which your data is sorted in the PDB. Use blanks to separate the variables in the list. A separate graph is produced for each value of the BY variable or for each combination of BY variable values, if you have multiple BY variables. For example, if you have four *diskids* on three machines, the following setting for the BY= parameter produces twelve reports, one for each of the twelve unique combinations of machine and *diskid* values.

```
by=machine diskid
```

For an alternate method of handling unique values of variables, refer to the description of class variables in the report you are producing.

If there is no BY= parameter, observations are sorted in the order that the variables are listed in the BY variable list or class variable list in the PDB. To check the order, follow this path from the main menu of the SAS/CPE interactive interface:

PDB Admin -> **Config Active PDB Dictionary** -> *select table*
-> **ItemActions** -> **Browse Definition**

or submit a batch job in which the **%CPDDUTL** macro runs a LIST TABLE control statement.

If you want to change the BY variables or their order for a one-time job, the fastest way to do so is to run a SAS program that contains the following statements:

```
proc sort data=level.table out=sasuser.table;
   by one-time-BY-variables-list;
```

where *level* is the reduction level on which to base the report, *table* is the table that you want to base the report on, *cpe-pdb* is the complete directory path or high-level-qualifiers and the name of the PDB you want to base your report on, and *one-time-BY-variables-list* is a list of the BY variables you want to use in the report. Order the variables from major to minor and separate the variables by blanks. After you run this program, run the report definition on the data in SASUSER.*table*.

Before changing the BY-variables or their order in the data dictionary you should be aware of the following:

- Changes to the BY-variables will not take effect in the data until the next process or reduce task runs or you execute the %CPDDUTL macro with the BUILD VIEWS control statement.
- The BY-variables list specified on any reports must match the current BY-variables list in the PDB. Therefore, if you have updated the BY-variables for a table in the PDB, you should examine all report definitions that use this table to see if the definition should be

changed to match the new BY-variables list.

- When the BY-variables list is updated (via the process or reduce task or the BUILD VIEWS statement), the data in the PDB is physically sorted. Depending on the number of observations in the tables being sorted, this can take a considerable amount of time.
- It is not good practice to change the BY-variables list frequently. If you are changing the BY-variables list regularly in order to produce reports, you either have not chosen a good set of BY-variables or you have an incomplete understanding of how to create the report you want.

To change the BY variables list using the interactive interface, invoke SAS/CPE with update access to the PDB and then follow this path from the primary menu:

PDB Admin -> Config Active PDB Dictionary -> ***select table***
-> ItemActions -> Edit Definition

You can also use the **UPDATE TABLE** statement in the %CPDDUTL macro to change the BY variables list in batch mode.

DOWN=*number*

specifies the number of star or pie charts to place vertically on a single graph page. **The default is 1.**

END=*SAS-datetime-value*

represents the last date and time for data to include in the report. The *sas-datetime-value* must be in the DATETIME13. SAS format or in the today[-*nnnn*]@*hh:mm* format. For example, END=01jul96:17:00 or END=today-1@17:00.

Use this parameter in combination with BEGIN= to define the range for subsetting data for the report. Refer to **BEGIN=** for more information on using these parameters.

GROUP=*grouping-variable*

is the name of a variable that subsets the observations. The analysis variables are represented by bars and display in groups, with one group for each value of the group variable. If the TYPE= parameter for this macro is BAR or BLOCK, the groups of bars display in the form of a chart, with all groups on one chart. If TYPE= STAR or PIE, the analysis variables are represented by stars or pieces of pie and a separate chart displays for each unique value of the group variable.

GRP_LAB=*label*

is the label (as many as 16 characters) for the variable specified by the GROUP= parameter. You may use blank characters. You may enclose the label in single quotes, but the quotes are not required.

Caution: *Do not include commas, equal signs, parentheses, or ampersands in the label.*

ORDER=DESCENDING | ASCENDING | MIDPOINT

indicates the order to chart values.

DESCENDING

order from the highest value of the chart statistic to the lowest.

ASCENDING

order from the lowest value of the chart statistic to the highest.

MIDPOINT

displays a specific character value, a range of numeric values, or a specific numeric value. The midpoint is represented in different ways, based on the type of report you are producing, such as pie chart or horizontal bar chart. MIDPOINT is not valid if you specify the **TOPN=** parameter, since the TOPN= parameter displays a specified number of values in ascending or descending order. For more information, see "Chart Variables and Midpoint Selection" in Chapter 23 of *SAS/GRAPH Software: Reference, Version 6, First Edition, Volume 2.*

If the TOPN= parameter is specified, the default value is ORDER=DESCENDING; otherwise, the default value is ORDER=MIDPOINT.

OUTDESC=*text*

is a description (as many as 40 characters) of the output.

If OUTMODE=CATALOG, the description is stored with the entry in the SAS catalog specified in the OUTLOC= parameter. Otherwise, the description is ignored.

OUTLOC=*output-location*

is the physical location of a graphics stream file, a SAS catalog name, or the physical location of the file or catalog member (for text reports only). The value of the OUTNAME= parameter is appended to the value of this parameter to specify the complete output location. Specify this parameter if you specify the OUTMODE= parameter.

OUTMODE=*output-format*

specifies the format for the output. **The default value is GWINDOW for all reports except %CPTABRPT. The default for %CPTABRPT is the output window.**

Valid values for this parameter are:

LP

stores the output as a text file. If you specify OUTMODE=LP, you should also specify the OUTLOC and OUTNAME parameters for the text report. If you do not specify the output location (OUTLOC=), the output is sent to the output window or standard SASLIST file. **This value is not valid for the %CPSPEC, %CPG3D, or %CPGTPLT macros.**

GSF

stores the output as a graphics stream file. If you specify OUTMODE=GSF, you must also specify the OUTLOC and OUTNAME parameters. **This value is not valid for the %CPXTAB and %CPTABRPT macros.**

CATALOG

stores the output as a GRSEG entry in a SAS catalog. If you are producing a graph report and you specify OUTMODE=CATALOG, you should also specify the OUTLOC, OUTNAME, and OUTDESC parameters. **This value is not valid for the %CPXTAB and %CPTABRPT macros.**

The following table summarizes which parameters should be specified in addition to OUTMODE=, based on the report type and the value of the OUTMODE= parameter.

When OUTMODE=	Specify these additional parameters			Not valid for these macros
LP	-	OUTLOC	OUTNAME	%CPSPEC, %CPG3D %CPGTPLT
GSF	-	OUTLOC	OUTNAME	%CPXTAB, %CPTABRPT
CATALOG	OUTDESC	OUTLOC	OUTNAME	%CPXTAB, %CPTABRPT

For more information on using OUTMODE= with OUTNAME= and OUTLOC=, see **Examples of the OUTMODE= Parameter**.

Caution: *OUTMODE=LP is the only valid option for reports that produce text output, for example those that use procedures such as TABULATE, REPORT, or PRINT. If you specify OUTMODE=CATALOG for a text report, the OUTLOC= and OUTNAME= parameters are ignored.*

The OUTNAME and OUTLOC parameters execute PROC PRINTTO in the background to set the output filename and location. When PROC PRINTTO is set, it stays in effect for subsequent text reports for the current SAS session until it is reset by another PROC PRINTTO. Therefore, after you set the OUTNAME and OUTLOC parameters and run your report, you must reset these values if you want the output from future reports to go to another location.

Furthermore, unless you have experience using PROC PRINTTO, you should not use the OUTNAME and OUTLOC parameters when PROC PRINTTO is executed because the commands may override each other and send your output to a location other than the one you expected. PROC PRINTTO does not produce a data set or printed output. It is useful when you want to route output from different steps in a SAS job to different files.

For more information on using PROC PRINTTO, refer to Chapter 28 of the *SAS Procedures Guide, Version 6, Third Edition.*

Note: The SAS/CPE interactive interface handles report output different from the OUTMODE=, OUTLOC=, and OUTNAME= batch parameters. In the interactive interface, use the value GWINDOW to display the report output in a GRAPH window, and use the value LP to display the report output in an OUTPUT window. In both cases, omit the OUTDESC=, OUTLOC=, and OUTNAME= parameters. Specify these parameters only if you use OUTMODE=GSF or CATALOG.

If you are running SAS/CPE in batch mode (i.e., you have executed it from within a cron job or from the MVS batch scheduler) and are running a graph report, you should specify an output location other than the graph window.

OUTNAME=*physical-filename* | *entry-name*
: is the name of the external file or the entry-name in the SAS catalog where you want to store output results. Catalog entries are stored as GRSEG type entries. The value of this parameter is appended to the value of the OUTLOC= parameter to specify the complete output location.

Specify this parameter whenever you specify the OUTMODE= parameter, except when you specify OUTMODE=CATALOG.

PERIOD=*time-interval*

is the summarization period for the report. **The default is ASIS**. For values other than ASIS, the values for the time period within a class or category are combined to form a single point on a plot, a bar on a chart, or a row or column in a table.

Notes: For the %CPCHART and %CPXTAB macros, PERIOD= is only valid if the class variable is DATETIME. For the %CPCCHRT macro, PERIOD= is only valid if the DATETIME variable is selected in any category.

Period	Effect	Example
ASIS	leaves datetime in its present form.	09Jun94:14:37:25
15MIN	transforms the time to the first minute of the 15-minute period in the hour and retains the date.	09Jun94:14:30
HOUR	transforms the time to the first minute of the hour and retains the date.	09Jun94:14:00
24HOUR	transforms the time to its hour component and omits the date. Range: 0-23.	14
DATE	omits the time and retains the date.	09Jun94
WHOLEDAY	same as DATE.	
WEEKDAY	transforms the day to the day of the week (where 1=Sunday, 2=Monday, and so on) and omits the month, year, and time. Range: 1-7, which displays as Sunday-Saturday.	Thursday
MONTHDAY	omits everything but the day of the month. Range: 1-31.	9
YEARDAY	transforms the day to the day of the year and omits the month, year, and time. Range: 1-366.	160
WEEK	transforms the date to first date in the week (where the week begins on	04Jun94

	`the day on which January 1 falls in the year) and omits the time.`	
MONTH	`omits the day and the time`	`Jun94`
YEARMONTH	`omits everything but the month of the year. Range: 1-12.`	`6`
QTR	`transforms the month to the first month of the quarter and omits the day and time.`	`Apr94`

SGRP_LAB=*label*

is the label (as many as 16 characters) for the variable specified by the SUBGROUP= parameter for this macro. You may use blank characters. You may enclose the label in single quotes, but the quotes are not required.

Caution: *Do not include commas, equal signs, parentheses, or ampersands in the label.*

STAT=*statistic*

specifies what statistic to use to summarize data. **The default statistic is MEAN**. Valid values for STAT= in the %CPCHART macro are:

MEAN

is the arithmetic average. Mean is one measure used to describe the center of a distribution of values. Other measures include mode and median.

SUM

is the sum of values for all observations.

SUBGROUP=*variable*

is the name of a variable by which to subdivide the groups that are specified by the value of the GROUP= parameter. Each subdivision becomes a section of a bar. You cannot specify a subgroup variable if the TYPE= parameter value is PIE or STAR.

TABTYPE=INTERVAL | EVENT

specifies whether the data cover a specified interval of time or whether they are logged in response to an event that occurs, such as when a job begins or ends. **INTERVAL is the default value.**

INTERVAL

each observation represents an interval of time.

EVENT

each observation represents an event.

TOPN=*number*

specifies the maximum number of bars to chart. This produces a chart that displays the top *number* values and does not display lower values. For example,

- ☐ If ORDER=DESCENDING and neither the GROUP= parameter nor the SUBGROUP= parameter is set, TOPN=10 generates a chart of the largest ten values of the analysis variable.

- ☐ Under the same conditions, except that the GROUP=parameter is set, the largest ten values of the analysis variable are found, without respect to group, and then the ten are displayed within their groups.

- ☐ Under the same conditions, except that the GROUP= parameter is set and the SUBGROUP= parameter is set, the ten largest values of the analysis variable are found, without regard to group and subgroup, and then the ten are displayed within their groups and subgroups.

If you specify the TOPN= parameter, the default value for the **ORDER=** parameter is DESCENDING; you may use ORDER=DESCENDING or ORDER=ASCENDING, but do not use ORDER=MIDPOINT. Specifying ORDER=ASCENDING and TOPN=*number* allows you to create a "bottomN" report of the lowest *number* of values of the analysis variable.

TYPE=*chart-type*
: is the type of chart to produce. **The default type is HBAR.** Valid values are:

BLOCK
: creates a three-dimensional block chart in which the height of each block represents the statistic for the variable being charted.

HBAR
: creates a horizontal bar chart in which the length of each bar represents the statistic for the variable being charted.

PIE
: creates a circular pie chart in which the size of each piece represents the statistic for the variable being charted.

STAR
: creates a star chart in which the size of each piece represents the statistic for the variable being charted.

VBAR
: creates a vertical bar chart in which the height of each bar represents the statistic for the variable being charted.

WHERE=*where-expression*
: specifies an expression that subsets the data to be reported on. Valid operators include, but are not limited to, BETWEEN AND, CONTAINS, LIKE, IN, IS NULL or IS MISSING. For example, the following statement limits the included observations to only those where the value of machine is 'host1' or 'host2':

```
where=machine in ('host1','host2')
```

For more information on these and other where operators, see the WHERE statement in Chapter 9 of *SAS Language: Reference, Version 6, First Edition.*

YVAL=*number*

is the number of Y values to print on one page of the graph. For example, if the graph TYPE= BLOCK, HBAR or PIE for this macro, this parameter specifies the number of block, bar, or pie charts to print on one page. **The default number is based on the output device type**. If the number of specified variables, groups, sub-groups, or stack variables is greater than the value of YVAL=, the chart is broken into multiple pages. For example, if you specfied a group variable that had nine instances, such as nine different machines, and you set YVAL=6, your graph would print on two pages. The first page would contain a graph with the first six bars or slices of pie and the second page would contain a graph with the last three bars or slices of pie.

%CPGTPLT

Graph Templates

Purpose

The %CPGTPLT macro constructs a template in which you can display from one to four plots or charts generated by any of the other report macros, although generally you specify two or more. The positional parameters *graph1* through *graph4* are calls to report macros without the percent sign and are separated by a comma.

If you specify one or two *graph* parameters, the reports are vertically stacked, like this:

Two-Part Template for One or Two Graphs

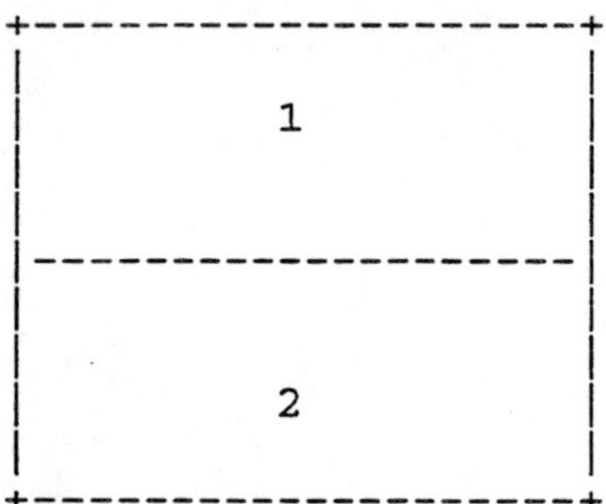

Each of the reports is half-height and full width. If you specify three or four *graph* parameters, the reports are arranged like this:

Four-Part Template for Three or Four Graphs

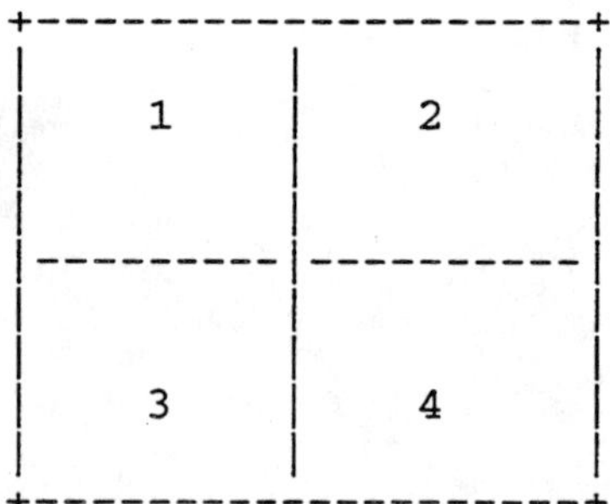

If you specify three graph parameters the lower right corner remains blank. For more information about the underlying procedure, see Chapter 36, "The GREPLAY Procedure," in *SAS/GRAPH Software: Reference, Version 6, First Edition, Volume 2.*

Syntax

```
%CPGTPLT(graph1, ..., graph4,
         <OUTDESC=text>,
         <OUTLOC=output-location>,
         <OUTMODE=output-format>,
```

```
<OUTNAME=physical-filename|entry-name> ) ;
```

%CPGTPLT Parameters

graph1, ..., graph4

specifies up to four calls to other report macros. **This positional parameter is required.** Each *graphn* value is a complete invocation of another report macro, except that you do not use the % sign in front of the macro name. The graphs you invoke are displayed in a multipart window, so you can see multiple reports on the same page or in the same window.

Optional Keyword Parameters

OUTDESC=*text*

is a description (as many as 40 characters) of the output.

If OUTMODE=CATALOG, the description is stored with the entry in the SAS catalog specified in the OUTLOC= parameter. Otherwise, the description is ignored.

OUTLOC=*output-location*

is the physical location of a graphics stream file, a SAS catalog name, or the physical location of the file or catalog member (for text reports only). The value of the OUTNAME= parameter is appended to the value of this parameter to specify the complete output location. Specify this parameter if you specify the OUTMODE= parameter.

OUTMODE=*output-format*

specifies the format for the output. **The default value is GWINDOW for all reports except %CPTABRPT. The default for %CPTABRPT is the output window.**

Valid values for this parameter are:

LP

stores the output as a text file. If you specify OUTMODE=LP, you should also specify the OUTLOC and OUTNAME parameters for the text report. If you do not specify the output location (OUTLOC=), the output is sent to the output window or standard SASLIST file. **This value is not valid for the %CPSPEC, %CPG3D, or %CPGTPLT macros.**

GSF

stores the output as a graphics stream file. If you specify OUTMODE=GSF, you must also specify the OUTLOC and OUTNAME parameters. **This value is not valid for the %CPXTAB and %CPTABRPT macros.**

CATALOG

stores the output as a GRSEG entry in a SAS catalog. If you are producing a graph report and you specify OUTMODE=CATALOG, you should also specify the OUTLOC, OUTNAME, and OUTDESC parameters. **This value is not valid for the %CPXTAB and %CPTABRPT macros.**

The following table summarizes which parameters should be specified in addition to OUTMODE=, based on the report type and the value of the OUTMODE= parameter.

When OUTMODE=	Specify these additional parameters			Not valid for these macros
LP	-	OUTLOC	OUTNAME	%CPSPEC, %CPG3D %CPGTPLT
GSF	-	OUTLOC	OUTNAME	%CPXTAB, %CPTABRPT
CATALOG	OUTDESC	OUTLOC	OUTNAME	%CPXTAB, %CPTABRPT

For more information on using OUTMODE= with OUTNAME= and OUTLOC=, see **Examples of the OUTMODE= Parameter**.

Caution: *OUTMODE=LP is the only valid option for reports that produce text output, for example those that use procedures such as TABULATE, REPORT, or PRINT. If you specify OUTMODE=CATALOG for a text report, the OUTLOC= and OUTNAME= parameters are ignored.*

The OUTNAME and OUTLOC parameters execute PROC PRINTTO in the background to set the output filename and location. When PROC PRINTTO is set, it stays in effect for subsequent text reports for the current SAS session until it is reset by another PROC PRINTTO. Therefore, after you set the OUTNAME and OUTLOC parameters and run your report, you must reset these values if you want the output from future reports to go to another location.

Furthermore, unless you have experience using PROC PRINTTO, you should not use the OUTNAME and OUTLOC parameters when PROC PRINTTO is executed because the commands may override each other and send your output to a location other than the one you expected. PROC PRINTTO does not produce a data set or printed output. It is useful when you want to route output from different steps in a SAS job to different files.

For more information on using PROC PRINTTO, refer to Chapter 28 of the *SAS Procedures Guide, Version 6, Third Edition.*

Note: The SAS/CPE interactive interface handles report output different from the OUTMODE=, OUTLOC=, and OUTNAME= batch parameters. In the interactive interface, use the value GWINDOW to display the report output in a GRAPH window, and use the value LP to display the report output in an OUTPUT window. In both cases, omit the OUTDESC=, OUTLOC=, and OUTNAME= parameters. Specify these parameters only if you use OUTMODE=GSF or CATALOG.

If you are running SAS/CPE in batch mode (i.e., you have executed it from within a cron job or from the MVS batch scheduler) and are running a graph report, you should specify an output location other than the graph window.

OUTNAME=*physical-filename* | *entry-name*
is the name of the external file or the entry-name in the SAS catalog where you want to store output results. Catalog entries are stored as GRSEG type entries. The value of this parameter is appended to the value of the OUTLOC= parameter to specify the complete output location.

Specify this parameter whenever you specify the OUTMODE= parameter, except when you specify OUTMODE=CATALOG.

Example: %CPGTPLT

This example generates a two-part report.

```
GOPTIONS reset=title reset=footnote;
TITLE1 "Application Volume Quality Values";
%CPGTPLT
   (CPCHART(UUDCV, CLVAR1, CLLAB1, VAR1, LAB1,
            TYPE=VBAR,
            REDLVL=DAY,
            STAT=MEAN,
            ),
   CPCHART(UUDCV, CLVAR1, CLLAB1, VAR1, LAB1,
            TYPE=HBAR,
            REDLVL=DAY,
            STAT=MEAN,
           ),
    OUTMODE=CATALOG,
    OUTLOC=physical-output-location
    OUTNAME=RESULTS,
    OUTDESC=Application Volume Quality Values
    );
```

Notes

The default OUTMODE= value is GWINDOW for this macro.

The %CPGTPLT macro calls other report macros using the *graph1,..., graph4* positional parmeter. When you include those macro calls in this report, you must specify all of the parameters you would normally specify when you invoke those report macros indvidually, except you should not specify the OUTDESC=, OUTLOC=, OUTMODE=, and OUTNAME= parameters. These parameters are specified for the multipart report, not the underlying reports.

The macro calls within %CPGTPLT should not include the percent (%) sign.

For multipart reports, each report must have the same number of graphs. The number of graphs is determined by the number of BY variables, class variables, group variables, and the number of pages in each report. For example, if report one has five BY variables, reports 2 and 3 also must have five BY variables.

%CPG3D

3-D (X, Y, Z) Plot

Purpose

The %CPG3D macro produces a three-dimensional scatter plot that displays multidimensional trends or concentrations in data.

You can select a maximum of 15 analysis variables. If you select multiple analysis variables *(var1, lab1,...var15, lab15)*, the variable names display on the Y axis, the values for those variables display on the Z axis, and the X variable (XVAR=) displays on the X axis.

If you specify a class variable (CL_NAM=) then you can only select one analysis variable. The class variable displays on the Y axis, the analysis variable (*var1, lab1*) displays on the Z axis, and the X variable (XVAR=) displays on the X axis.

For more information about the underlying procedure, refer to "The G3D Procedure," in Chapter 39 of *SAS/GRAPH Software: Reference, Version 6, First Edition, Volume 2*.

Syntax

```
%CPG3D(dataset,
        var1,lab1,...,var15,lab15,
        REDLVL=reduction-level,
       <BEGIN=SAS-datetime-value>,
       <BY=BY-variable-list>,
       <CL_LAB=label>,
       <CL_NAM=class-variable-name>,
       <CTEXT=color>,
       <END=SAS-datetime-value>,
       <NEEDLE=NO|YES>,
       <OUTDESC=text>,
       <OUTLOC=output-location>,
       <OUTMODE=output-format>,
       <OUTNAME=physical-filename|entry-name>,
       <PERIOD=time-interval>,
       <ROTATE=angle-list>,
       <STAT=statistic>,
       <TABTYPE=INTERVAL|EVENT>,
       <TILT=angle-list>,
       <TYPE=plot-type>,
       <WHERE=where-expression>,
       <XLAB=label>,
       <XVAR=variable>,
       <YLAB=>,
       <YVAR=> ) ;
```

%CPG3D Parameters

dataset

specifies the table name from which to generate the report. **This positional parameter is**

required and it can be specified in one of three ways.

If the data are in the DETAIL, DAY, WEEK, MONTH, or YEAR levels of the active PDB:

- ☐ Specify a tablename via the *dataset* parameter and a level via the **REDLVL=** parameter. If the REDLVL= parameter is not specified for the table name, REDLVL=DETAIL.

- ☐ Specify the name in the format of *REDLVL.TABLE*, in which case the REDLVL= parameter is not required.

If the data are in a SAS library that is not in the DETAIL, DAY, WEEK, MONTH, or YEAR level of the active PDB:

- ☐ Specify a two-level name in the format *libref.data-set-name* and specify REDLVL=OTHER.

Note: When specifying the data set name using the *libref* format, you must assign a *libref* before this macro is invoked. For more information see the LIBNAME statement in Chapter 9 of *SAS Language: Reference, Version 6, First Edition.*

var1,lab1 . . . var15,lab15

specifies a paired list of analysis variable names and labels (up to 16 characters) for the analysis axis. The maximum number of pairs you can specify is 15. **This positional parameter is required.** You must specify at least one variable and one label.

The analysis variable typically displays on the left (Y) axis. However, certain combinations of parameters may affect the axis on which the analysis variable is displayed or the number of variables that can be specified for a specific report. For a detailed explanation of the variables displayed on each axis and the maximum number of variables that can be specified for the report, refer to the *Purpose* section of the macro description.

If you specify multiple analysis variables, the unit of measure for all of the variables should be the same and the range of values should be similar. You may use blank characters in the label and you may enclose the label in single quotes, but the quotes are not required.

Caution: *Do not include commas, equal signs, parentheses, or ampersands in the labels.*

REDLVL=*reduction-level*

specifies which level of the table you are reporting on: DETAIL, DAY, WEEK, MONTH, YEAR, or OTHER. **The default is DETAIL**. The value of this parameter is used as a libref. You should specify REDLVL=OTHER if you want to select a SAS data set. The SAS data set should contain a variable named DATETIME, which represents the datetime stamp for each observation.

Note: When specifying the data set name using the *libref* format, you must assign a *libref* before this macro is invoked. For more information see the LIBNAME statement in Chapter 9 of *SAS Language: Reference, Version 6, First Edition.*

Optional Keyword Parameters

BEGIN=*SAS-datetime-value*

represents the first date and time for data to include in the report. The *sas-datetime-value* must be in the DATETIME13. SAS format. For example, BEGIN=01jul96:08:45. Use this parameter in combination with END= to define the range for subsetting data for the report. You can also use the TODAY[-*nnnn*]@*hh:mm* format, which uses the current date value minus *nnnn* days at the specified hour. This format supports the symbol or the word (@ or at) for the "at" instruction. For example, the following combination of values reports on the last three days of data, beginning at 8:00 a.m. three days ago and ending today at 5:00 p.m.

```
begin=today-3@08:00, end=todayat17:00
```

If you omit the time, the default time for the BEGIN= parameter is 00:00 on the specified date and the default time for the END= parameter is 23:59 on the specified date.

This example illustrates specific dates:

```
begin=01jul96:08:00, end=31jul96:17:00
```

If you omit the BEGIN= and END= parameters, the macro uses the information stored with the table definition (in the data dictionary) for the earliest and most recent datetime values at the specified level. The values stored with the table definition are based on the data currently in that level of the table. Exception: If the level is set to OTHER, the macro reads the data to determine the earliest and most recent datetime values (because there is not a table definition).

If you use only one parameter, BEGIN= or END=, that datetime is restricted and the other value is based on the data.

BY=*BY-variable-list*

lists the variables by which your data is sorted in the PDB. Use blanks to separate the variables in the list. A separate graph is produced for each value of the BY variable or for each combination of BY variable values, if you have multiple BY variables. For example, if you have four *diskids* on three machines, the following setting for the BY= parameter produces twelve reports, one for each of the twelve unique combinations of machine and *diskid* values.

```
by=machine diskid
```

For an alternate method of handling unique values of variables, refer to the description of class variables in the report you are producing.

If there is no BY= parameter, observations are sorted in the order that the variables are listed in the BY variable list or class variable list in the PDB. To check the order, follow this path from the main menu of the SAS/CPE interactive interface:

PDB Admin -> **Config Active PDB Dictionary** -> *select table*
-> **ItemActions** -> **Browse Definition**

or submit a batch job in which the %CPDDUTL macro runs a LIST TABLE control statement.

If you want to change the BY variables or their order for a one-time job, the fastest way to do so is to run a SAS program that contains the following statements:

```
proc sort data=level.table out=sasuser.table;
   by one-time-BY-variables-list;
```

where *level* is the reduction level on which to base the report, *table* is the table that you want to base the report on, *cpe-pdb* is the complete directory path or high-level-qualifiers and the name of the PDB you want to base your report on, and *one-time-BY-variables-list* is a list of the BY variables you want to use in the report. Order the variables from major to minor and separate the variables by blanks. After you run this program, run the report definition on the data in SASUSER.*table*.

Before changing the BY-variables or their order in the data dictionary you should be aware of the following:

- □ Changes to the BY-variables will not take effect in the data until the next process or reduce task runs or you execute the %CPDDUTL macro with the BUILD VIEWS control statement.
- □ The BY-variables list specified on any reports must match the current BY-variables list in the PDB. Therefore, if you have updated the BY-variables for a table in the PDB, you should examine all report definitions that use this table to see if the definition should be changed to match the new BY-variables list.
- □ When the BY-variables list is updated (via the process or reduce task or the BUILD VIEWS statement), the data in the PDB is physically sorted. Depending on the number of observations in the tables being sorted, this can take a considerable amount of time.
- □ It is not good practice to change the BY-variables list frequently. If you are changing the BY-variables list regularly in order to produce reports, you either have not chosen a good set of BY-variables or you have an incomplete understanding of how to create the report you want.

To change the BY variables list using the interactive interface, invoke SAS/CPE with update access to the PDB and then follow this path from the primary menu:

PDB Admin -> Config Active PDB Dictionary -> ***select table***
-> ItemActions -> Edit Definition

You can also use the **UPDATE TABLE** statement in the %CPDDUTL macro to change the BY variables list in batch mode.

CL_LAB=*label*

is the label (a maximum of 16 characters) for the class variable. You may use blank characters. You may enclose the label in single quotes, but the quotes are not required.

Caution: *Do not include commas, equal signs, parentheses, or ampersands in the label.*

CL_NAM=*variable-name*

specifies the name of the class variable for the report. For each unique value of the class variable, the macro creates a separate portion or group on the graph.

Compare this type of variable to the BY variable. The BY variable creates separate graphs for each unique value of the variable. For example, the following combination of parameters produces one report or plot for each unique value of MACHINE, the BY variable.

```
cl_nam=diskid, by=machine
```

Each of the graphs for MACHINE includes all possible values of DISKID, the class variable. If you are producing a plot, each unique value of DISKID is represented by a different color or plot symbol. If you are producing a chart each value of DISKID is represented in a separate column or row.

CTEXT=*color*

indicates the color of the text on a plot. **The default text color is white.** You can specify the background color with the CBACK= parameter in the SAS GOPTIONS statement. The default background color is device dependent. Refer to the information on your output device in *SAS/GRAPH Software: Using Graphics Devices, Version 6, First Edition* for your specific host.

Notes: If the color of the text is the same as the color of the background, the text appears to be missing. If you specify this parameter and the COLORLST= parameter, the value of this parameter is ignored.

END=*SAS-datetime-value*

represents the last date and time for data to include in the report. The *sas-datetime-value* must be in the DATETIME13. SAS format or in the today[*-nnnn*]@*hh:mm* format. For example, END=01jul96:17:00 or END=today-1@17:00.

Use this parameter in combination with BEGIN= to define the range for subsetting data for the report. Refer to **BEGIN=** for more information on using these parameters.

NEEDLE=NO|YES

specifies whether plot points have lines that connect the points to the X-Y plane. If you specify NEEDLE=NO, you produce a three-dimensional scatter plot. NEEDLE=YES connects the plot points to the plane using lines. **The default is NEEDLE=YES when the X variable is DATETIME; otherwise the default is NEEDLE=NO.**

See the TYPE= parameter for examples of the symbols that can be used for scatter plots.

Note: NEEDLE=NO has no effect on prism or pillar plots.

OUTDESC=*text*

is a description (as many as 40 characters) of the output.

If OUTMODE=CATALOG, the description is stored with the entry in the SAS catalog specified in the OUTLOC= parameter. Otherwise, the description is ignored.

OUTLOC=*output-location*

is the physical location of a graphics stream file, a SAS catalog name, or the physical location of the file or catalog member (for text reports only). The value of the OUTNAME= parameter is appended to the value of this parameter to specify the complete output location.

Specify this parameter if you specify the OUTMODE= parameter.

OUTMODE=*output-format*

specifies the format for the output. **The default value is GWINDOW for all reports except %CPTABRPT. The default for %CPTABRPT is the output window.**

Valid values for this parameter are:

LP

stores the output as a text file. If you specify OUTMODE=LP, you should also specify the OUTLOC and OUTNAME parameters for the text report. If you do not specify the output location (OUTLOC=), the output is sent to the output window or standard SASLIST file. **This value is not valid for the %CPSPEC, %CPG3D, or %CPGTPLT macros.**

GSF

stores the output as a graphics stream file. If you specify OUTMODE=GSF, you must also specify the OUTLOC and OUTNAME parameters. **This value is not valid for the %CPXTAB and %CPTABRPT macros.**

CATALOG

stores the output as a GRSEG entry in a SAS catalog. If you are producing a graph report and you specify OUTMODE=CATALOG, you should also specify the OUTLOC, OUTNAME, and OUTDESC parameters. **This value is not valid for the %CPXTAB and %CPTABRPT macros.**

The following table summarizes which parameters should be specified in addition to OUTMODE=, based on the report type and the value of the OUTMODE= parameter.

When OUTMODE=	Specify these additional parameters			Not valid for these macros
LP	-	OUTLOC	OUTNAME	%CPSPEC, %CPG3D %CPGTPLT
GSF	-	OUTLOC	OUTNAME	%CPXTAB, %CPTABRPT
CATALOG	OUTDESC	OUTLOC	OUTNAME	%CPXTAB, %CPTABRPT

For more information on using OUTMODE= with OUTNAME= and OUTLOC=, see Examples of the OUTMODE= Parameter.

Caution: *OUTMODE=LP is the only valid option for reports that produce text output, for example those that use procedures such as TABULATE, REPORT, or PRINT. If you specify OUTMODE=CATALOG for a text report, the OUTLOC= and OUTNAME= parameters are ignored.*

The OUTNAME and OUTLOC parameters execute PROC PRINTTO in the background to set the output filename and location. When PROC PRINTTO is set, it stays in effect for subsequent text reports for the current SAS session until it is reset by another PROC

PRINTTO. Therefore, after you set the OUTNAME and OUTLOC parameters and run your report, you must reset these values if you want the output from future reports to go to another location.

Furthermore, unless you have experience using PROC PRINTTO, you should not use the OUTNAME and OUTLOC parameters when PROC PRINTTO is executed because the commands may override each other and send your output to a location other than the one you expected. PROC PRINTTO does not produce a data set or printed output. It is useful when you want to route output from different steps in a SAS job to different files.

For more information on using PROC PRINTTO, refer to Chapter 28 of the *SAS Procedures Guide, Version 6, Third Edition.*

Note: The SAS/CPE interactive interface handles report output different from the OUTMODE=, OUTLOC=, and OUTNAME= batch parameters. In the interactive interface, use the value GWINDOW to display the report output in a GRAPH window, and use the value LP to display the report output in an OUTPUT window. In both cases, omit the OUTDESC=, OUTLOC=, and OUTNAME= parameters. Specify these parameters only if you use OUTMODE=GSF or CATALOG.

If you are running SAS/CPE in batch mode (i.e., you have executed it from within a cron job or from the MVS batch scheduler) and are running a graph report, you should specify an output location other than the graph window.

OUTNAME=*physical-filename* | *entry-name*

is the name of the external file or the entry-name in the SAS catalog where you want to store output results. Catalog entries are stored as GRSEG type entries. The value of this parameter is appended to the value of the OUTLOC= parameter to specify the complete output location.

Specify this parameter whenever you specify the OUTMODE= parameter, except when you specify OUTMODE=CATALOG.

PERIOD=*time-interval*

is the summarization period for the report. **The default is ASIS**. For values other than ASIS, the values for the time period within a class or category are combined to form a single point on a plot, a bar on a chart, or a row or column in a table.

Notes: For the %CPCHART and %CPXTAB macros, PERIOD= is only valid if the class variable is DATETIME. For the %CPCCHRT macro, PERIOD= is only valid if the DATETIME variable is selected in any category.

Period	Effect	Example
ASIS	leaves datetime in its present form.	09Jun94:14:37:25
15MIN	transforms the time to the first minute of the	09Jun94:14:30

	15-minute period in the hour and retains the date.	
HOUR	transforms the time to the first minute of the hour and retains the date.	09Jun94:14:00
24HOUR	transforms the time to its hour component and omits the date. Range: 0-23.	14
DATE	omits the time and retains the date.	09Jun94
WHOLEDAY	same as DATE.	
WEEKDAY	transforms the day to the day of the week (where 1=Sunday, 2=Monday, and so on) and omits the month, year, and time. Range: 1-7, which displays as Sunday-Saturday.	Thursday
MONTHDAY	omits everything but the day of the month. Range: 1-31.	9
YEARDAY	transforms the day to the day of the year and omits the month, year, and time. Range: 1-366.	160
WEEK	transforms the date to first date in the week (where the week begins on the day on which January 1 falls in the year) and omits the time.	04Jun94
MONTH	omits the day and the time	Jun94
YEARMONTH	omits everything but the month of the year. Range: 1-12.	6
QTR	transforms the month to the first month of the quarter and omits the day and time.	Apr94

ROTATE=*angle-list*

specifies one or more angles at which to rotate the X-Y plane about the perpendicular Z axis. A separate graph is produced for each angle listed. The units of measure for *angle-list* are degrees. **In SAS/CPE software, the default value is -20**.

angle-list can be specified in the following ways:

n n . . . n

```
n TO n <BY increment> <n . . . n> <n,. . .,n>
n n . . . n TO n <BY increment> <n . . . n>
```

The values specified in *angle-list* can be negative or positive and can be greater than 360 degrees. For example, a rotation angle of 45 degrees can also be expressed as

```
rotate=45
rotate=405
rotate=-315
```

Specifying a sequence of angles produces a graph for each pair of rotate and tilt angles. The angles specified in the ROTATE= option are paired with any angles specified with the **TILT=** parameter. Therefore, you must specify the same number of angle values for both the rotate and tilt parameters.

For more information about the *angle-list* value, see the ORDER= parameter in "AXIS Statement Options," Chapter 9 of *SAS/GRAPH Software: Reference, Version 6, First Edition, Volume 1.*

For more information about rotating the plot, see "Rotating and Tilting the Plot" in Chapter 39 of *SAS/GRAPH Software: Reference, Version 6, First Edition, Volume 1.*

STAT=*statistic*

specifies what statistic to use to summarize data that span the time interval specified by **PERIOD=**. The selected statistic is used for all variables in the report. **The default statistic is MEAN**. The STAT= parameter is not valid if PERIOD=ASIS. Valid values for STAT= are:

CSS

is the sum of squares corrected for the mean.

CV

is the coefficient of variation. It is calculated as the standard deviation divided by the mean and multiplied by 100.

MAX

is the maximum value for all observations.

MEAN

is the arithmetic average. Mean is one measure used to describe the center of a distribution of values.

MIN

is the minimum value for all observations.

N

or COUNT, is the number of observations with nonmissing values for the variables being summarized.

NMISS

the number of observations with missing values for the variable being summarized.

RANGE
: is the maximum of the difference between the maximum and minimum values for the variables, RANGE=MAX-MIN.

STD
: is the standard deviation or square root of variance. Like the variance, it is a measure of the dispersion about the mean, but in the same unit of measure as the data.

STDERR
: is the positive square root of the variance of a statistic.

SUM
: is the sum of values for all observations.

USS
: is the uncorrected sum of squares.

VAR
: is a measure of the dispersion or variability of the data about the mean. When values are close to the mean, the variance is small. When values are scattered widely about the mean, the variance is large.

Note: If you specify the **BY=** parameter, the statistics are calculated separately for each value of the BY variable or for each combination of the BY variable values, if you specified multiple BY variables.

TABTYPE=INTERVAL | EVENT
: specifies whether the data cover a specified interval of time or whether they are logged in response to an event that occurs, such as when a job begins or ends. **INTERVAL is the default value.**

INTERVAL
: each observation represents an interval of time.

EVENT
: each observation represents an event.

TILT=*angle-list*
: specifies one or more angles at which to tilt the graph toward you. A separate graph is produced for each angle listed. **The default tilt for SAS/CPE software is 80**. The units for *angle-list* are degrees. Specify *angle-list* using the same format described for ROTATE=. The values for *angle-list* must be in the range of 0 through 90. Refer to the description of the ROTATE= parameter on this macro for an explanation of the interaction between ROTATE= and TILT=.

For more information about tilting the plot, see "Rotating and Tilting the Plot" in Chapter 39 of *SAS/GRAPH Software: Reference, Version 6, First Edition, Volume 1*.

TYPE=*plot-type*
: specifies one of the following shapes to represent the analysis variable on the graph:

BALLOON	FLAG	SPADE
CLUB	HEART	SQUARE
CROSS	PILLAR	STAR
CUBE	POINT	
CYLINDER	PRISM	
DIAMOND	PYRAMID	

The default value is BALLOON. The following figure illustrates the various plot symbols that are available.

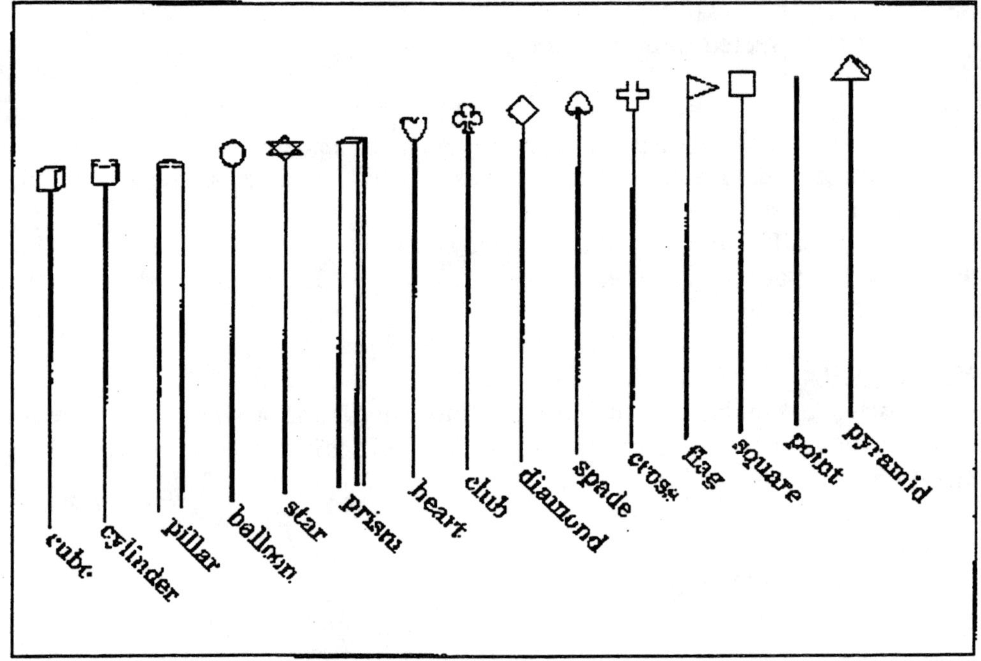

WHERE=*where-expression*

specifies an expression that subsets the data to be reported on. Valid operators include, but are not limited to, BETWEEN AND, CONTAINS, LIKE, IN, IS NULL or IS MISSING. For example, the following statement limits the included observations to only those where the value of machine is 'host1' or 'host2':

```
where=machine in ('host1','host2')
```

For more information on these and other where operators, see the WHERE statement in Chapter 9 of *SAS Language: Reference, Version 6, First Edition.*

XLAB=*label*

provides a label (not more than 16 characters) for the X axis of a plot. **By default, the label is the name of the X variable.** You may use blank characters. You may enclose the label in single quotes, but the quotes are not required.

Caution: *Do not include commas, equal signs, parenthesis, or ampersands in the label.*

XVAR=*variable*
specifies the variable for the X axis of a plot. **This parameter is required.** If you do not provide a value, the variable defaults to DATETIME.

YLAB=
not currently used.

YVAR=
not currently used.

Note

All variables for the chart should have the same unit of measurement.

%CPPLOT1

One Y-Axis Plot

Purpose

The %CPPLOT1 macro plots a maximum of 15 analysis (Y) variables against an X variable. However, if you specify a class or grouping variable (CL_NAM=) you can only specify one analysis (Y) variable. This macro supports a number of plot types, which are defined in the description of the TYPE= parameter.

Only one axis is used to display all analysis (Y) variable values, therefore, multiple analysis (Y) variables should be of the same unit of measurement.

For more information on the underlying procedure, refer to "The GPLOT Procedure" in Chapter 31 of *SAS/GRAPH Software: Reference, Version 6, First Edition, Volume 2.*

Syntax

```
%CPPLOT1(dataset,
         var1,lab1,...,var15,lab15,
         REDLVL=reduction-level,
         XVAR=variable,
        <BEGIN=SAS-datetime-value>,
        <BY=BY-variable-list>,
        <CL_LAB=char-label>,
        <CL_NAM=class-variable-name>,
        <END=SAS-datetime-value>,
        <OUTDESC=text>,
        <OUTLOC=output-location>,
        <OUTMODE=output-format>,
        <OUTNAME=physical-filename|entry-name>,
        <PERCENTS=>,
        <PERIOD=time-interval>,
        <STAT=statistic>,
        <TABTYPE=INTERVAL|EVENT>,
        <TYPE=plot-type>,
        <VAXIS=value-list>,
        <VREF=value-list>,
        <VZERO=NO|YES>,
        <WHERE=where-expression>,
        <XLAB=label> ) ;
```

%CPPLOT1 Parameters

dataset

specifies the table name from which to generate the report. **This positional parameter is required** and it can be specified in one of three ways.

If the data are in the DETAIL, DAY, WEEK, MONTH, or YEAR levels of the active PDB:

- ☐ Specify a tablename via the *dataset* parameter and a level via the **REDLVL=** parameter. If the REDLVL= parameter is not specified for the table name,

REDLVL=DETAIL.

- Specify the name in the format of *REDLVL.TABLE*, in which case the REDLVL= parameter is not required.

If the data are in a SAS library that is not in the DETAIL, DAY, WEEK, MONTH, or YEAR level of the active PDB:

- Specify a two-level name in the format *libref.data-set-name* and specify REDLVL=OTHER.

Note: When specifying the data set name using the *libref* format, you must assign a *libref* before this macro is invoked. For more information see the LIBNAME statement in Chapter 9 of *SAS Language: Reference, Version 6, First Edition.*

var1,lab1 . . . var15,lab15

specifies a paired list of analysis variable names and labels (up to 16 characters) for the analysis axis. The maximum number of pairs you can specify is 15. **This positional parameter is required.** You must specify at least one variable and one label.

The analysis variable typically displays on the left (Y) axis. However, certain combinations of parameters may affect the axis on which the analysis variable is displayed or the number of variables that can be specified for a specific report. For a detailed explanation of the variables displayed on each axis and the maximum number of variables that can be specified for the report, refer to the *Purpose* section of the macro description.

If you specify multiple analysis variables, the unit of measure for all of the variables should be the same and the range of values should be similar. You may use blank characters in the label and you may enclose the label in single quotes, but the quotes are not required.

Caution: *Do not include commas, equal signs, parentheses, or ampersands in the labels.*

REDLVL=*reduction-level*

specifies which level of the table you are reporting on: DETAIL, DAY, WEEK, MONTH, YEAR, or OTHER. **The default is DETAIL**. The value of this parameter is used as a libref. You should specify REDLVL=OTHER if you want to select a SAS data set. The SAS data set should contain a variable named DATETIME, which represents the datetime stamp for each observation.

Note: When specifying the data set name using the *libref* format, you must assign a *libref* before this macro is invoked. For more information see the LIBNAME statement in Chapter 9 of *SAS Language: Reference, Version 6, First Edition.*

XVAR=*variable*

specifies the variable for the X axis of a plot. **This parameter is required.** If you do not provide a value, the variable defaults to DATETIME.

Optional Keyword Parameters

BEGIN=*SAS-datetime-value*

represents the first date and time for data to include in the report. The *sas-datetime-value* must be in the DATETIME13. SAS format. For example, BEGIN=01jul96:08:45. Use this parameter in combination with **END=** to define the range for subsetting data for the report. You can also use the TODAY[-*nnnn*]@*hh:mm* format, which uses the current date value minus *nnnn* days at the specified hour. This format supports the symbol or the word (@ or at) for the "at" instruction. For example, the following combination of values reports on the last three days of data, beginning at 8:00 a.m. three days ago and ending today at 5:00 p.m.

```
begin=today-3@08:00, end=todayat17:00
```

If you omit the time, the default time for the BEGIN= parameter is 00:00 on the specified date and the default time for the END= parameter is 23:59 on the specified date.

This example illustrates specific dates:

```
begin=01jul96:08:00, end=31jul96:17:00
```

If you omit the BEGIN= and END= parameters, the macro uses the information stored with the table definition (in the data dictionary) for the earliest and most recent datetime values at the specified level. The values stored with the table definition are based on the data currently in that level of the table. Exception: If the level is set to OTHER, the macro reads the data to determine the earliest and most recent datetime values (because there is not a table definition).

If you use only one parameter, BEGIN= or END=, that datetime is restricted and the other value is based on the data.

BY=*BY-variable-list*

lists the variables by which your data is sorted in the PDB. Use blanks to separate the variables in the list. A separate graph is produced for each value of the BY variable or for each combination of BY variable values, if you have multiple BY variables. For example, if you have four *diskids* on three machines, the following setting for the BY= parameter produces twelve reports, one for each of the twelve unique combinations of machine and *diskid* values.

```
by=machine diskid
```

For an alternate method of handling unique values of variables, refer to the description of class variables in the report you are producing.

If there is no BY= parameter, observations are sorted in the order that the variables are listed in the BY variable list or class variable list in the PDB. To check the order, follow this path from the main menu of the SAS/CPE interactive interface:

PDB Admin -> **Config Active PDB Dictionary** -> *select table*
-> **ItemActions** -> **Browse Definition**

or submit a batch job in which the **%CPDDUTL** macro runs a LIST TABLE control statement.

If you want to change the BY variables or their order for a one-time job, the fastest way to do so is to run a SAS program that contains the following statements:

```
proc sort data=level.table out=sasuser.table;
   by one-time-BY-variables-list;
```

where *level* is the reduction level on which to base the report, *table* is the table that you want to base the report on, *cpe-pdb* is the complete directory path or high-level-qualifiers and the name of the PDB you want to base your report on, and *one-time-BY-variables-list* is a list of the BY variables you want to use in the report. Order the variables from major to minor and separate the variables by blanks. After you run this program, run the report definition on the data in SASUSER.*table*.

Before changing the BY-variables or their order in the data dictionary you should be aware of the following:

- Changes to the BY-variables will not take effect in the data until the next process or reduce task runs or you execute the %CPDDUTL macro with the BUILD VIEWS control statement.
- The BY-variables list specified on any reports must match the current BY-variables list in the PDB. Therefore, if you have updated the BY-variables for a table in the PDB, you should examine all report definitions that use this table to see if the definition should be changed to match the new BY-variables list.
- When the BY-variables list is updated (via the process or reduce task or the BUILD VIEWS statement), the data in the PDB is physically sorted. Depending on the number of observations in the tables being sorted, this can take a considerable amount of time.
- It is not good practice to change the BY-variables list frequently. If you are changing the BY-variables list regularly in order to produce reports, you either have not chosen a good set of BY-variables or you have an incomplete understanding of how to create the report you want.

To change the BY variables list using the interactive interface, invoke SAS/CPE with update access to the PDB and then follow this path from the primary menu:

PDB Admin -> Config Active PDB Dictionary -> ***select table***
-> ItemActions -> Edit Definition

You can also use the UPDATE TABLE statement in the %CPDDUTL macro to change the BY variables list in batch mode.

CL_LAB=*label*
: is the label (a maximum of 16 characters) for the class variable. You may use blank characters. You may enclose the label in single quotes, but the quotes are not required.

Caution: *Do not include commas, equal signs, parentheses, or ampersands in the label.*

CL_NAM=*variable-name*
: specifies the name of the class variable for the report. For each unique value of the class variable, the macro creates a separate portion or group on the graph.

Compare this type of variable to the BY variable. The BY variable creates separate graphs for each unique value of the variable. For example, the following combination of parameters produces one report or plot for each unique value of MACHINE, the BY variable.

```
cl_nam=diskid, by=machine
```

Each of the graphs for MACHINE includes all possible values of DISKID, the class variable. If you are producing a plot, each unique value of DISKID is represented by a different color or plot symbol. If you are producing a chart each value of DISKID is represented in a separate column or row.

END=*SAS-datetime-value*
represents the last date and time for data to include in the report. The *sas-datetime-value* must be in the DATETIME13. SAS format or in the today[*-nnnn*]@*hh:mm* format. For example, END=01jul96:17:00 or END=today-1@17:00.

Use this parameter in combination with BEGIN= to define the range for subsetting data for the report. Refer to **BEGIN=** for more information on using these parameters.

OUTDESC=*text*
is a description (as many as 40 characters) of the output.

If OUTMODE=CATALOG, the description is stored with the entry in the SAS catalog specified in the OUTLOC= parameter. Otherwise, the description is ignored.

OUTLOC=*output-location*
is the physical location of a graphics stream file, a SAS catalog name, or the physical location of the file or catalog member (for text reports only). The value of the OUTNAME= parameter is appended to the value of this parameter to specify the complete output location. Specify this parameter if you specify the OUTMODE= parameter.

OUTMODE=*output-format*
specifies the format for the output. **The default value is GWINDOW for all reports except %CPTABRPT. The default for %CPTABRPT is the output window.**

Valid values for this parameter are:

LP
stores the output as a text file. If you specify OUTMODE=LP, you should also specify the OUTLOC and OUTNAME parameters for the text report. If you do not specify the output location (OUTLOC=), the output is sent to the output window or standard SASLIST file. **This value is not valid for the %CPSPEC, %CPG3D, or %CPGTPLT macros.**

GSF
stores the output as a graphics stream file. If you specify OUTMODE=GSF, you must also specify the OUTLOC and OUTNAME parameters. **This value is not valid for the %CPXTAB and %CPTABRPT macros.**

CATALOG
stores the output as a GRSEG entry in a SAS catalog. If you are producing a graph

report and you specify OUTMODE=CATALOG, you should also specify the OUTLOC, OUTNAME, and OUTDESC parameters. **This value is not valid for the %CPXTAB and %CPTABRPT macros.**

The following table summarizes which parameters should be specified in addition to OUTMODE=, based on the report type and the value of the OUTMODE= parameter.

When OUTMODE=	Specify these additional parameters			Not valid for these macros
LP	-	OUTLOC	OUTNAME	%CPSPEC, %CPG3D %CPGTPLT
GSF	-	OUTLOC	OUTNAME	%CPXTAB, %CPTABRPT
CATALOG	OUTDESC	OUTLOC	OUTNAME	%CPXTAB, %CPTABRPT

For more information on using OUTMODE= with OUTNAME= and OUTLOC=, see **Examples of the OUTMODE= Parameter**.

Caution: *OUTMODE=LP is the only valid option for reports that produce text output, for example those that use procedures such as TABULATE, REPORT, or PRINT. If you specify OUTMODE=CATALOG for a text report, the OUTLOC= and OUTNAME= parameters are ignored.*

The OUTNAME and OUTLOC parameters execute PROC PRINTTO in the background to set the output filename and location. When PROC PRINTTO is set, it stays in effect for subsequent text reports for the current SAS session until it is reset by another PROC PRINTTO. Therefore, after you set the OUTNAME and OUTLOC parameters and run your report, you must reset these values if you want the output from future reports to go to another location.

Furthermore, unless you have experience using PROC PRINTTO, you should not use the OUTNAME and OUTLOC parameters when PROC PRINTTO is executed because the commands may override each other and send your output to a location other than the one you expected. PROC PRINTTO does not produce a data set or printed output. It is useful when you want to route output from different steps in a SAS job to different files.

For more information on using PROC PRINTTO, refer to Chapter 28 of the *SAS Procedures Guide, Version 6, Third Edition.*

Note: The SAS/CPE interactive interface handles report output different from the OUTMODE=, OUTLOC=, and OUTNAME= batch parameters. In the interactive interface, use the value GWINDOW to display the report output in a GRAPH window, and use the value LP to display the report output in an OUTPUT window. In both cases, omit the OUTDESC=, OUTLOC=, and OUTNAME= parameters. Specify these parameters only if you use OUTMODE=GSF or CATALOG.

If you are running SAS/CPE in batch mode (i.e., you have executed it from within a cron job or from the MVS batch scheduler) and are running a graph report, you should specify an output location other than the graph window.

OUTNAME=*physical-filename* | *entry-name*
is the name of the external file or the entry-name in the SAS catalog where you want to store output results. Catalog entries are stored as GRSEG type entries. The value of this parameter is appended to the value of the OUTLOC= parameter to specify the complete output location.

Specify this parameter whenever you specify the OUTMODE= parameter, except when you specify OUTMODE=CATALOG.

PERCENTS=
is not currently used.

PERIOD=*time-interval*
is the summarization period for the report. **The default is ASIS**. For values other than ASIS, the values for the time period within a class or category are combined to form a single point on a plot, a bar on a chart, or a row or column in a table.

Notes: For the %CPCHART and %CPXTAB macros, PERIOD= is only valid if the class variable is DATETIME. For the %CPCCHRT macro, PERIOD= is only valid if the DATETIME variable is selected in any category.

Period	Effect	Example
ASIS	leaves datetime in its present form.	09Jun94:14:37:25
15MIN	transforms the time to the first minute of the 15-minute period in the hour and retains the date.	09Jun94:14:30
HOUR	transforms the time to the first minute of the hour and retains the date.	09Jun94:14:00
24HOUR	transforms the time to its hour component and omits the date. Range: 0-23.	14
DATE	omits the time and retains the date.	09Jun94
WHOLEDAY	same as DATE.	
WEEKDAY	transforms the day to the day of the week (where 1=Sunday, 2=Monday, and so on) and omits the month, year, and time. Range: 1-7, which displays as Sunday-Saturday.	Thursday

MONTHDAY	omits everything but the day of the month. Range: 1-31.	9
YEARDAY	transforms the day to the day of the year and omits the month, year, and time. Range: 1-366.	160
WEEK	transforms the date to first date in the week (where the week begins on the day on which January 1 falls in the year) and omits the time.	04Jun94
MONTH	omits the day and the time	Jun94
YEARMONTH	omits everything but the month of the year. Range: 1-12.	6
QTR	transforms the month to the first month of the quarter and omits the day and time.	Apr94

STAT=*statistic*

specifies what statistic to use to summarize data that span the time interval specified by **PERIOD=**. The selected statistic is used for all variables in the report. **The default statistic is MEAN**. The STAT= parameter is not valid if PERIOD=ASIS. Valid values for STAT= are:

CSS

is the sum of squares corrected for the mean.

CV

is the coefficient of variation. It is calculated as the standard deviation divided by the mean and multiplied by 100.

MAX

is the maximum value for all observations.

MEAN

is the arithmetic average. Mean is one measure used to describe the center of a distribution of values.

MIN

is the minimum value for all observations.

N

or COUNT, is the number of observations with nonmissing values for the variables being summarized.

NMISS

the number of observations with missing values for the variable being summarized.

RANGE

is the maximum of the difference between the maximum and minimum values for the variables, RANGE=MAX-MIN.

STD

is the standard deviation or square root of variance. Like the variance, it is a measure of the dispersion about the mean, but in the same unit of measure as the data.

STDERR

is the positive square root of the variance of a statistic.

SUM

is the sum of values for all observations.

USS

is the uncorrected sum of squares.

VAR

is a measure of the dispersion or variability of the data about the mean. When values are close to the mean, the variance is small. When values are scattered widely about the mean, the variance is large.

Note: If you specify the **BY=** parameter, the statistics are calculated separately for each value of the BY variable or for each combination of the BY variable values, if you specified multiple BY variables.

TABTYPE=INTERVAL | EVENT

specifies whether the data cover a specified interval of time or whether they are logged in response to an event that occurs, such as when a job begins or ends. **INTERVAL is the default value.**

INTERVAL

each observation represents an interval of time.

EVENT

each observation represents an event.

TYPE=*plot-type*

specifies the type of plot to produce. **The default value is LINE.**

Valid values are described below. The value you specify for the TYPE= parameter is passed to the GPLOT procedure. For more detailed information about how the GPLOT procedure uses these values, refer to "SYMBOL Statement Options" in Chapter 16 of *SAS/GRAPH Software: Reference, Version 6, First Edition, Volume 1.*

BOX produces a box and whiskers plot that shows the mean and standard deviation of the values being plotted. Refer to the description of the INTERPOL=BOX option of the GPLOT procedure.

HILO*xx*
: plots maximum and minimum values of combined data values as a vertical line. Refer to the description of the INTERPOL=HILO option of the GPLOT procedure.

JOIN joins data points using straight lines. See also RC*xxxxx*, RL*xxxxx*, RQ*xxxxx*, SM*xxx*, and SPLINE*x* for joining techniques that use smoothing. Refer to the description of the INTERPOL=JOIN option of the GPLOT procedure.

LINE joins adjacent data points with a straight line.

LINEDOT
: joins adjacent data points with a straight line and uses a large DOT to represent the data points. Refer to the description of the VALUE=DOT option of the GPLOT procedure.

LINESTAR
: joins adjacent data points with a straight line and uses a large asterisk to represent the data points. Refer to the description of the VALUE=STAR option of the GPLOT procedure.

LINEX
: joins adjacent data points with a straight line and uses a large X to represent the data points. Refer to the description of the VALUE=X option of the GPLOT procedure.

NEEDLE
: plots the data points as a vertical line that drops from the point to the Y axis. Refer to the description of the INTERPOL=NEEDLE option of the GPLOT procedure.

PERCENT
: plots each value of the variable as a percent of the total value for that variable. For example, the values of 9 and 11 are converted to 45% and 55% and plotted at 45 and 55. This option is available only with SAS/CPE software.

RC*xxxxx*
: joins data points by using cubic regression as a smoothing technique. Refer to the description of the INTERPOL=RC option of the GPLOT procedure.

RL*xxxxx*
: joins data points by using linear regression as a smoothing technique. Refer to the description of the INTERPOL=RL option of the GPLOT procedure.

RQ*xxxxx*
: joins data points by using quadratic regression as a smoothing technique. Refer to the description of the INTERPOL=RQ option of the GPLOT procedure.

SCATTER
: plots only the data points and does not join the points. Refer to the description of the INTERPOL=NONE option of the GPLOT procedure.

SM*xxx*
: joins data points by using a cubic spline that minimizes a linear combination of the

sum of squares of the residuals of fit and the integral of the square of the second derivation. The greater the *xxx* value, the smoother the fitted curve. The value of *xxx* can be from 0 to 99P, or you can omit *xxx*. Refer to the description of the INTERPOL=SM option of the GPLOT procedure.

SPLINE*x*
: joins data points by using cubic spline interpolation with continuous second derivatives. This method uses a piecewise third-degree polynomial for each set of two adjacent points. Refer to the description of the INTERPOL=SPLINE option of the GPLOT procedure.

STACK
: plots the value or statistic in the first class and fills under the line, plots the value or statistic in the second class starting from the line for the first class and fills between the two lines, and so on. For example, the values of 9 and 11 are plotted at 9 and 20 (the sum of 9 + 11). This option is available only with SAS/CPE software.

STACKPCT
: same as STACK except plots each value or statistic of the variable as a percent of the total value or statistic for that variable. For example, the values of 9 and 11 are converted to 45% and 55% and plotted at 45 and 100 (the sum of 45 + 55). This option is available only with SAS/CPE software.

STD*xx*
: uses a solid line to connect, for each X value, the mean Y value's statistic with the Y value's statistics that are two standard deviations away from the mean Y value's statistic. Refer to the description of the INTERPOL=STD option of the GPLOT procedure.

STEP*cxx*
: plots the data with a step function. Refer to the description of the INTERPOL=STEP option of the GPLOT procedure.

VAXIS=*value-list*
: specifies the value for the major tick marks on the left Y axis (the vertical axis). These examples illustrate ways you can specify the *value-list*:

```
n n . . . n
n TO n <BY increment>
n n . . . n TO n <BY increment> <n . . . n>
```

Note: The values for VAXIS= must be specified as actual values, not formatted values. Thus, the tick marks for time values must be either a count of seconds or a SAS time constant, such as '12:20:01.8't. You must specify percentages as decimal values, such as .10 to .80 for 10% to 80%.

For more information about the *value-list*, see the ORDER= parameter in the "AXIS Statement Options" in Chapter 9 of *SAS/GRAPH Software: Reference, Version 6, First Edition, Volume 1*.

VREF=*value-list*

indicates values on the left Y axis (vertical axis) where you want to draw one or more horizontal lines to use as reference lines. Separate items in the *value-list* with blanks.

VZERO=NO | YES

specifies whether or not the tick marks on the vertical axis should begin with zero. The VZERO request is ignored if negative values are present for the vertical variable or if the vertical axis has been specified with the VAXIS= option. If you specify VZERO=NO or omit the VZERO= parameter, the tick marks begin with a value that is appropriate to the range of the data values.

The default value is NO.

WHERE=*where-expression*

specifies an expression that subsets the data to be reported on. Valid operators include, but are not limited to, BETWEEN AND, CONTAINS, LIKE, IN, IS NULL or IS MISSING. For example, the following statement limits the included observations to only those where the value of machine is 'host1' or 'host2':

```
where=machine in ('host1','host2')
```

For more information on these and other where operators, see the WHERE statement in Chapter 9 of *SAS Language: Reference, Version 6, First Edition.*

XLAB=*label*

provides a label (not more than 16 characters) for the X axis of a plot. **By default, the label is the name of the X variable.** You may use blank characters. You may enclose the label in single quotes, but the quotes are not required.

Caution: *Do not include commas, equal signs, parenthesis, or ampersands in the label.*

%CPPLOT2

Two Y-Axis Plot

Purpose

The %CPPLOT2 macro plots two Y variables on two Y axes, over time. The first variable specified is plotted against the left vertical axis, and the second is plotted against the right vertical axis. The two analysis variables do not have to share the same unit of measurement or have a similar range.

For more information on the underlying procedure, refer to "The GPLOT Procedure" in Chapter 31 of *SAS/GRAPH Software: Reference, Version 6, First Edition, Volume 2.*

Syntax

```
%CPPLOT2(dataset,
         y1 var,y1 lab,y2 var,y2 lab,
         REDLVL=reduction-level,
        <BEGIN=sas-datetime-value>,
        <BY=by-variable-list>,
        <END=sas-datetime-value>,
        <OUTDESC=text>,
        <OUTLOC=output-location>,
        <OUTMODE=output-format>,
        <OUTNAME=physical-filename|entry-name>,
        <PERIOD=time-interval>,
        <STAT=statistic>,
        <TABTYPE=INTERVAL|EVENT>,
        <VAXIS=value-list>,
        <VREF=value-list>,
        <VZERO=NO|YES>,
        <WHERE=where-expression> ) ;
```

%CPPLOT2 Parameters

dataset

specifies the table name from which to generate the report. **This positional parameter is required** and it can be specified in one of three ways.

If the data are in the DETAIL, DAY, WEEK, MONTH, or YEAR levels of the active PDB:

- ☐ Specify a tablename via the *dataset* parameter and a level via the **REDLVL=** parameter. If the REDLVL= parameter is not specified for the table name, REDLVL=DETAIL.

- ☐ Specify the name in the format of *REDLVL.TABLE*, in which case the REDLVL= parameter is not required.

If the data are in a SAS library that is not in the DETAIL, DAY, WEEK, MONTH, or YEAR level of the active PDB:

- ☐ Specify a two-level name in the format *libref.data-set-name* and specify REDLVL=OTHER.

Note: When specifying the data set name using the *libref* format, you must assign a *libref* before this macro is invoked. For more information see the LIBNAME statement in Chapter 9 of *SAS Language: Reference, Version 6, First Edition.*

y1_var,y1_lab, y2_var,y2_lab

specifies a paired list of analysis (Y) variable names and labels (up to 16 characters) for the left and right vertical axes, respectively. These variables do not have to have the same unit of measure or similar ranges of values. **This positional parameter is required**.

REDLVL=*reduction-level*

specifies which level of the table you are reporting on: DETAIL, DAY, WEEK, MONTH, YEAR, or OTHER. **The default is DETAIL**. The value of this parameter is used as a libref. You should specify REDLVL=OTHER if you want to select a SAS data set. The SAS data set should contain a variable named DATETIME, which represents the datetime stamp for each observation.

Note: When specifying the data set name using the *libref* format, you must assign a *libref* before this macro is invoked. For more information see the LIBNAME statement in Chapter 9 of *SAS Language: Reference, Version 6, First Edition.*

Optional Keyword Parameters

BEGIN=*SAS-datetime-value*

represents the first date and time for data to include in the report. The *sas-datetime-value* must be in the DATETIME13. SAS format. For example, BEGIN=01jul96:08:45. Use this parameter in combination with END= to define the range for subsetting data for the report. You can also use the TODAY[*-nnnn*]@*hh:mm* format, which uses the current date value minus *nnnn* days at the specified hour. This format supports the symbol or the word (@ or at) for the "at" instruction. For example, the following combination of values reports on the last three days of data, beginning at 8:00 a.m. three days ago and ending today at 5:00 p.m.

```
begin=today-3@08:00, end=todayat17:00
```

If you omit the time, the default time for the BEGIN= parameter is 00:00 on the specified date and the default time for the END= parameter is 23:59 on the specified date.

This example illustrates specific dates:

```
begin=01jul96:08:00, end=31jul96:17:00
```

If you omit the BEGIN= and END= parameters, the macro uses the information stored with the table definition (in the data dictionary) for the earliest and most recent datetime values at the specified level. The values stored with the table definition are based on the data currently in that level of the table. Exception: If the level is set to OTHER, the macro reads the data to determine the earliest and most recent datetime values (because there is not a table definition).

If you use only one parameter, BEGIN= or END=, that datetime is restricted and the other value is based on the data.

BY=*BY-variable-list*

lists the variables by which your data is sorted in the PDB. Use blanks to separate the variables in the list. A separate graph is produced for each value of the BY variable or for each combination of BY variable values, if you have multiple BY variables. For example, if you have four *diskids* on three machines, the following setting for the BY= parameter produces twelve reports, one for each of the twelve unique combinations of machine and *diskid* values.

```
by=machine diskid
```

For an alternate method of handling unique values of variables, refer to the description of class variables in the report you are producing.

If there is no BY= parameter, observations are sorted in the order that the variables are listed in the BY variable list or class variable list in the PDB. To check the order, follow this path from the main menu of the SAS/CPE interactive interface:

PDB Admin -> **Config Active PDB Dictionary** -> *select table*
-> **ItemActions** -> **Browse Definition**

or submit a batch job in which the **%CPDDUTL** macro runs a LIST TABLE control statement.

If you want to change the BY variables or their order for a one-time job, the fastest way to do so is to run a SAS program that contains the following statements:

```
proc sort data=level.table out=sasuser.table;
   by one-time-BY-variables-list;
```

where *level* is the reduction level on which to base the report, *table* is the table that you want to base the report on, *cpe-pdb* is the complete directory path or high-level-qualifiers and the name of the PDB you want to base your report on, and *one-time-BY-variables-list* is a list of the BY variables you want to use in the report. Order the variables from major to minor and separate the variables by blanks. After you run this program, run the report definition on the data in SASUSER.*table*.

Before changing the BY-variables or their order in the data dictionary you should be aware of the following:

- Changes to the BY-variables will not take effect in the data until the next process or reduce task runs or you execute the %CPDDUTL macro with the BUILD VIEWS control statement.
- The BY-variables list specified on any reports must match the current BY-variables list in the PDB. Therefore, if you have updated the BY-variables for a table in the PDB, you should examine all report definitions that use this table to see if the definition should be changed to match the new BY-variables list.
- When the BY-variables list is updated (via the process or reduce task or the BUILD VIEWS statement), the data in the PDB is physically sorted. Depending on the number of observations in the tables being sorted, this can take a considerable amount of time.

- ☐ It is not good practice to change the BY-variables list frequently. If you are changing the BY-variables list regularly in order to produce reports, you either have not chosen a good set of BY-variables or you have an incomplete understanding of how to create the report you want.

To change the BY variables list using the interactive interface, invoke SAS/CPE with update access to the PDB and then follow this path from the primary menu:

PDB Admin -> Config Active PDB Dictionary -> ***select table***
-> ItemActions -> Edit Definition

You can also use the **UPDATE TABLE** statement in the %CPDDUTL macro to change the BY variables list in batch mode.

END=*SAS-datetime-value*

represents the last date and time for data to include in the report. The *sas-datetime-value* must be in the DATETIME13. SAS format or in the today[-*nnnn*]@*hh:mm* format. For example, END=01jul96:17:00 or END=today-1@17:00.

Use this parameter in combination with BEGIN= to define the range for subsetting data for the report. Refer to **BEGIN=** for more information on using these parameters.

OUTDESC=*text*

is a description (as many as 40 characters) of the output.

If OUTMODE=CATALOG, the description is stored with the entry in the SAS catalog specified in the OUTLOC= parameter. Otherwise, the description is ignored.

OUTLOC=*output-location*

is the physical location of a graphics stream file, a SAS catalog name, or the physical location of the file or catalog member (for text reports only). The value of the OUTNAME= parameter is appended to the value of this parameter to specify the complete output location. Specify this parameter if you specify the OUTMODE= parameter.

OUTMODE=*output-format*

specifies the format for the output. **The default value is GWINDOW for all reports except %CPTABRPT. The default for %CPTABRPT is the output window.**

Valid values for this parameter are:

LP

stores the output as a text file. If you specify OUTMODE=LP, you should also specify the OUTLOC and OUTNAME parameters for the text report. If you do not specify the output location (OUTLOC=), the output is sent to the output window or standard SASLIST file. **This value is not valid for the %CPSPEC, %CPG3D, or %CPGTPLT macros.**

GSF

stores the output as a graphics stream file. If you specify OUTMODE=GSF, you must also specify the OUTLOC and OUTNAME parameters. **This value is not valid for the %CPXTAB and %CPTABRPT macros.**

CATALOG

stores the output as a GRSEG entry in a SAS catalog. If you are producing a graph report and you specify OUTMODE=CATALOG, you should also specify the OUTLOC, OUTNAME, and OUTDESC parameters. **This value is not valid for the %CPXTAB and %CPTABRPT macros.**

The following table summarizes which parameters should be specified in addition to OUTMODE=, based on the report type and the value of the OUTMODE= parameter.

When OUTMODE=	Specify these additional parameters			Not valid for these macros
LP	-	OUTLOC	OUTNAME	%CPSPEC, %CPG3D %CPGTPLT
GSF	-	OUTLOC	OUTNAME	%CPXTAB, %CPTABRPT
CATALOG	OUTDESC	OUTLOC	OUTNAME	%CPXTAB, %CPTABRPT

For more information on using OUTMODE= with OUTNAME= and OUTLOC=, see **Examples of the OUTMODE= Parameter**.

Caution: *OUTMODE=LP is the only valid option for reports that produce text output, for example those that use procedures such as TABULATE, REPORT, or PRINT. If you specify OUTMODE=CATALOG for a text report, the OUTLOC= and OUTNAME= parameters are ignored.*

The OUTNAME and OUTLOC parameters execute PROC PRINTTO in the background to set the output filename and location. When PROC PRINTTO is set, it stays in effect for subsequent text reports for the current SAS session until it is reset by another PROC PRINTTO. Therefore, after you set the OUTNAME and OUTLOC parameters and run your report, you must reset these values if you want the output from future reports to go to another location.

Furthermore, unless you have experience using PROC PRINTTO, you should not use the OUTNAME and OUTLOC parameters when PROC PRINTTO is executed because the commands may override each other and send your output to a location other than the one you expected. PROC PRINTTO does not produce a data set or printed output. It is useful when you want to route output from different steps in a SAS job to different files.

For more information on using PROC PRINTTO, refer to Chapter 28 of the *SAS Procedures Guide, Version 6, Third Edition.*

Note: The SAS/CPE interactive interface handles report output different from the OUTMODE=, OUTLOC=, and OUTNAME= batch parameters. In the interactive interface, use the value GWINDOW to display the report output in a GRAPH window, and use the value LP to display the report output in an OUTPUT window. In both cases, omit the OUTDESC=, OUTLOC=, and OUTNAME= parameters. Specify these parameters only if you use OUTMODE=GSF or CATALOG.

If you are running SAS/CPE in batch mode (i.e., you have executed it from within a cron job or from the MVS batch scheduler) and are running a graph report, you should specify an output location other than the graph window.

OUTNAME=*physical-filename* | *entry-name*

is the name of the external file or the entry-name in the SAS catalog where you want to store output results. Catalog entries are stored as GRSEG type entries. The value of this parameter is appended to the value of the OUTLOC= parameter to specify the complete output location.

Specify this parameter whenever you specify the OUTMODE= parameter, except when you specify OUTMODE=CATALOG.

PERIOD=*time-interval*

is the summarization period for the report. **The default is ASIS.** For values other than ASIS, the values for the time period within a class or category are combined to form a single point on a plot, a bar on a chart, or a row or column in a table.

Notes: For the %CPCHART and %CPXTAB macros, PERIOD= is only valid if the class variable is DATETIME. For the %CPCCHRT macro, PERIOD= is only valid if the DATETIME variable is selected in any category.

Period	Effect	Example
ASIS	leaves datetime in its present form.	09Jun94:14:37:25
15MIN	transforms the time to the first minute of the 15-minute period in the hour and retains the date.	09Jun94:14:30
HOUR	transforms the time to the first minute of the hour and retains the date.	09Jun94:14:00
24HOUR	transforms the time to its hour component and omits the date. Range: 0-23.	14
DATE	omits the time and retains the date.	09Jun94
WHOLEDAY	same as DATE.	
WEEKDAY	transforms the day to the day of the week (where 1=Sunday, 2=Monday, and so on) and omits the month, year, and time. Range: 1-7, which displays as Sunday-Saturday.	Thursday

MONTHDAY	omits everything but the day of the month. Range: 1-31.	9
YEARDAY	transforms the day to the day of the year and omits the month, year, and time. Range: 1-366.	160
WEEK	transforms the date to first date in the week (where the week begins on the day on which January 1 falls in the year) and omits the time.	04Jun94
MONTH	omits the day and the time	Jun94
YEARMONTH	omits everything but the month of the year. Range: 1-12.	6
QTR	transforms the month to the first month of the quarter and omits the day and time.	Apr94

STAT=*statistic*

specifies what statistic to use to summarize data that span the time interval specified by **PERIOD=**. The selected statistic is used for all variables in the report. **The default statistic is MEAN**. The STAT= parameter is not valid if PERIOD=ASIS. Valid values for STAT= are:

CSS

is the sum of squares corrected for the mean.

CV

is the coefficient of variation. It is calculated as the standard deviation divided by the mean and multiplied by 100.

MAX

is the maximum value for all observations.

MEAN

is the arithmetic average. Mean is one measure used to describe the center of a distribution of values.

MIN

is the minimum value for all observations.

N

or COUNT, is the number of observations with nonmissing values for the variables being summarized.

NMISS
: the number of observations with missing values for the variable being summarized.

RANGE
: is the maximum of the difference between the maximum and minimum values for the variables, RANGE=MAX-MIN.

STD
: is the standard deviation or square root of variance. Like the variance, it is a measure of the dispersion about the mean, but in the same unit of measure as the data.

STDERR
: is the positive square root of the variance of a statistic.

SUM
: is the sum of values for all observations.

USS
: is the uncorrected sum of squares.

VAR
: is a measure of the dispersion or variability of the data about the mean. When values are close to the mean, the variance is small. When values are scattered widely about the mean, the variance is large.

Note: If you specify the **BY=** parameter, the statistics are calculated separately for each value of the BY variable or for each combination of the BY variable values, if you specified multiple BY variables.

TABTYPE=INTERVAL | EVENT
: specifies whether the data cover a specified interval of time or whether they are logged in response to an event that occurs, such as when a job begins or ends. **INTERVAL is the default value.**

INTERVAL
: each observation represents an interval of time.

EVENT
: each observation represents an event.

VAXIS=*value-list*
: specifies the value for the major tick marks on the left Y axis (the vertical axis). These examples illustrate ways you can specify the *value-list*:

```
n n . . . n
n TO n <BY increment>
n n . . . n TO n <BY increment> <n . . . n>
```

Note: The values for VAXIS= must be specified as actual values, not formatted values. Thus, the tick marks for time values must be either a count of seconds or a SAS time constant, such as '12:20:01.8't. You must specify percentages as decimal values, such as .10 to .80 for 10% to 80%.

For more information about the *value-list*, see the ORDER= parameter in the "AXIS Statement Options" in Chapter 9 of *SAS/GRAPH Software: Reference, Version 6, First Edition, Volume 1.*

VREF=*value-list*
: indicates values on the left Y axis (vertical axis) where you want to draw one or more horizontal lines to use as reference lines. Separate items in the *value-list* with blanks.

VZERO=NO | YES
: specifies whether or not the tick marks on the vertical axis should begin with zero. The VZERO request is ignored if negative values are present for the vertical variable or if the vertical axis has been specified with the VAXIS= option. If you specify VZERO=NO or omit the VZERO= parameter, the tick marks begin with a value that is appropriate to the range of the data values.

  The default value is NO.

WHERE=*where-expression*
: specifies an expression that subsets the data to be reported on. Valid operators include, but are not limited to, BETWEEN AND, CONTAINS, LIKE, IN, IS NULL or IS MISSING. For example, the following statement limits the included observations to only those where the value of machine is 'host1' or 'host2':

```
where=machine in ('host1','host2')
```

  For more information on these and other where operators, see the WHERE statement in Chapter 9 of *SAS Language: Reference, Version 6, First Edition.*

%CPSPEC

Three-Dimensional Plot with Color as the Third Dimension (Spectrum Plot)

Purpose

The %CPSPEC macro generates a two-dimensional surface plot in which the values of the analysis variable are grouped by percentiles or specified data values and represented on the graph by color. The plot resembles a multiline spectrograph.

You can specify a maximum of 15 analysis variables for this report. If you specify a class variable (CL_NAM=) by which to group the analyisis variable on the plot, you can only specify one analysis *(var1,lab1)* variable.

By default, the colors on the graph represent the data values of the analysis variables using a cool-to-hot spectrum, with blue being cool or low values, green to orange being warm or mid-range values, and red being hot or high values. However, you can use the COLORLST= parameter to change the colors used in your Spectrum Plot.

Syntax

```
%CPSPEC(dataset,
        var1,lab1,...,var15,lab15,
        REDLVL=reduction-level,
       <BEGIN=SAS-datetime-value>,
       <BY=BY-variable-list>,
       <CL_LAB=label>,
       <CL_NAM=class-variable-name>,
       <COLORLST=color-list>,
       <CTEXT=color>,
       <END=SAS-datetime-value>,
       <OUTDESC=text>,
       <OUTLOC=output-location>,
       <OUTMODE=output-format>,
       <OUTNAME=physical-filename|entry-name>,
       <PERCENTS=list-of-ranges> | <DATAVALS= value list>,
       <PERIOD=time-interval>,
       <STAT=statistic>,
       <TABTYPE=INTERVAL|EVENT>,
       <WHERE=where-expression>,
       <YVAL=number> ) ;
```

%CPSPEC Parameters

dataset

specifies the table name from which to generate the report. **This positional parameter is required** and it can be specified in one of three ways.

If the data are in the DETAIL, DAY, WEEK, MONTH, or YEAR levels of the active PDB:

- ☐ Specify a tablename via the *dataset* parameter and a level via the **REDLVL=** parameter. If the REDLVL= parameter is not specified for the table name,

REDLVL=DETAIL.

- Specify the name in the format of *REDLVL.TABLE*, in which case the REDLVL= parameter is not required.

If the data are in a SAS library that is not in the DETAIL, DAY, WEEK, MONTH, or YEAR level of the active PDB:

- Specify a two-level name in the format *libref.data-set-name* and specify REDLVL=OTHER.

Note: When specifying the data set name using the *libref* format, you must assign a *libref* before this macro is invoked. For more information see the LIBNAME statement in Chapter 9 of *SAS Language: Reference, Version 6, First Edition.*

var1,lab1 . . . var15,lab15

specifies a paired list of analysis variable names and labels (up to 16 characters) for the analysis axis. The maximum number of pairs you can specify is 15. **This positional parameter is required.** You must specify at least one variable and one label.

The analysis variable typically displays on the left (Y) axis. However, certain combinations of parameters may affect the axis on which the analysis variable is displayed or the number of variables that can be specified for a specific report. For a detailed explanation of the variables displayed on each axis and the maximum number of variables that can be specified for the report, refer to the *Purpose* section of the macro description.

If you specify multiple analysis variables, the unit of measure for all of the variables should be the same and the range of values should be similar. You may use blank characters in the label and you may enclose the label in single quotes, but the quotes are not required.

Caution: *Do not include commas, equal signs, parentheses, or ampersands in the labels.*

REDLVL=*reduction-level*

specifies which level of the table you are reporting on: DETAIL, DAY, WEEK, MONTH, YEAR, or OTHER. **The default is DETAIL**. The value of this parameter is used as a libref. You should specify REDLVL=OTHER if you want to select a SAS data set. The SAS data set should contain a variable named DATETIME, which represents the datetime stamp for each observation.

Note: When specifying the data set name using the *libref* format, you must assign a *libref* before this macro is invoked. For more information see the LIBNAME statement in Chapter 9 of *SAS Language: Reference, Version 6, First Edition.*

Optional Keyword Parameters

BEGIN=*SAS-datetime-value*

represents the first date and time for data to include in the report. The *sas-datetime-value* must be in the DATETIME13. SAS format. For example, BEGIN=01jul96:08:45. Use this parameter in combination with **END=** to define the range for subsetting data for the report. You can also use the TODAY[*-nnnn*]@*hh:mm* format, which uses the current date value minus *nnnn* days at the specified hour. This format supports the symbol or the word (@ or at) for the "at" instruction. For example, the following combination of values reports on the last three days of data, beginning at 8:00 a.m. three days ago and ending today at 5:00 p.m.

```
begin=today-3@08:00, end=todayat17:00
```

If you omit the time, the default time for the BEGIN= parameter is 00:00 on the specified date and the default time for the END= parameter is 23:59 on the specified date.

This example illustrates specific dates:

```
begin=01jul96:08:00, end=31jul96:17:00
```

If you omit the BEGIN= and END= parameters, the macro uses the information stored with the table definition (in the data dictionary) for the earliest and most recent datetime values at the specified level. The values stored with the table definition are based on the data currently in that level of the table. Exception: If the level is set to OTHER, the macro reads the data to determine the earliest and most recent datetime values (because there is not a table definition).

If you use only one parameter, BEGIN= or END=, that datetime is restricted and the other value is based on the data.

BY=*BY-variable-list*

lists the variables by which your data is sorted in the PDB. Use blanks to separate the variables in the list. A separate graph is produced for each value of the BY variable or for each combination of BY variable values, if you have multiple BY variables. For example, if you have four *diskids* on three machines, the following setting for the BY= parameter produces twelve reports, one for each of the twelve unique combinations of machine and *diskid* values.

```
by=machine diskid
```

For an alternate method of handling unique values of variables, refer to the description of class variables in the report you are producing.

If there is no BY= parameter, observations are sorted in the order that the variables are listed in the BY variable list or class variable list in the PDB. To check the order, follow this path from the main menu of the SAS/CPE interactive interface:

PDB Admin -> **Config Active PDB Dictionary** -> *select table*
-> **ItemActions** -> **Browse Definition**

or submit a batch job in which the **%CPDDUTL** macro runs a LIST TABLE control statement.

If you want to change the BY variables or their order for a one-time job, the fastest way to do so is to run a SAS program that contains the following statements:

```
proc sort data=level.table out=sasuser.table;
   by one-time-BY-variables-list;
```

where *level* is the reduction level on which to base the report, *table* is the table that you want to base the report on, *cpe-pdb* is the complete directory path or high-level-qualifiers and the name of the PDB you want to base your report on, and *one-time-BY-variables-list* is a list of the BY variables you want to use in the report. Order the variables from major to minor and separate the variables by blanks. After you run this program, run the report definition on the data in SASUSER.*table*.

Before changing the BY-variables or their order in the data dictionary you should be aware of the following:

- ☐ Changes to the BY-variables will not take effect in the data until the next process or reduce task runs or you execute the %CPDDUTL macro with the BUILD VIEWS control statement.
- ☐ The BY-variables list specified on any reports must match the current BY-variables list in the PDB. Therefore, if you have updated the BY-variables for a table in the PDB, you should examine all report definitions that use this table to see if the definition should be changed to match the new BY-variables list.
- ☐ When the BY-variables list is updated (via the process or reduce task or the BUILD VIEWS statement), the data in the PDB is physically sorted. Depending on the number of observations in the tables being sorted, this can take a considerable amount of time.
- ☐ It is not good practice to change the BY-variables list frequently. If you are changing the BY-variables list regularly in order to produce reports, you either have not chosen a good set of BY-variables or you have an incomplete understanding of how to create the report you want.

To change the BY variables list using the interactive interface, invoke SAS/CPE with update access to the PDB and then follow this path from the primary menu:

PDB Admin -> **Config Active PDB Dictionary** -> *select table*
-> **ItemActions** -> **Edit Definition**

You can also use the **UPDATE TABLE** statement in the %CPDDUTL macro to change the BY variables list in batch mode.

CL_LAB=*label*

is the label (a maximum of 16 characters) for the class variable. You may use blank characters. You may enclose the label in single quotes, but the quotes are not required.

Caution: *Do not include commas, equal signs, parentheses, or ampersands in the label.*

CL_NAM=*variable-name*

specifies the name of the class variable for the report. For each unique value of the class variable, the macro creates a separate portion or group on the graph.

Compare this type of variable to the BY variable. The BY variable creates separate graphs for each unique value of the variable. For example, the following combination of parameters produces one report or plot for each unique value of MACHINE, the BY variable.

```
cl_nam=diskid, by=machine
```

Each of the graphs for MACHINE includes all possible values of DISKID, the class variable. If you are producing a plot, each unique value of DISKID is represented by a different color or plot symbol. If you are producing a chart each value of DISKID is represented in a separate column or row.

COLORLST=*value-list*

specifies the colors to use for this spectrum plot. **By default, the color list is represented by a blue to red color spectrum and the number of colors used is based on the number of values specified in the <u>PERCENTS=</u> or <u>DATAVALS=</u> parameter.**

Specify the names of the colors that you want to use on your report, such as blue, green, yellow, orange, or red, using the following guidelines:

- ☐ Use blanks to separate the items in the list, but do not enclose the list in quotes.
- ☐ SAS/CPE uses the colors in ascending order exactly as you list them in this parameter.
- ☐ The first color specified will be used as the text color and as the color for your first data category. Therefore, you should not specify this color to be the same color as your background or your text will appear to be missing.
- ☐ The number of colors specified must be equal to $n + 1$, where n is the number of values specified in the DATAVALS= or PERCENTS= parameter. If the number of colors is incorrect, the macro stops and a message is printed in the SAS log.

If you specify this parameter the **<u>CTEXT=</u>** parameter is ignored.

For a complete list of available colors, see SAS/GRAPH Colors in Chapter 7 of *SAS/GRAPH Software: Reference, Version 6, First Edition.*

CTEXT=*color*

indicates the color of the text on a plot. **The default text color is white**. You can specify the background color with the CBACK= parameter in the SAS GOPTIONS statement. The default background color is device dependent. Refer to the information on your output device in *SAS/GRAPH Software: Using Graphics Devices, Version 6, First Edition* for your specific host.

Notes: If the color of the text is the same as the color of the background, the text appears to be missing. If you specify this parameter and the COLORLST= parameter, the value of this parameter is ignored.

END=*SAS-datetime-value*

represents the last date and time for data to include in the report. The *sas-datetime-value* must be in the DATETIME13. SAS format or in the today[-*nnnn*]@*hh:mm* format. For example, END=01jul96:17:00 or END=today-1@17:00.

Use this parameter in combination with BEGIN= to define the range for subsetting data for the report. Refer to **<u>BEGIN=</u>** for more information on using these parameters.

OUTDESC=*text*

is a description (as many as 40 characters) of the output.

If OUTMODE=CATALOG, the description is stored with the entry in the SAS catalog specified in the OUTLOC= parameter. Otherwise, the description is ignored.

OUTLOC=*output-location*
: is the physical location of a graphics stream file, a SAS catalog name, or the physical location of the file or catalog member (for text reports only). The value of the OUTNAME= parameter is appended to the value of this parameter to specify the complete output location. Specify this parameter if you specify the OUTMODE= parameter.

OUTMODE=*output-format*
: specifies the format for the output. **The default value is GWINDOW for all reports except %CPTABRPT. The default for %CPTABRPT is the output window.**

Valid values for this parameter are:

LP
: stores the output as a text file. If you specify OUTMODE=LP, you should also specify the OUTLOC and OUTNAME parameters for the text report. If you do not specify the output location (OUTLOC=), the output is sent to the output window or standard SASLIST file. **This value is not valid for the %CPSPEC, %CPG3D, or %CPGTPLT macros.**

GSF
: stores the output as a graphics stream file. If you specify OUTMODE=GSF, you must also specify the OUTLOC and OUTNAME parameters. **This value is not valid for the %CPXTAB and %CPTABRPT macros.**

CATALOG
: stores the output as a GRSEG entry in a SAS catalog. If you are producing a graph report and you specify OUTMODE=CATALOG, you should also specify the OUTLOC, OUTNAME, and OUTDESC parameters. **This value is not valid for the %CPXTAB and %CPTABRPT macros.**

The following table summarizes which parameters should be specified in addition to OUTMODE=, based on the report type and the value of the OUTMODE= parameter.

When OUTMODE=	Specify these additional parameters			Not valid for these macros
LP	-	OUTLOC	OUTNAME	%CPSPEC, %CPG3D %CPGTPLT
GSF	-	OUTLOC	OUTNAME	%CPXTAB, %CPTABRPT
CATALOG	OUTDESC	OUTLOC	OUTNAME	%CPXTAB, %CPTABRPT

For more information on using OUTMODE= with OUTNAME= and OUTLOC=, see Examples of the OUTMODE= Parameter.

Caution: *OUTMODE=LP is the only valid option for reports that produce text output, for example those that use procedures such as TABULATE, REPORT, or PRINT. If you specify OUTMODE=CATALOG for a text report, the OUTLOC= and OUTNAME= parameters are ignored.*

The OUTNAME and OUTLOC parameters execute PROC PRINTTO in the background to set the output filename and location. When PROC PRINTTO is set, it stays in effect for subsequent text reports for the current SAS session until it is reset by another PROC PRINTTO. Therefore, after you set the OUTNAME and OUTLOC parameters and run your report, you must reset these values if you want the output from future reports to go to another location.

Furthermore, unless you have experience using PROC PRINTTO, you should not use the OUTNAME and OUTLOC parameters when PROC PRINTTO is executed because the commands may override each other and send your output to a location other than the one you expected. PROC PRINTTO does not produce a data set or printed output. It is useful when you want to route output from different steps in a SAS job to different files.

For more information on using PROC PRINTTO, refer to Chapter 28 of the *SAS Procedures Guide, Version 6, Third Edition.*

Note: The SAS/CPE interactive interface handles report output different from the OUTMODE=, OUTLOC=, and OUTNAME= batch parameters. In the interactive interface, use the value GWINDOW to display the report output in a GRAPH window, and use the value LP to display the report output in an OUTPUT window. In both cases, omit the OUTDESC=, OUTLOC=, and OUTNAME= parameters. Specify these parameters only if you use OUTMODE=GSF or CATALOG.

If you are running SAS/CPE in batch mode (i.e., you have executed it from within a cron job or from the MVS batch scheduler) and are running a graph report, you should specify an output location other than the graph window.

OUTNAME=*physical-filename* | *entry-name*

is the name of the external file or the entry-name in the SAS catalog where you want to store output results. Catalog entries are stored as GRSEG type entries. The value of this parameter is appended to the value of the OUTLOC= parameter to specify the complete output location.

Specify this parameter whenever you specify the OUTMODE= parameter, except when you specify OUTMODE=CATALOG.

PERCENTS=*range-list*

lists the percentile ranges to which the data points are mapped. You can select a maximum of 13 percentile range categories or groups. Analysis variables display in percentile groups and the groups are represented by color (see the **COLORLST=** parameter) on the graph. **The default range list is 25 50 75 95 99.**

Use blanks to separate the values in the list, but do not enclose the list in quotes. You can specify this parameter or the **DATAVALS=** parameter, but not both.

DATAVALS=*value-list*

specifies the list of numeric values by which to group your data in this report. For example, if you specify a value list of 50 100 150 200, and the values in your data range from less than 50 to above 200, data values that are less than or equal to 50 would fall in the first category and would be represented in the first color in the color spectrum (see the **COLORLST=** parameter) for this report. Data values greater than 50 and less than or equal to 100 would fall in the second category and would be represented by the next color in the color spectrum for this report, and so on. The last group would represent data values greater than 200 and would be represented by the last color in the color spectrum for this report.

You can specify a maximum of 13 values. Use blanks to separate the values in the list, but do not enclose the list in quotes. You can specify this parameter or the **PERCENTS=** parameter, but not both. **If you do not specify this parameter, the values in the PERCENTS= parameter are used. If you do not specify values for the PERCENTS= parameter, the default values for that parameter are used.**

PERIOD=*time-interval*

is the summarization period for the report. **The default is ASIS**. For values other than ASIS, the values for the time period within a class or category are combined to form a single point on a plot, a bar on a chart, or a row or column in a table.

Notes: For the %CPCHART and %CPXTAB macros, PERIOD= is only valid if the class variable is DATETIME. For the %CPCCHRT macro, PERIOD= is only valid if the DATETIME variable is selected in any category.

Period	Effect	Example
ASIS	leaves datetime in its present form.	09Jun94:14:37:25
15MIN	transforms the time to the first minute of the 15-minute period in the hour and retains the date.	09Jun94:14:30
HOUR	transforms the time to the first minute of the hour and retains the date.	09Jun94:14:00
24HOUR	transforms the time to its hour component and omits the date. Range: 0-23.	14
DATE	omits the time and retains the date.	09Jun94
WHOLEDAY	same as DATE.	
WEEKDAY	transforms the day to the day of the week (where 1=Sunday, 2=Monday, and so on) and omits the month, year, and time. Range:	Thursday

	1-7, which displays as Sunday-Saturday.	
MONTHDAY	omits everything but the day of the month. Range: 1-31.	9
YEARDAY	transforms the day to the day of the year and omits the month, year, and time. Range: 1-366.	160
WEEK	transforms the date to first date in the week (where the week begins on the day on which January 1 falls in the year) and omits the time.	04Jun94
MONTH	omits the day and the time	Jun94
YEARMONTH	omits everything but the month of the year. Range: 1-12.	6
QTR	transforms the month to the first month of the quarter and omits the day and time.	Apr94

STAT=*statistic*

specifies what statistic to use to summarize data that span the time interval specified by **PERIOD=**. The selected statistic is used for all variables in the report. **The default statistic is MEAN**. The STAT= parameter is not valid if PERIOD=ASIS. Valid values for STAT= are:

CSS

is the sum of squares corrected for the mean.

CV

is the coefficient of variation. It is calculated as the standard deviation divided by the mean and multiplied by 100.

MAX

is the maximum value for all observations.

MEAN

is the arithmetic average. Mean is one measure used to describe the center of a distribution of values.

MIN

is the minimum value for all observations.

N

or COUNT, is the number of observations with nonmissing values for the variables being summarized.

NMISS
the number of observations with missing values for the variable being summarized.

RANGE
is the maximum of the difference between the maximum and minimum values for the variables, RANGE=MAX-MIN.

STD
is the standard deviation or square root of variance. Like the variance, it is a measure of the dispersion about the mean, but in the same unit of measure as the data.

STDERR
is the positive square root of the variance of a statistic.

SUM
is the sum of values for all observations.

USS
is the uncorrected sum of squares.

VAR
is a measure of the dispersion or variability of the data about the mean. When values are close to the mean, the variance is small. When values are scattered widely about the mean, the variance is large.

Note: If you specify the **BY=** parameter, the statistics are calculated separately for each value of the BY variable or for each combination of the BY variable values, if you specified multiple BY variables.

TABTYPE=INTERVAL | EVENT
specifies whether the data cover a specified interval of time or whether they are logged in response to an event that occurs, such as when a job begins or ends. **INTERVAL is the default value.**

INTERVAL
each observation represents an interval of time.

EVENT
each observation represents an event.

WHERE=*where-expression*
specifies an expression that subsets the data to be reported on. Valid operators include, but are not limited to, BETWEEN AND, CONTAINS, LIKE, IN, IS NULL or IS MISSING. For example, the following statement limits the included observations to only those where the value of machine is 'host1' or 'host2':

```
where=machine in ('host1','host2')
```

For more information on these and other where operators, see the WHERE statement in Chapter 9 of *SAS Language: Reference, Version 6, First Edition.*

YVAL=*number*

is the number of Y values to print on one page of the plot. **The default number is based on the output device type.** If the number of analysis variables is greater than the value of YVAL=, the chart is broken into multiple pages.

Note

All variables for the plot should have the same unit of measurement.

For more information on the underlying procedure, refer to "The GPLOT Procedure" in Chapter 31 of *SAS/GRAPH Software: Reference, Version 6, First Edition, Volume 2.*

%CPSRCRPT

Runs a predefined SAS program using global macro variables

Purpose

The %CPSRCRPT macro runs any SAS program stored in a SOURCE catalog entry. This macro enables you to run complex reports that may require multiple steps to manipulate your data, while still using the global macro variable values such as beginning and ending dates and WHERE expressions.

The SOURCE code that is run by %CPSRCRPT is specified using the *rptname* parameter and can be any source code that you want to run. It can be source code that you have saved from one of the SAS/CPE sample reports or source code that you have written. For example, you may have an existing data set that you want to read and further subset or summarize using %CPSRCRPT parameters. You can use the data set as input to %CPSRCRPT (*dataset*), manipulate the data using %CPSRCRPT parameters (such as BY=, BEGIN=, END=), output the summarized data to a new data set (*outdata*), which is then used as input to your existing source code (*rptname*). That source code is read and submitted by %CPSRCRPT to create your report.

Syntax

```
%CPSRCRPT(dataset,
          outdata,
          rptname,
          <p4,...p31>,
          REDLVL=reduction-level,
          <BEGIN=SAS-datetime-value>,
          <BY=BY-variable-list>,
          <CL_NAM=variable-name>,
          <END=SAS-datetime-value>,
          <OUTDESC=text>,
          <OUTLOC=output-location>,
          <OUTMODE=output-format>,
          <OUTNAME=physical-filename|entry-name>,
          <PERIOD=time-interval>,
          <WHERE=where-expression> ) ;
```

%CPSRCRPT Parameters

dataset

specifies the table name from which to generate the report. **This positional parameter is required** and it can be specified in one of three ways.

If the data are in the DETAIL, DAY, WEEK, MONTH, or YEAR levels of the active PDB:

- ☐ Specify a tablename via the *dataset* parameter and a level via the **REDLVL=** parameter. If the REDLVL= parameter is not specified for the table name, REDLVL=DETAIL.

- ☐ Specify the name in the format of *REDLVL.TABLE*, in which case the REDLVL= parameter is not required.

If the data are in a SAS library that is not in the DETAIL, DAY, WEEK, MONTH, or YEAR level of the active PDB:

- ☐ Specify a two-level name in the format *libref.data-set-name* and specify REDLVL=OTHER.

Note: When specifying the data set name using the *libref* format, you must assign a *libref* before this macro is invoked. For more information see the LIBNAME statement in Chapter 9 of *SAS Language: Reference, Version 6, First Edition.*

outdata

is the name of the SAS data set that is created when you run %CPSRCRPT. When you run the %CPSRCRPT macro, the data set specified in the *outdata* parameter is created based on the values specified in the data set, BEGIN, END, REDLVL, WHERE, BY, and CL_NAM, parameters. The *outdata* data set can then be used as input to your source code (*rptname*). **This positional parameter is required.**

rptname

is the name of the SAS catalog entry that contains your source code, which will produce your report when this SOURCE entry is run by %CPSRCRPT. **This positional parameter is required.**

p4,...p31

identifies values that you want to use in your source code. **These positional parameters are optional**, but when used, the items must be specified in positions 4 through 31. The information is not used by %CPSRCRPT, but using these parameters provides you the option of passing additional information into your source code (*rptname*) when %CPSRCRPT runs that code.

You must separate items in the list with commas, but you do not need to use commas as placeholders if you are not using all 31 of these positional parameters. For example, if you are using four positional parameters (p4-p7) you would separate the four parameters with commas, but do not need to include the additional commas for parameters p8 through p31. For an example of how to use these parameters, refer to the %CPSRCRPT macro examples.

The parameters specified here should be referenced in your source code as macro variables with names such as &p4, &p5, and so on.

REDLVL=*reduction-level*

specifies which level of the table you are reporting on: DETAIL, DAY, WEEK, MONTH, YEAR, or OTHER. **The default is DETAIL**. The value of this parameter is used as a libref. You should specify REDLVL=OTHER if you want to select a SAS data set. The SAS data set should contain a variable named DATETIME, which represents the datetime stamp for each observation.

Note: When specifying the data set name using the *libref* format, you must assign a *libref* before this macro is invoked. For more information see the LIBNAME statement in Chapter 9 of *SAS Language: Reference, Version 6, First Edition.*

Optional Keyword Parameters

BEGIN=*SAS-datetime-value*

represents the first date and time for data to include in the report. The *sas-datetime-value* must be in the DATETIME13. SAS format. For example, BEGIN=01jul96:08:45. Use this parameter in combination with **END=** to define the range for subsetting data for the report. You can also use the TODAY[-*nnnn*]@*hh:mm* format, which uses the current date value minus *nnnn* days at the specified hour. This format supports the symbol or the word (@ or at) for the "at" instruction. For example, the following combination of values reports on the last three days of data, beginning at 8:00 a.m. three days ago and ending today at 5:00 p.m.

```
begin=today-3@08:00, end=todayat17:00
```

If you omit the time, the default time for the BEGIN= parameter is 00:00 on the specified date and the default time for the END= parameter is 23:59 on the specified date.

This example illustrates specific dates:

```
begin=01jul96:08:00, end=31jul96:17:00
```

If you omit the BEGIN= and END= parameters, the macro uses the information stored with the table definition (in the data dictionary) for the earliest and most recent datetime values at the specified level. The values stored with the table definition are based on the data currently in that level of the table. Exception: If the level is set to OTHER, the macro reads the data to determine the earliest and most recent datetime values (because there is not a table definition).

If you use only one parameter, BEGIN= or END=, that datetime is restricted and the other value is based on the data.

BY=*BY-variable-list*

lists the variables by which your data is sorted in the PDB. Use blanks to separate the variables in the list. A separate graph is produced for each value of the BY variable or for each combination of BY variable values, if you have multiple BY variables. For example, if you have four *diskids* on three machines, the following setting for the BY= parameter produces twelve reports, one for each of the twelve unique combinations of machine and *diskid* values.

```
by=machine diskid
```

For an alternate method of handling unique values of variables, refer to the description of class variables in the report you are producing.

If there is no BY= parameter, observations are sorted in the order that the variables are listed in the BY variable list or class variable list in the PDB. To check the order, follow this path from the main menu of the SAS/CPE interactive interface:

PDB Admin -> **Config Active PDB Dictionary** -> *select table*
-> **ItemActions** -> **Browse Definition**

or submit a batch job in which the **%CPDDUTL** macro runs a LIST TABLE control statement.

If you want to change the BY variables or their order for a one-time job, the fastest way to do so is to run a SAS program that contains the following statements:

```
proc sort data=level.table out=sasuser.table;
   by one-time-BY-variables-list;
```

where *level* is the reduction level on which to base the report, *table* is the table that you want to base the report on, *cpe-pdb* is the complete directory path or high-level-qualifiers and the name of the PDB you want to base your report on, and *one-time-BY-variables-list* is a list of the BY variables you want to use in the report. Order the variables from major to minor and separate the variables by blanks. After you run this program, run the report definition on the data in SASUSER.*table*.

Before changing the BY-variables or their order in the data dictionary you should be aware of the following:

- Changes to the BY-variables will not take effect in the data until the next process or reduce task runs or you execute the %CPDDUTL macro with the BUILD VIEWS control statement.
- The BY-variables list specified on any reports must match the current BY-variables list in the PDB. Therefore, if you have updated the BY-variables for a table in the PDB, you should examine all report definitions that use this table to see if the definition should be changed to match the new BY-variables list.
- When the BY-variables list is updated (via the process or reduce task or the BUILD VIEWS statement), the data in the PDB is physically sorted. Depending on the number of observations in the tables being sorted, this can take a considerable amount of time.
- It is not good practice to change the BY-variables list frequently. If you are changing the BY-variables list regularly in order to produce reports, you either have not chosen a good set of BY-variables or you have an incomplete understanding of how to create the report you want.

To change the BY variables list using the interactive interface, invoke SAS/CPE with update access to the PDB and then follow this path from the primary menu:

PDB Admin -> Config Active PDB Dictionary -> ***select table***
-> ItemActions -> Edit Definition

You can also use the **UPDATE TABLE** statement in the %CPDDUTL macro to change the BY variables list in batch mode.

CL_NAM=*variable-list*

specifies the list of class variables used in this table. Separate multiple variables with blanks. You can specify up to five variables. If the data is summarized, a separate observation will be created for each value of the CL_NAM variable, however, the data is not sorted by these variables.

END=*SAS-datetime-value*

represents the last date and time for data to include in the report. The *sas-datetime-value* must be in the DATETIME13. SAS format or in the today[-*nnnn*]@*hh:mm* format. For example, END=01jul96:17:00 or END=today-1@17:00.

Use this parameter in combination with BEGIN= to define the range for subsetting data for the report. Refer to **BEGIN=** for more information on using these parameters.

OUTDESC=*text*

is a description (as many as 40 characters) of the output.

If OUTMODE=CATALOG, the description is stored with the entry in the SAS catalog specified in the OUTLOC= parameter. Otherwise, the description is ignored.

OUTLOC=*output-location*

is the physical location of a graphics stream file, a SAS catalog name, or the physical location of the file or catalog member (for text reports only). The value of the OUTNAME= parameter is appended to the value of this parameter to specify the complete output location. Specify this parameter if you specify the OUTMODE= parameter.

OUTMODE=*output-format*

specifies the format for the output. **The default value is GWINDOW**. Values for batch mode are:

LP

stores the output as a text file. If you specify OUTMODE=LP, you should also specify the OUTLOC and OUTNAME parameters for the text report. If you do not specify the output location, the output is sent to the output window or standard SASLIST file.

GSF

stores the output as a graphics stream file. If you specify OUTMODE=GSF, you must also specify the OUTLOC and OUTNAME parameters.

CATALOG

stores the output as a GRSEG entry in a SAS catalog. If you are producing a graph report and you specify OUTMODE=CATALOG, you should also specify the OUTLOC, OUTNAME, and OUTDESC parameters. If you are producing a text report and you specify OUTMODE=CATALOG, you only need to specify the OUTDESC parameter.

If you are generating graphic output from %CPSRCRPT (such as OUTMODE=CATALOG or GSF), you must reference in your source code the OUTNAME= and OUTLOC= parameters specified on %CPSRCRPT.

The following tables summarize which parameters should be specified in addition to OUTMODE=, based on the report type and the value of the OUTMODE= parameter.

```
For GRAPH Reports:
                                  Specify these additional
     When OUTMODE=                       parameters
```

LP	-	OUTLOC	OUTNAME
GSF	-	OUTLOC	OUTNAME
CATALOG	OUTDESC	OUTLOC	OUTNAME

For TEXT Reports:

When OUTMODE=	Specify these additional parameters		
LP	-	OUTLOC	OUTNAME
GSF	-	OUTLOC	OUTNAME
CATALOG	OUTDESC	-	-

For more information on using OUTMODE= with OUTNAME= and OUTLOC=, see **Examples of the OUTMODE= Parameter**.

Caution: *OUTMODE=LP is the only valid option for reports that produce text output, for example, those that use procedures such as TABULATE, REPORT, PRINT, and others. If you specify OUTMODE=CATALOG for a text report the OUTLOC= and OUTNAME= parameters are ignored.*

The OUTNAME and OUTLOC parameters execute PROC PRINTTO in the background to set the output filename and location. When PROC PRINTTO is set, it stays in effect for subsequent text reports for the current SAS session until it is reset by another PROC PRINTTO. Therefore, after you set the OUTNAME and OUTLOC parameters and run your report, you must reset these values if you want the output from future reports to go to another location.

Furthermore, unless you have experience using PROC PRINTTO, you should not use the OUTNAME and OUTLOC parameters when PROC PRINTTO is executed because the commands may override each other and send your output to a location other than the one you expected. PROC PRINTTO does not produce a data set or printed output. It is useful when you want to route output from different steps in a SAS job to different files.

For more information on using PROC PRINTTO, refer to Chapter 28 of *SAS Procedures Guide, Version 6, Third Edition.*

Note: The SAS/CPE interactive interface handles report output different from these output parameters for batch mode. In the interactive interface, use the value GWINDOW to display the report output in a GRAPH window, and use the value LP to display the report output in an OUTPUT window. In both cases, omit the OUTDESC=, OUTLOC=, and OUTNAME= parameters. Specify these parameters only if you use OUTMODE=GSF or CATALOG.

OUTNAME=*physical-filename* | *entry-name*
: is the name of the external file or the entry-name in the SAS catalog where you want to store

output results. Catalog entries are stored as GRSEG type entries. The value of this parameter is appended to the value of the OUTLOC= parameter to specify the complete output location.

Specify this parameter whenever you specify the OUTMODE= parameter, except when you specify OUTMODE=CATALOG.

PERIOD=*time-interval*

is the summarization period for the report. **The default is ASIS**. For values other than ASIS, the values for the time period within a class or category are combined to form a single point on a plot, a bar on a chart, or a row or column in a table.

Notes: For the %CPCHART and %CPXTAB macros, PERIOD= is only valid if the class variable is DATETIME. For the %CPCCHRT macro, PERIOD= is only valid if the DATETIME variable is selected in any category.

Period	Effect	Example
ASIS	leaves datetime in its present form.	09Jun94:14:37:25
15MIN	transforms the time to the first minute of the 15-minute period in the hour and retains the date.	09Jun94:14:30
HOUR	transforms the time to the first minute of the hour and retains the date.	09Jun94:14:00
24HOUR	transforms the time to its hour component and omits the date. Range: 0-23.	14
DATE	omits the time and retains the date.	09Jun94
WHOLEDAY	same as DATE.	
WEEKDAY	transforms the day to the day of the week (where 1=Sunday, 2=Monday, and so on) and omits the month, year, and time. Range: 1-7, which displays as Sunday-Saturday.	Thursday
MONTHDAY	omits everything but the day of the month. Range: 1-31.	9
YEARDAY	transforms the day to the day of the year and omits the month, year, and time.	160

	Range: 1-366.	
WEEK	transforms the date to first date in the week (where the week begins on the day on which January 1 falls in the year) and omits the time.	04Jun94
MONTH	omits the day and the time	Jun94
YEARMONTH	omits everything but the month of the year. Range: 1-12.	6
QTR	transforms the month to the first month of the quarter and omits the day and time.	Apr94

WHERE=*where-expression*

specifies an expression that subsets the data to be reported on. Valid operators include, but are not limited to, BETWEEN AND, CONTAINS, LIKE, IN, IS NULL or IS MISSING. For example, the following statement limits the included observations to only those where the value of machine is 'host1' or 'host2':

```
where=machine in ('host1','host2')
```

For more information on these and other where operators, see the WHERE statement in Chapter 9 of *SAS Language: Reference, Version 6, First Edition.*

Examples: CPSRCRPT

Example 1

This program plots the values of variables IFIOCTS and DATETIME from the input data set TMPDATA and stores the resulting graph in the SAS catalog MYGRAPHS in the SAS library WORK. The %CPCAT macro stores the PROC GPLOT code in WORK.MYPGMS.INOCTS.SOURCE.

```
%CPSTART( pdb="!sasroot/saspgm/cpe/pdb-hpo", mode=batch );
%cpcat(); cards4;
proc gplot data=tmpdata gout=work.mygraphs;
     title 'Input Octets';
     plot ifiocts * datetime = 'x';
     run;
;;;;

%cpcat(cat=work.mypgms.inocts.source);
```

You can then use the SAS/CPE report macro %CPSRCRPT to run the following program to compute hourly averages, such as 24HOUR, and subset data based on DATETIME. The following example reports on data from the past seven days, summarized by hour of the day. The source file created above (WORK.MYPGMS.INOCTS.SOURCE) is used as the source file for %CPSRCRPT in the following code.

```
%CPSTART( pdb="!sasroot/saspgm/cpe/pdb-hpo", mode=batch );
%CPSRCRPT   ( hn2ift,
              tmpdata,
              work.mypgms.inocts.source,
              redlvl=detail,
              period=24hour,
              outmode=catalog,
              begin=TODAY-7,
              end=TODAY-1,
              where=machine='bigapple.net.sas.com' );
```

Example 2

The following example stores SAS code in the SAS catalog member WORK.MYPGMS.TEMP.SOURCE and then executes it using %CPSRCRPT. This example uses macro programming (%if-%then logic), therefore, the code must be contained in a macro. The code is first defined in the macro and then invoked. This example also uses the values passed in the OUTLOC= and OUTNAME= parameters and the positional parameter p4.

This example also shows how your SOURCE might include references to the OUTLOC= and OUTNAME= parameters that are specified on %CPSRCRPT.

```
%CPCAT ; cards4;

%macro temp();
  /* if outloc was specified, put it into the right syntax for use
     on PROC GPLOT stmt */
%if &outloc ne %str() %then %let rptout = GOUT=&outloc ;
  /* if outname was specified, put it into the right syntax for use
     on PLOT stmt */
%if &outname ne %str() %then %let rptnm = NAME="&outname" ;
%if &p4 eq %str() %then %let p4 = * ;              <--- use an '*' if user
                                                         doesn't specify one
proc gplot data=tmpdata &rptout ;                  <--- adds GOUT=&outloc to
     title 'Input Octets';                               GPLOT statement
     plot ifiocts * datetime = "&p4" /             <--- user can specify plot
                                                         char
          &rptnm                                   <--- adds NAME="&outname"
                                                         to PLOT stmt
          description = "&outdesc" ;               <--- use description if
                                                         given
     run;
%mend temp;
%temp();

;;;;
%CPCAT( cat=work.mypgms.temp.source) ;

%CPSRCRPT   ( hn2ift,
              tmpdata,
              work.mypgms.temp.source,
              +,                                   <--- want plot char to
              redlvl=detail,                             be a '+'
              period=24hour,
              outmode=catalog,
              outloc=work.mystuff,
```

```
outname=inocts,
outdesc=My Important Graph,
begin=01Jun94:00:00:00,
end=TODAY-1,
where=machine='bigapple.net.sas.com' );
```

In this example, the code is written to expect that the user will specify the plot character to be used as the fourth positional parameter, or &p4. It also checks whether the macro was invoked with the OUTNAME and OUTLOC parameters, and if so it will use these values in the invocation of PROC GPLOT.

NOTE: Once you direct text output to an external location using OUTLOC and OUTNAME, all subsequent text reports will go to the same location until you specify a different location. This is true both interactively and in batch. This is because SAS/CPE generates a PROC PRINTTO, which stays in effect until another PROC PRINTTO redirects standard text output.

Note

You cannot use the SAS/CPE interactive interface to construct or modify reports using %CPSRCRPT. However, you can run the report through the interactive interface.

The output data set created by %CPSRCRPT *outdata* contains data based on the parameters and values specified when you submitted the %CPSRCRPT macro. However, when you use this data set as input to the source code (*rptname*) that is run by %CPSRCRPT, you may also need to specify some of these parameters in that source code, such as BY, CL_NAM, OUTLOC, OUTNAME, OUTDESC, and OUTMODE, in order to further manipulate or redirect output for the data. For example, if you specify a list of BY variables, %CPSRCRPT creates a BY variables list, but you must also specify the list in the source code that is being run by %CPSRCRPT (*rptname*), in order to produce separate graphs or reports based on those BY variables.

%CPTABRPT

Tabular Reports

Purpose

The %CPTABRPT macro generates tabular reports by executing the TABULATE procedure. This macro can generate any of six different tabular reports. You can specify a maximum of 10 analysis variables for this report, and the other parameters that you specify depend on your report type.

For more information on the underlying procedure, refer to the *SAS Guide to TABULATE Processing, Second Edition.*

Syntax

```
%CPTABRPT(dataset,
          var1,lab1,fmt1,...,var10,lab10,fmt10,
          CL_NAM=class-variable-name,
          REDLVL=reduction-level,
          STAT=statistic,
         <ACROSS=class-variable-list>,
         <BEGIN=SAS-datetime-value>,
         <BOX='text'>,
         <BY=BY-variable-list>,
         <CL_LAB=label-list>,
         <END=SAS-datetime-value>,
         <MISS=YES|NO>,
         <MISSTEXT='text'>,
         <NCOLS=line-size>,
         <NROWS=page-size>,
         <ORDER=DATA|FORMATTED|FREQ|INTERNAL>,
         <OUTDESC=text>,
         <OUTLOC=output-location>,
         <OUTMODE=output-format>,
         <OUTNAME=physical-filename|entry-name>,
         <PRTMISS=YES|NO>,
         <ROTATE=LANDSCAPE|PORTRAIT>,
         <RTS=number>,
         <SEPS=YES|NO>,
         <STATFMT=format>,
         <STATLAB='label'>,
         <SUMMARY=ALL|NONE|LAST>,
         <TABTYPE=INTERVAL|EVENT>,
         <TYPE=TYPE1|TYPE2|TYPE3|TYPE4|TYPE5|TYPE6>,
         <WHERE=where-expression> ) ;
```

%CPTABRPT Parameters

dataset

specifies the table name from which to generate the report. **This positional parameter is required** and it can be specified in one of three ways.

If the data are in the DETAIL, DAY, WEEK, MONTH, or YEAR levels of the active PDB:

- ☐ Specify a tablename via the *dataset* parameter and a level via the **REDLVL=** parameter. If the REDLVL= parameter is not specified for the table name, REDLVL=DETAIL.

- ☐ Specify the name in the format of *REDLVL.TABLE*, in which case the REDLVL= parameter is not required.

If the data are in a SAS library that is not in the DETAIL, DAY, WEEK, MONTH, or YEAR level of the active PDB:

- ☐ Specify a two-level name in the format *libref.data-set-name* and specify REDLVL=OTHER.

Note: When specifying the data set name using the *libref* format, you must assign a *libref* before this macro is invoked. For more information see the LIBNAME statement in Chapter 9 of *SAS Language: Reference, Version 6, First Edition.*

var1,lab1,fmt1, . . . , var10,lab10,fmt10

specifies a triplet list of analysis variable names, labels (up to 16 characters), and SAS formats for the report. The maximum number of triplets you can specify is ten. **This positional parameter is required.**

For more information concerning SAS formats, refer to "SAS Formats" in Chapter 3 of *SAS Language: Reference, Version 6, First Edition.*

CL_NAM=*variable-list*

specifies the class variables for this report. A separate row or group of analysis variables displays for each unique value of the class variable. **This parameter is required for all report styles except TYPE1**. Separate multiple variables with blanks. You can specify a maximum of five variables.

REDLVL=*reduction-level*

specifies which level of the table you are reporting on: DETAIL, DAY, WEEK, MONTH, YEAR, or OTHER. **The default is DETAIL**. The value of this parameter is used as a libref. You should specify REDLVL=OTHER if you want to select a SAS data set. The SAS data set should contain a variable named DATETIME, which represents the datetime stamp for each observation.

Note: When specifying the data set name using the *libref* format, you must assign a *libref* before this macro is invoked. For more information see the LIBNAME statement in Chapter 9 of *SAS Language: Reference, Version 6, First Edition.*

STAT=*statistic*

specifies a maximum of five statistics to calculate for the analysis variables in this report. **For %CPTABRPT, this parameter is required for all report styles except TYPE4.** Valid values for STAT= are:

CSS

is the sum of squares corrected for the mean.

CV

is the coefficient of variation. It is calculated as the standard deviation divided by the mean and multiplied by 100.

MAX
: is the maximum value for all observations.

MEAN
: is the arithmetic average. Mean is one measure used to describe the center of a distribution of values. Other measures include mode and median.

MIN
: is the minimum value for all observations.

N
: or COUNT, is the number of observations with nonmissing values for the variables being summarized.

NMISS
: the number of observations with missing variable values.

RANGE
: is the maximum of the difference between the maximum and minimum values for the variable MAX-MIN.

STD
: is the standard deviation or square root of variance. Like the variance, it is a measure of the dispersion about the mean, but in the same unit of measure as the data.

STDERR
: is the positive square root of the variance of a statistic.

SUM
: is the sum of values for all observations.

USS
: is the uncorrected sum of squares.

VAR
: is a measure of the dispersion or variability of the data about the mean. When values are close to the mean, the variance is small. When values are scattered widely about the mean, the variance is large.

Optional Keyword Parameters

ACROSS=*class-variable-list*
: specifies the variables to use for column headers. **This parameter is required for report TYPE5**. You can specify a maximum of five variables. Use blanks to separate the values in the list.

BEGIN=*SAS-datetime-value*
: represents the first date and time for data to include in the report. The *sas-datetime-value*

must be in the DATETIME13. SAS format. For example, BEGIN=01jul96:08:45. Use this parameter in combination with END= to define the range for subsetting data for the report. You can also use the TODAY[*-nnnn*]@*hh:mm* format, which uses the current date value minus *nnnn* days at the specified hour. This format supports the symbol or the word (@ or at) for the "at" instruction. For example, the following combination of values reports on the last three days of data, beginning at 8:00 a.m. three days ago and ending today at 5:00 p.m.

```
begin=today-3@08:00, end=todayat17:00
```

If you omit the time, the default time for the BEGIN= parameter is 00:00 on the specified date and the default time for the END= parameter is 23:59 on the specified date.

This example illustrates specific dates:

```
begin=01jul96:08:00, end=31jul96:17:00
```

If you omit the BEGIN= and END= parameters, the macro uses the information stored with the table definition (in the data dictionary) for the earliest and most recent datetime values at the specified level. The values stored with the table definition are based on the data currently in that level of the table. Exception: If the level is set to OTHER, the macro reads the data to determine the earliest and most recent datetime values (because there is not a table definition).

If you use only one parameter, BEGIN= or END=, that datetime is restricted and the other value is based on the data.

BOX='*text*'
: places text in the box above the row titles on the left side of the table.

BY=*BY-variable-list*
: lists the variables by which your data is sorted in the PDB. Use blanks to separate the variables in the list. A separate graph is produced for each value of the BY variable or for each combination of BY variable values, if you have multiple BY variables. For example, if you have four *diskids* on three machines, the following setting for the BY= parameter produces twelve reports, one for each of the twelve unique combinations of machine and *diskid* values.

```
by=machine diskid
```

For an alternate method of handling unique values of variables, refer to the description of class variables in the report you are producing.

If there is no BY= parameter, observations are sorted in the order that the variables are listed in the BY variable list or class variable list in the PDB. To check the order, follow this path from the main menu of the SAS/CPE interactive interface:

PDB Admin -> Config Active PDB Dictionary -> *select table*
-> ItemActions -> Browse Definition

or submit a batch job in which the %CPDDUTL macro runs a LIST TABLE control statement.

If you want to change the BY variables or their order for a one-time job, the fastest way to do so is to run a SAS program that contains the following statements:

```
proc sort data=level.table out=sasuser.table;
   by one-time-BY-variables-list;
```

where *level* is the reduction level on which to base the report, *table* is the table that you want to base the report on, *cpe-pdb* is the complete directory path or high-level-qualifiers and the name of the PDB you want to base your report on, and *one-time-BY-variables-list* is a list of the BY variables you want to use in the report. Order the variables from major to minor and separate the variables by blanks. After you run this program, run the report definition on the data in SASUSER.*table*.

Before changing the BY-variables or their order in the data dictionary you should be aware of the following:

- ☐ Changes to the BY-variables will not take effect in the data until the next process or reduce task runs or you execute the %CPDDUTL macro with the BUILD VIEWS control statement.
- ☐ The BY-variables list specified on any reports must match the current BY-variables list in the PDB. Therefore, if you have updated the BY-variables for a table in the PDB, you should examine all report definitions that use this table to see if the definition should be changed to match the new BY-variables list.
- ☐ When the BY-variables list is updated (via the process or reduce task or the BUILD VIEWS statement), the data in the PDB is physically sorted. Depending on the number of observations in the tables being sorted, this can take a considerable amount of time.
- ☐ It is not good practice to change the BY-variables list frequently. If you are changing the BY-variables list regularly in order to produce reports, you either have not chosen a good set of BY-variables or you have an incomplete understanding of how to create the report you want.

To change the BY variables list using the interactive interface, invoke SAS/CPE with update access to the PDB and then follow this path from the primary menu:

PDB Admin -> **Config Active PDB Dictionary** -> ***select table***
-> **ItemActions** -> **Edit Definition**

You can also use the **UPDATE TABLE** statement in the %CPDDUTL macro to change the BY variables list in batch mode.

CL_LAB=*label-list*

specifies the labels for the class variables used in the table. Separate multiple labels with blanks. If you specify this parameter, the number of labels should match the number of class variables. You can use a period to indicate a missing label, for example:

```
cl_nam=var1 var2 var3,
cl_lab=lab2 .    lab3
```

Note that commas separate parameters, not labels. Use blanks to separate the labels in the list.

Caution: *Do not include blanks, commas, equal signs, parentheses, or ampersands in the labels.*

END=*SAS-datetime-value*

represents the last date and time for data to include in the report. The *sas-datetime-value* must be in the DATETIME13. SAS format or in the today[*-nnnn*]@*hh:mm* format. For example, END=01jul96:17:00 or END=today-1@17:00.

Use this parameter in combination with BEGIN= to define the range for subsetting data for the report. Refer to **BEGIN=** for more information on using these parameters.

MISS=YES | NO

includes missing values as valid levels for class variables. A heading displays to identify the missing value information that appears in the table. **The default value is YES**.

MISSTEXT=*'text'*

supplies text to be printed in table cells that contain missing values. The text can be a maximum length of 200 characters.

NCOLS=*line-size*

is the number of characters that fit across the page for printed reports. This value is not the number of columns that appear in a tabular report.

NROWS=*page-size*

is the number of lines on the page for printed reports. This value is not the number of rows that appear in a tabular report.

ORDER=DATA | FORMATTED | FREQ | INTERNAL

specifies the order in which headings for class variable values are displayed in the table. **In SAS/CPE software, the default setting is ORDER=INTERNAL.**

DATA

keeps values of class variables in the order in which they were read in from the data set.

FORMATTED

orders the values by their formatted representation.

FREQ

orders the values by descending frequency count so that values that occur more frequently appear first in the table.

INTERNAL

orders values by the same order that they would be ordered by the SORT procedure.

OUTDESC=*text*

is a description (as many as 40 characters) of the output.

If OUTMODE=CATALOG, the description is stored with the entry in the SAS catalog

specified in the OUTLOC= parameter. Otherwise, the description is ignored.

OUTLOC=*output-location*
is the physical location of a graphics stream file, a SAS catalog name, or the physical location of the file or catalog member (for text reports only). The value of the OUTNAME= parameter is appended to the value of this parameter to specify the complete output location. Specify this parameter if you specify the OUTMODE= parameter.

OUTMODE=*output-format*
specifies the format for the output. **The default value is GWINDOW for all reports except %CPTABRPT. The default for %CPTABRPT is the output window.**

Valid values for this parameter are:

LP
stores the output as a text file. If you specify OUTMODE=LP, you should also specify the OUTLOC and OUTNAME parameters for the text report. If you do not specify the output location (OUTLOC=), the output is sent to the output window or standard SASLIST file. **This value is not valid for the %CPSPEC, %CPG3D, or %CPGTPLT macros.**

GSF
stores the output as a graphics stream file. If you specify OUTMODE=GSF, you must also specify the OUTLOC and OUTNAME parameters. **This value is not valid for the %CPXTAB and %CPTABRPT macros.**

CATALOG
stores the output as a GRSEG entry in a SAS catalog. If you are producing a graph report and you specify OUTMODE=CATALOG, you should also specify the OUTLOC, OUTNAME, and OUTDESC parameters. **This value is not valid for the %CPXTAB and %CPTABRPT macros.**

The following table summarizes which parameters should be specified in addition to OUTMODE=, based on the report type and the value of the OUTMODE= parameter.

When OUTMODE=	Specify these additional parameters			Not valid for these macros
LP	-	OUTLOC	OUTNAME	%CPSPEC, %CPG3D %CPGTPLT
GSF	-	OUTLOC	OUTNAME	%CPXTAB, %CPTABRPT
CATALOG	OUTDESC	OUTLOC	OUTNAME	%CPXTAB, %CPTABRPT

For more information on using OUTMODE= with OUTNAME= and OUTLOC=, see Examples of the OUTMODE= Parameter.

Caution: *OUTMODE=LP is the only valid option for reports that produce text output, for example those that use procedures such as TABULATE, REPORT, or PRINT. If you specify*

OUTMODE=CATALOG for a text report, the OUTLOC= and OUTNAME= parameters are ignored.

The OUTNAME and OUTLOC parameters execute PROC PRINTTO in the background to set the output filename and location. When PROC PRINTTO is set, it stays in effect for subsequent text reports for the current SAS session until it is reset by another PROC PRINTTO. Therefore, after you set the OUTNAME and OUTLOC parameters and run your report, you must reset these values if you want the output from future reports to go to another location.

Furthermore, unless you have experience using PROC PRINTTO, you should not use the OUTNAME and OUTLOC parameters when PROC PRINTTO is executed because the commands may override each other and send your output to a location other than the one you expected. PROC PRINTTO does not produce a data set or printed output. It is useful when you want to route output from different steps in a SAS job to different files.

For more information on using PROC PRINTTO, refer to Chapter 28 of the *SAS Procedures Guide, Version 6, Third Edition.*

Note: The SAS/CPE interactive interface handles report output different from the OUTMODE=, OUTLOC=, and OUTNAME= batch parameters. In the interactive interface, use the value GWINDOW to display the report output in a GRAPH window, and use the value LP to display the report output in an OUTPUT window. In both cases, omit the OUTDESC=, OUTLOC=, and OUTNAME= parameters. Specify these parameters only if you use OUTMODE=GSF or CATALOG.

If you are running SAS/CPE in batch mode (i.e., you have executed it from within a cron job or from the MVS batch scheduler) and are running a graph report, you should specify an output location other than the graph window.

OUTNAME=*physical-filename* | *entry-name*

is the name of the external file or the entry-name in the SAS catalog where you want to store output results. Catalog entries are stored as GRSEG type entries. The value of this parameter is appended to the value of the OUTLOC= parameter to specify the complete output location.

Specify this parameter whenever you specify the OUTMODE= parameter, except when you specify OUTMODE=CATALOG.

PRTMISS=YES | NO

forces all row and column headings to be the same for all pages of the table. **The default value is NO**.

ROTATE=LANDSCAPE | PORTRAIT

indicates whether the output should be displayed in landscape or portrait mode. This parameter is only valid for tabular reports that have been produced in graphics mode, such as those output to the graph window. **The default value is device dependent**.

RTS=*number*

specifies the number of print positions available for printing all levels of row headings.

SEPS=YES | NO

places horizontal lines to separate the column titles and body of the table. Specifying SEPS=NO completely removes these lines from the table; it does not print blank lines. **The default value is YES.**

STATFMT=*format*

specifies the format for the stastical values in the table cells.

STATLAB=*label*

specifies the labels (as many as 16 characters) to print in the row or column headers instead of the name of the statistic. Use blanks to separate multiple labels. If you specify this parameter, the number of labels should match the number of statistics in the value of the STAT= parameter on this macro. Use a period to indicate a missing label, for example,

```
stat=min mean max,
statlab=least. most
```

Caution: *Do not enclose the label in single or double quotes. Also, do not include commas, equal signs, parenthesis, or ampersands in the labels.*

SUMMARY=ALL | NONE | LAST

indicates the type of summary statistics to provide for this report. If the value of TYPE= parameter for this report macro is TYPE2, TYPE3, TYPE4, TYPE5, or TYPE6, then valid values for SUMMARY= are ALL or NONE. SUMMARY=LAST is only valid when TYPE=TYPE5 or TYPE6 and you select multiple class variables for this report. The SUMMARY= parameter is not valid if TYPE=TYPE1.

NONE

no summary information is provided for the report.

ALL

summary information is provided after each class variable and a summary total for all class variables is listed at the bottom of the report matrix. Example:

```
+--------------------------+
|             |   Variables|
|             |------------|
|             |  Statistics|
+-------------+------------+
|Class (nested)|     |     |
|Summary      |      |     |
|Class (nested)|     |     |
|Summary      |      |     |
|Summary Total|      |     |
+-------------+------+-----+
```

LAST

summary information is provided for the last class variable. Example:

```
+--------------------------+
|             |   Variables|
|             |------------|
|             |  Statistics|
+-------------+------------+
```

```
|Class (nested)|     |     |
|Class (nested)|     |     |
|Summary       |     |     |
+--------------+-----+-----+
```

TABTYPE=INTERVAL | EVENT

specifies whether the data cover a specified interval of time or whether they are logged in response to an event that occurs, such as when a job begins or ends. **INTERVAL is the default value.**

INTERVAL

each observation represents an interval of time.

EVENT

each observation represents an event.

TYPE=TYPE1 | TYPE2 | TYPE3 | TYPE4 | TYPE5 | TYPE6

indicates which type of TABULATE table you want to produce. The types are described here and are followed by diagrams of each type.

TYPE1

produces a table with summary statistics listed horizontally for each of the analysis variables listed vertically. Use the **STAT=** parameter to specify the statistics and the *var1* through *var10* parameters to specify the analysis variables.

TYPE2

produces a table with summary statistics listed under each of the analysis variables in columns of the table. In the rows of the table, you can specify a maximum of five class variables. For each class variable, the table has one row for each unique value of that variable and a final row to summarize all values of that variable. Use the **CL_NAM=** parameter to specify the class variables. Use the **STAT=** parameter to specify the statistics and the *var1* through *var10* parameters to specify the analysis variables.

TYPE3

is similar to TYPE2 except that the column headings group the statistics and list individual variables for each statistic.

TYPE4

is similar to TYPE2 except that the analysis variables are the only column headings and the SUM is the only statistic.

TYPE5

produces a table with class variables in both the row and column dimensions of the table. Use the **ACROSS=** parameter to specify a maximum of five class variables for the column dimension. For each value of each ACROSS= variable, the table lists summary statistics for the analysis variables. In the row dimension, the variables you specify for the **CL_NAM=** parameter are nested, therefore, for each value of the first class variable, the report lists all values of the second class variable, and so on. For example, if you specify MACHINE and SHIFT, and you have three machines and two shifts, the report lists shifts 1 and 2 for machine 1; then, shifts 1 and 2 for machine 2;

and finally, shifts 1 and 2 for machine 3.

TYPE6
: produces a table like TYPE5 except there are no ACROSS variables.

TYPE 1

	Statistics		
variable 1 variable *n*			

TYPE 2

	Variable		
	Statistics		
Class Summary			

TYPE 3

	Statistics		
	Variables		
Class Summary			

TYPE 4

	Variables		
Class Summary			

TYPE 5

	Across		
	Variables		
	Statistics		
Class (nest) Summary			

TYPE 6

	Variable		
	Statistics		
Class (nest) Summary			

WHERE=*where-expression*
: specifies an expression that subsets the data to be reported on. Valid operators include, but are not limited to, BETWEEN AND, CONTAINS, LIKE, IN, IS NULL or IS MISSING. For example, the following statement limits the included observations to only those where the value of machine is 'host1' or 'host2':

```
where=machine in ('host1','host2')
```

For more information on these and other where operators, see the WHERE statement in Chapter 9 of *SAS Language: Reference, Version 6, First Edition.*

Notes

You can specify both a label and a format for each analysis variable you include in this report.

The OUTNAME and OUTLOC parameters execute PROC PRINTTO in the background to set the output filename and location. When PROC PRINTTO is set, it stays in effect for subsequent text reports for the current SAS session for this user ID, until it is reset by another PROC PRINTTO. Therefore, after you set the OUTNAME and OUTLOC parameters and run your report, you must reset these values if you want the output from future reports to go to another location.

Furthermore, unless you have experience using PROC PRINTTO, you should not use the OUTNAME and OUTLOC parameters when PROC PRINTTO is executed because the commands may override each other and send your output to a location other than the one you expected. PROC PRINTTO does not produce a data set or printed output. It is useful when you want to route output from different steps in a SAS job, to different files.

For more information on using PROC PRINTTO, refer to Chapter 28 of *SAS Procedures Guide, Version 6, Third Edition.*

%CPXTAB

Exception Reports Format

Purpose

The %CPXTAB macro generates a tabular report that meets user-defined exception criteria. You can specify a maximum of 15 exception variables (the exception criteria) for this report. The report indicates the amount and type of failures of the specified tests. Specify the tests as formulas that compare the value of a variable to a set value or calculated amount. You can combine several comparisons into one test. The tests shown here illustrate some formats you might use:

- server>50
- cpubusy>98
- input error/input packet error>.0025

Syntax

```
%CPXTAB(dataset,
        test1,lab1,...,test15,lab15,
        REDLVL=reduction-level,
       <BEGIN=SAS-datetime-value>,
       <BY=BY-variable-list>,
       <CL_LAB=label-list>,
       <CL_NAM=variable-name>,
       <END=SAS-datetime-value>,
       <NCOLS=line-size>,
       <NROWS=page-size>,
       <OUTDESC=text>,
       <OUTLOC=output-location>,
       <OUTMODE=output-format>,
       <OUTNAME=physical-filename|entry-name>,
       <PERIOD=time-interval>,
       <ROTATE=LANDSCAPE|PORTRAIT>,
       <TABTYPE=INTERVAL|EVENT>,
       <WHERE=where-expression> ) ;
```

%CPXTAB Parameters

dataset

specifies the table name from which to generate the report. **This positional parameter is required** and it can be specified in one of three ways.

If the data are in the DETAIL, DAY, WEEK, MONTH, or YEAR levels of the active PDB:

- Specify a tablename via the *dataset* parameter and a level via the **REDLVL=** parameter. If the REDLVL= parameter is not specified for the table name, REDLVL=DETAIL.

- Specify the name in the format of *REDLVL.TABLE*, in which case the REDLVL= parameter is not required.

If the data are in a SAS library that is not in the DETAIL, DAY, WEEK, MONTH, or

YEAR level of the active PDB:

- Specify a two-level name in the format *libref.data-set-name* and specify REDLVL=OTHER.

Note: When specifying the data set name using the *libref* format, you must assign a *libref* before this macro is invoked. For more information see the LIBNAME statement in Chapter 9 of *SAS Language: Reference, Version 6, First Edition.*

test1,lab1 . . . test15,lab15

specifies up to 15 paired lists of tests to perform and the label (up to 16 characters) to attach to the tests for the report. **This positional parameter is required**. You may use blank characters in the label. You may enclose the label in single quotes, but quotes are not required.

Caution: *Do not include commas, equal signs, parenthesis or ampersands in the labels.*

REDLVL=*reduction-level*

specifies which level of the table you are reporting on: DETAIL, DAY, WEEK, MONTH, YEAR, or OTHER. **The default is DETAIL**. The value of this parameter is used as a libref. You should specify REDLVL=OTHER if you want to select a SAS data set. The SAS data set should contain a variable named DATETIME, which represents the datetime stamp for each observation.

Note: When specifying the data set name using the *libref* format, you must assign a *libref* before this macro is invoked. For more information see the LIBNAME statement in Chapter 9 of *SAS Language: Reference, Version 6, First Edition.*

Optional Keyword Parameters

BEGIN=*SAS-datetime-value*

represents the first date and time for data to include in the report. The *sas-datetime-value* must be in the DATETIME13. SAS format. For example, BEGIN=01jul96:08:45. Use this parameter in combination with **END=** to define the range for subsetting data for the report. You can also use the TODAY[*-nnnn*]@*hh:mm* format, which uses the current date value minus *nnnn* days at the specified hour. This format supports the symbol or the word (@ or at) for the "at" instruction. For example, the following combination of values reports on the last three days of data, beginning at 8:00 a.m. three days ago and ending today at 5:00 p.m.

```
begin=today-3@08:00, end=todayat17:00
```

If you omit the time, the default time for the BEGIN= parameter is 00:00 on the specified date and the default time for the END= parameter is 23:59 on the specified date.

This example illustrates specific dates:

```
begin=01jul96:08:00, end=31jul96:17:00
```

If you omit the BEGIN= and END= parameters, the macro uses the information stored with the table definition (in the data dictionary) for the earliest and most recent

datetime values at the specified level. The values stored with the table definition are based on the data currently in that level of the table. Exception: If the level is set to OTHER, the macro reads the data to determine the earliest and most recent datetime values (because there is not a table definition).

If you use only one parameter, BEGIN= or END=, that datetime is restricted and the other value is based on the data.

BY=*BY-variable-list*

lists the variables by which your data is sorted in the PDB. Use blanks to separate the variables in the list. A separate graph is produced for each value of the BY variable or for each combination of BY variable values, if you have multiple BY variables. For example, if you have four *diskids* on three machines, the following setting for the BY= parameter produces twelve reports, one for each of the twelve unique combinations of machine and *diskid* values.

```
by=machine diskid
```

For an alternate method of handling unique values of variables, refer to the description of class variables in the report you are producing.

If there is no BY= parameter, observations are sorted in the order that the variables are listed in the BY variable list or class variable list in the PDB. To check the order, follow this path from the main menu of the SAS/CPE interactive interface:

PDB Admin -> **Config Active PDB Dictionary** -> *select table*
-> **ItemActions** -> **Browse Definition**

or submit a batch job in which the <u>**%CPDDUTL**</u> macro runs a LIST TABLE control statement.

If you want to change the BY variables or their order for a one-time job, the fastest way to do so is to run a SAS program that contains the following statements:

```
proc sort data=level.table out=sasuser.table;
   by one-time-BY-variables-list;
```

where *level* is the reduction level on which to base the report, *table* is the table that you want to base the report on, *cpe-pdb* is the complete directory path or high-level-qualifiers and the name of the PDB you want to base your report on, and *one-time-BY-variables-list* is a list of the BY variables you want to use in the report. Order the variables from major to minor and separate the variables by blanks. After you run this program, run the report definition on the data in SASUSER.*table*.

Before changing the BY-variables or their order in the data dictionary you should be aware of the following:

- Changes to the BY-variables will not take effect in the data until the next process or reduce task runs or you execute the %CPDDUTL macro with the BUILD VIEWS control statement.
- The BY-variables list specified on any reports must match the current BY-variables

list in the PDB. Therefore, if you have updated the BY-variables for a table in the PDB, you should examine all report definitions that use this table to see if the definition should be changed to match the new BY-variables list.

- When the BY-variables list is updated (via the process or reduce task or the BUILD VIEWS statement), the data in the PDB is physically sorted. Depending on the number of observations in the tables being sorted, this can take a considerable amount of time.
- It is not good practice to change the BY-variables list frequently. If you are changing the BY-variables list regularly in order to produce reports, you either have not chosen a good set of BY-variables or you have an incomplete understanding of how to create the report you want.

To change the BY variables list using the interactive interface, invoke SAS/CPE with update access to the PDB and then follow this path from the primary menu:

PDB Admin -> Config Active PDB Dictionary -> ***select table***
-> ItemActions -> Edit Definition

You can also use the **UPDATE TABLE** statement in the %CPDDUTL macro to change the BY variables list in batch mode.

CL_LAB=*label*
is the label (a maximum of 16 characters) for the class variable. You may use blank characters. You may enclose the label in single quotes, but the quotes are not required.

Caution: *Do not include commas, equal signs, parentheses, or ampersands in the label.*

CL_NAM=*variable-name*
specifies the name of the class variable for the report. A separate row displays for each unique value of the class variable.

END=*SAS-datetime-value*
represents the last date and time for data to include in the report. The *sas-datetime-value* must be in the DATETIME13. SAS format or in the today[-*nnnn*]@*hh:mm* format. For example, END=01jul96:17:00 or END=today-1@17:00.

Use this parameter in combination with BEGIN= to define the range for subsetting data for the report. Refer to **BEGIN=** for more information on using these parameters.

NCOLS=*line-size*
is the number of characters that fit across the page for printed reports. This value is not the number of columns that appear in a tabular report.

NROWS=*page-size*
is the number of lines on the page for printed reports. This value is not the number of rows that appear in a tabular report.

OUTDESC=*text*
is a description (as many as 40 characters) of the output.

If OUTMODE=CATALOG, the description is stored with the entry in the SAS catalog

specified in the OUTLOC= parameter. Otherwise, the description is ignored.

OUTLOC=*output-location*
is the physical location of a graphics stream file, a SAS catalog name, or the physical location of the file or catalog member (for text reports only). The value of the OUTNAME= parameter is appended to the value of this parameter to specify the complete output location. Specify this parameter if you specify the OUTMODE= parameter.

OUTMODE=*output-format*
specifies the format for the output. **The default value is GWINDOW for all reports except %CPTABRPT. The default for %CPTABRPT is the output window.**

Valid values for this parameter are:

LP
stores the output as a text file. If you specify OUTMODE=LP, you should also specify the OUTLOC and OUTNAME parameters for the text report. If you do not specify the output location (OUTLOC=), the output is sent to the output window or standard SASLIST file. **This value is not valid for the %CPSPEC, %CPG3D, or %CPGTPLT macros.**

GSF
stores the output as a graphics stream file. If you specify OUTMODE=GSF, you must also specify the OUTLOC and OUTNAME parameters. **This value is not valid for the %CPXTAB and %CPTABRPT macros.**

CATALOG
stores the output as a GRSEG entry in a SAS catalog. If you are producing a graph report and you specify OUTMODE=CATALOG, you should also specify the OUTLOC, OUTNAME, and OUTDESC parameters. **This value is not valid for the %CPXTAB and %CPTABRPT macros.**

The following table summarizes which parameters should be specified in addition to OUTMODE=, based on the report type and the value of the OUTMODE= parameter.

When OUTMODE=	Specify these additional parameters			Not valid for these macros
LP	-	OUTLOC	OUTNAME	%CPSPEC, %CPG3D %CPGTPLT
GSF	-	OUTLOC	OUTNAME	%CPXTAB, %CPTABRPT
CATALOG	OUTDESC	OUTLOC	OUTNAME	%CPXTAB, %CPTABRPT

For more information on using OUTMODE= with OUTNAME= and OUTLOC=, see **Examples of the OUTMODE= Parameter**.

Caution: *OUTMODE=LP is the only valid option for reports that produce text output, for example those that use procedures such as TABULATE, REPORT, or PRINT. If you specify*

OUTMODE=CATALOG for a text report, the OUTLOC= and OUTNAME= parameters are ignored.

The OUTNAME and OUTLOC parameters execute PROC PRINTTO in the background to set the output filename and location. When PROC PRINTTO is set, it stays in effect for subsequent text reports for the current SAS session until it is reset by another PROC PRINTTO. Therefore, after you set the OUTNAME and OUTLOC parameters and run your report, you must reset these values if you want the output from future reports to go to another location.

Furthermore, unless you have experience using PROC PRINTTO, you should not use the OUTNAME and OUTLOC parameters when PROC PRINTTO is executed because the commands may override each other and send your output to a location other than the one you expected. PROC PRINTTO does not produce a data set or printed output. It is useful when you want to route output from different steps in a SAS job to different files.

For more information on using PROC PRINTTO, refer to Chapter 28 of the *SAS Procedures Guide, Version 6, Third Edition.*

Note: The SAS/CPE interactive interface handles report output different from the OUTMODE=, OUTLOC=, and OUTNAME= batch parameters. In the interactive interface, use the value GWINDOW to display the report output in a GRAPH window, and use the value LP to display the report output in an OUTPUT window. In both cases, omit the OUTDESC=, OUTLOC=, and OUTNAME= parameters. Specify these parameters only if you use OUTMODE=GSF or CATALOG.

If you are running SAS/CPE in batch mode (i.e., you have executed it from within a cron job or from the MVS batch scheduler) and are running a graph report, you should specify an output location other than the graph window.

OUTNAME=*physical-filename* | *entry-name*

is the name of the external file or the entry-name in the SAS catalog where you want to store output results. Catalog entries are stored as GRSEG type entries. The value of this parameter is appended to the value of the OUTLOC= parameter to specify the complete output location.

Specify this parameter whenever you specify the OUTMODE= parameter, except when you specify OUTMODE=CATALOG.

PERIOD=*time-interval*

is the summarization period for the report. **The default is ASIS**. For values other than ASIS, the values for the time period within a class or category are combined to form a single point on a plot, a bar on a chart, or a row or column in a table.

Notes: For the %CPCHART and %CPXTAB macros, PERIOD= is only valid if the class variable is DATETIME. For the %CPCCHRT macro, PERIOD= is only valid if the DATETIME variable is selected in any category.

Period	Effect	Example

ASIS	leaves datetime in its present form.	09Jun94:14:37:25
15MIN	transforms the time to the first minute of the 15-minute period in the hour and retains the date.	09Jun94:14:30
HOUR	transforms the time to the first minute of the hour and retains the date.	09Jun94:14:00
24HOUR	transforms the time to its hour component and omits the date. Range: 0-23.	14
DATE	omits the time and retains the date.	09Jun94
WHOLEDAY	same as DATE.	
WEEKDAY	transforms the day to the day of the week (where 1=Sunday, 2=Monday, and so on) and omits the month, year, and time. Range: 1-7, which displays as Sunday-Saturday.	Thursday
MONTHDAY	omits everything but the day of the month. Range: 1-31.	9
YEARDAY	transforms the day to the day of the year and omits the month, year, and time. Range: 1-366.	160
WEEK	transforms the date to first date in the week (where the week begins on the day on which January 1 falls in the year) and omits the time.	04Jun94
MONTH	omits the day and the time	Jun94
YEARMONTH	omits everything but the month of the year. Range: 1-12.	6
QTR	transforms the month to the first month of the quarter and omits the day and time.	Apr94

ROTATE=LANDSCAPE | PORTRAIT

indicates whether the output should be displayed in landscape or portrait mode. This parameter is only valid for tabular reports that have been produced in graphics mode, such as those output to the graph window. **The default value is device dependent.**

TABTYPE=INTERVAL | EVENT

specifies whether the data cover a specified interval of time or whether they are logged in response to an event that occurs, such as when a job begins or ends. **INTERVAL is the default value.**

INTERVAL

each observation represents an interval of time.

EVENT

each observation represents an event.

WHERE=*where-expression*

specifies an expression that subsets the data to be reported on. Valid operators include, but are not limited to, BETWEEN AND, CONTAINS, LIKE, IN, IS NULL or IS MISSING. For example, the following statement limits the included observations to only those where the value of machine is 'host1' or 'host2':

```
where=machine in ('host1','host2')
```

For more information on these and other where operators, see the WHERE statement in Chapter 9 of *SAS Language: Reference, Version 6, First Edition.*

Note

Even though the default value for the OUTMODE= parameter on %CPXTAB is GWINDOW, you should specify OUTMODE=LP, which sends the output to the output window.

If you use an equal sign or percent sign in the test you specify, enclose the entire expression in a %QUOTE statement:

```
%QUOTE(expression-with-special-characters)
```

For more information on the underlying procedure, refer to the *SAS Guide to TABULATE Processing, Second Edition.*

Global and Local Report Macro Variables

Global Report Macro Variables

SAS/CPE software provides the following global report macro variables to control processing and to simplify your use of the system.

CPBEGIN
: sets the initial date and time so that you can subset data by a datetime range. Specify this value in the DATETIME13. format. For example, specify 1:30 p.m. on September 1, 1996, as 01SEP96:13:30. You can also use the TODAY*[-nnnn]@hh:mm* format, which uses the current date value, minus *nnnn* days at the specified hour. This allows you to set a begin time prior to the current date. Use this variable with the CPEND variable to set a datetime range.

    If you do not use this macro variable, SAS/CPE uses the date and time of the earliest observation in the specified level of the specified table, as stored in the PDB's data dictionary, or as obtained by SAS/CPE as it scans the data.

CPEND
: sets the final date and time when you subset data by a datetime range. Use the same date-time format as used for CPBEGIN.

    If you do not specify this macro variable, SAS/CPE uses the date and time of the latest observation in the specified level of the specified table in the PDB's data dictionary, or as obtained by SAS/CPE as it scans the data.

CPDREDLVL
: sets the global reduction level to DETAIL, DAY, WEEK, MONTH, or YEAR. This is useful if you want to run all of your reports based on the same reduction level.

    If this macro variable is null, SAS/CPE uses a global reduction level of DETAIL.

CPWHERE
: subsets data with a logical WHERE statement. Use the standard format for SAS WHERE expressions, documented in Chapter 9 of *SAS Language: Reference, Version 6, First Edition*. The following examples illustrate valid WHERE expressions:

```
%let cpwhere=machine='host1'
%let cpwhere=machine in ('host1','host2','host3')
%let cpwhere=machine is not missing
%let cpwhere=machine is like 'host%'
%let cpwhere=machine contains 'host'
%let cpwhere=errors > 200
%let cpwhere=datetime < '01jan94:00:00'dt
```

    If this macro variable is null, SAS/CPE does not use a global WHERE statement.

To set global macro variables in a batch job use the following format:

```
%let macro-variable = value
```

For example:

```
%let cpwhere = 'host' ;
```

Local Macro Variables

In addition to global macro variables, SAS/CPE software supports local macro variables for the report macros. You set the macros in batch mode by specifying the parameters on the macro you want to invoke, such as BEGIN= and END=. These variables temporarily override the values of the global macro variables, except when you specify a WHERE expression that begins with the key phrase SAME AND. In this case, the local WHERE expression temporarily appends to the global WHERE expression.

Refer to *SAS Language: Reference, Version 6, First Edition* for more information on WHERE expressions.

Other Global Options

You can set other global options for your SAS/CPE performance database by following this path from the main menu of the SAS/CPE interactive interface:

PDB Admin -> Set Active PDB Options

Refer to *SAS Guide to Macro Processing, Version 6, Second Edition* for more information on using macro variables.

Caution: *The values of SAS/CPE global macro variables are permanently stored.* If you change the value of a global macro variable in an interactive session, it also changes the value for batch jobs. (The reverse is not true.) The values of these variables are stored in your SAS user library.

You can change these values at any time, but each change you make is in effect until the next time you explicitly set the values. You can also set these values to missing, for example:

```
%let CPBEGIN=;
```

Examples of the OUTMODE= Parameter

The following examples illustrate the construction of the destination for a report, depending on the value of the OUTMODE= parameter. In these examples, the output location (OUTLOC=) is specified according to MVS naming conventions. In your code, you should use the appropriate file naming conventions for your platform.

OUTMODE=CATALOG: If OUTLOC=SASUSER.CPUPGMS and OUTNAME=RESULTS, the destination of your report is the SASUSER.CPUPGMS.RESULTS.GRSEG SAS catalog entry.

```
%CPCHART(tababc,machine,,pccpuby,,
        type=hbar,
        outmode=catalog,
        outdesc=All CPUs percent busy (dispatched),
        outloc=sasuser.cpupgms,
        outname=results);
```

OUTMODE=GSF: If OUTLOC=SASABC.WORK. and OUTNAME=RESULTS, the destination of your graphics stream file is the data set named SASABC.WORK.RESULTS.

```
%cpchart(tabxyz,machine,,pccpuby,,
     type=hbar,
     outmode=gsf,
     outloc=sasabc.work.,
     outname=results);
```

Note: The additional commas indicate positional parameters that are being ommitted.

OUTMODE=GSF: If OUTLOC=SYSOUT=B and OUTNAME=DEST=C269R1, the destination of your graphics stream file is the printer named C269R1. The print job is in the class defined by SYSOUT=B.

```
%cpchart(tababc,machine,,pccpuby,,
     type=hbar,
     outmode=gsf,
     outloc=sysout=b,
     outname=dest=c269r1);
```

OUTMODE=LP: If OUTLOC=SYSOUT=A and OUTNAME=DEST=C242R1, the destination of your text output is the printer named C242R1. The print job is in the class defined by SYSOUT=A.

```
%cpchart(tabxyz,machine,,pccpuby,,
    type=hbar,
    outmode=LP,
    outloc=sysout=a,
    outname=dest=c242r1);
```

OUTMODE=LP: If you do not specify the OUTLOC= or OUTNAME= parameter, the destination of your text file is specified in the SAS cataloged procedure by the SASLIST DDNAME statement, which routes the output wherever the job as a whole is routed.

```
%cpchart(tababc,machine,,pccpuby,,
      type=hbar,
      outmode=lp);
```

Chapter 4

Maintaining the Data Dictionary Using the %CPDDUTL Macro

%CPDDUTL

Manages the entire data dictionary in the active PDB

The %CPDDUTL macro allows you to change a data dictionary in batch mode. To run this macro, you write control statements and store them in an external file. When you run %CPDDUTL, the macro reads and acts on the control statements, which perform functions such as modifying or printing table, variable, and formula variable definitions, or the entire data dictionary in the active PDB. When %CPDDUTL macro runs, the data dictionary in the active PDB is updated and views are rebuilt for tables that were changed by the statements called during the %CPDDUTL statement stream.

For additional information about %CPDDUTL, see the following documents:
%CPDDUTL Macro Concepts
%CPDDUTL Syntax Guidelines .

Syntax

```
%CPDDUTL( ENTRYNAM=sas-catalog-entry | FILENAME='physical-filename',
         <LIST=Y | N> ) ;
```

%CPDDUTL Parameters

ENTRYNAM=*SAS-catalog-entry*
: is the name of a SAS catalog entry that contains the control statements to run the %CPDDUTL macro. The name must be a four-level entry name with a type of SOURCE, such as *libref.catalog.member.source*, and cannot be enclosed in quotes. You must specify either this parameter or the FILENAME= parameter, but not both.

FILENAME=*'physical-filename'*
: is the physical location and name of an external data set that contains the control statements to run the %CPDDUTL macro. This includes the complete directory path or high-level-qualifiers plus the filename. The name must be enclosed in single quotation marks. You must specify either this parameter or the ENTRYNAME= parameter, but not both.

Optional Keyword Parameters

LIST=Y | N
: indicates whether or not a listing of your control statements and their line numbers is to be produced on the SAS log. A listing can help you locate errors in your statements because error messages refer to the line numbers of the source lines that contain the errors. This parameter is optional.

: **The default is N, which does not produce a listing.**

Control Statements for %CPDDUTL

Example #1: %CPDDUTL Basic Example

The following examples run the data dictionary utility using the control statements from a SAS catalog entry:

Open Systems Example

```
%cpstart(mode=batch, system=osys, root='cpe/pgmlib',
        pdb=/your/PDB/,
        access=write);
libname stmts 'your-SAS-DATA-LIB' access=readonly;
%cpddutl(entrynam=stmts.stmtcat.tab1.source);
```

MVS Example

```
%cpstart(mode=batch, system=mvs, root='cpe.pgmlib',
        pdb='your.PDB',
        disp=old
        mxglib=mxg.mxg.formats,
        mxgsrc=('mxg.usrid.sourclib' 'mxg.mxg.sourcelib')
%cpddutl(entrynam=stmts.stmtcat.tab1.source);
```

Example #2: %CPDDUTL Long Example

This example runs the %CPDDUTL macro by specifying a SAS catalog entry that contains source statements and three other catalog entries.

Invoking the %CPDDUTL Macro

The example begins by submitting this macro call to a SAS session where the contents of the source entry is shown in

```
%cpddutl(entrynam=LIBREF.CATALOG.CPDDUTL.SOURCE);
```

where the contents of the source entry is shown in **The CPDDUTL Catalog Entry** and CPE is a catalog in the *libref* libref.

The CPDDUTL Catalog Entry

The CPDDUTL catalog entry contains the control statements to include the other files of control statements.

```
/* delete table definitions if they already exist */
include source
  entryname='libref.catalog.cpddutl1.source'
  noerror ;

/* create new table definitions with variables */
include source
  entryname='libref.catalog.cpddutl2.source'
  noerror ;

/* print out table definition and then remove them*/
include source
  entryname='libref.catalog.cpddutl3.source'
  noerror ;
```

```
/* -------------------- the end ------------------------ */
```

The three included source files submit statements to

- ☐ delete previously existing tables if they exist. If they do not exist, the NOERROR option ensures that the job continues processing. This step is illustrated in **The CPDDUTL1 Catalog Entry**.
- ☐ define the defaults for creating a new table, and then create two tables using these defaults. This step is illustrated in **The CPDDUTL2 Catalog Entry**. This step also includes another file to update the tables just created. This step is illustrated in **The CPDDUTL4 Catalog Entry**.
- ☐ print the table definitions just created. This step is illustrated in **The CPDDUTL3 Catalog Entry**.

The CPDDUTL1 Catalog Entry

The SAS catalog entry LIBREF.CATALOG.CPDDUTL1.SOURCE contains the control statements that delete pre-existing versions of the tables.

```
/*------------------------------------------------------------*
 * Deletes all the tables that are to be created later        *
 * even though the tables do not currently exist.             *
 *------------------------------------------------------------*/
 delete table name= ff2
   noerror
 ;

 delete table name= f42
   noerror
 ;
```

The CPDDUTL2 Catalog Entry

This SAS catalog entry LIBREF.CATALOG.CPDDUTL2.SOURCE contains the control statements that

- ☐ set defaults for creating new table definitions
- ☐ creates two new table definitions that use the defaults
- ☐ includes another SOURCE entry to update the tables.

```
/*------------------------------------------------------------*
 * Set default parameter values.                              *
 *                                                            *
 *------------------------------------------------------------*/

  set defaults
   extname=.
   collector = SPECTRUM
   Label=' '
   description=' '
   kept=YES
   detail= (agelimit=2
```

```
            )
    day   = (agelimit=60
             NOCOUNT NOSUM NOAVERAGE NOMINIMUM NOMAXIMUM
             NOUSS NOCV NORANGE NOVARIANCE NOSTD NONMISS
            )
    week  = (agelimit=0
             NOCOUNT NOSUM NOAVERAGE NOMINIMUM NOMAXIMUM
             NOUSS NOCV NORANGE NOVARIANCE NOSTD NONMISS
            )
    month = (agelimit=18
             NOCOUNT NOSUM NOAVERAGE NOMINIMUM NOMAXIMUM
             NOUSS NOCV NORANGE NOVARIANCE NOSTD NONMISS
            )
    year  = (agelimit=0
             NOCOUNT NOSUM NOAVERAGE NOMINIMUM NOMAXIMUM
             NOUSS NOCV NORANGE NOVARIANCE NOSTD NONMISS
            )

    length=8 format=best12.2 informat=.
    interpret=COUNT
    subject=' '
    ;

/*---------------------------------------------------------------*
 * Create table FF2 definition and its variable definitions     *
 *---------------------------------------------------------------*/

 create table
   name = ff2
     type=INTERVAL
     collector = SPECTRUM
     Label='The FF2 test table'
     extname = TYPEFF2
     description='The FF2 test table description'
     detail=(
       agelimit=5
       )
     day=(
       agelimit=90
       )
     month=(
       agelimit=18
       )
     ;
   create variable
     name = tvar1
       extname=tvar1longname
       type=NUMERIC length=8 format=5.1
       interpret=COUNT
       kept=YES
       label='Test var one'
       description='Test var one'
       subject='CPU DISK IO'
       day=(COUNT AVERAGE)
       month=(COUNT AVERAGE)
       ;
   create variable
     name = tvar2
       extname=tvar2longname
       type=NUMERIC length=8 format=9.3
```

```
      interpret=COUNT
      kept=YES
      label='Test var label'
      description='Test var description'
      subject='CPU DISK'
      day=(COUNT )
      month=(COUNT )
      ;
  create variable
    name = tvar3
      extname=tvar3longname
      type=CHARACTER length=20 format=$char10.
      interpret=STRING
      kept=YES
      label='Test var 3 label'
      description='Test var 3 description'
      subject='CPU DISK'
      ;


/*-------------------------------------------------------------*
 * Create table F42 definition and its variable definitions    *
 *-------------------------------------------------------------*/

 create table
   name = f42
     type=EVENT
     collector = SPECTRUM
     Label='The test table F42'
     extname = TYPEF42
     kept=NO
     description='The test table F42 description'
     detail=(
       agelimit=7
       )
     day=(
       agelimit=120
       )
     month=(
       agelimit=0
       )
     ;
   create variable
     name = wvar1
       extname=wvar1longname
       type=NUMERIC length=8 format=5.
       interpret=COUNT
       kept=YES
       label='Wvar label'
       description='Wvar description'
       subject='CPU IO'
       day=(COUNT AVERAGE)
       ;
   create variable
     name = wvar2
       extname=wvar2longname
       type=NUMERIC length=8 format=9.3
       interpret=COUNT
       kept=YES
       label='Wvar2 label'
```

```
        description='Wvar2 description'
        subject='CPU DISK'
        day=(COUNT )
        month=(COUNT )
        ;
create variable
    name = wvar3
        extname=wvar3longname
        type=NUMERIC length=8 format=9.
        interpret=COUNT
        kept=YES
        label='Wvar3 label'
        description='Wvar3 description'
        subject='CPU DISK'
        day=(COUNT )
        month=(COUNT )
        ;
create variable
    name = wvar4
        extname=wvar4longname
        type=CHARACTER length=20 format=$char30.
        interpret=STRING
        kept=YES
        label='Wvar4 label'
        description='Wvar4 description'
        subject='CPU DISK'
        ;

/*--------------------------------------------------------*
 *  Update current table and variable definitions        *
 *--------------------------------------------------------*/
set table name=ff2 ;

update variable
    name = tvar3
        extname=tvar3_longer_name_than_before
        format=$char15.
        interpret=NAME
        ;

update variable
    name = tvar1
        format=9.3
        description='Some other label'
        subject='CPU DISK MEMORY'
        ;

create variable
    name = tvar16
        extname=tvar16_long_name
        type=CHARACTER length=8 format=$hex4.
        interpret=HEXFLAGS
        kept=YES
        label='A label for tvar16'
        description='description for tvar16'
        subject='CPU'
        ;

/*--------------------------------------------------------*
 *  Change current table definitions                      *
```

```
*-----------------------------------------------------*/

set table name=f42 ;

delete variable name=wvar3 ;

/* include some updates to the bylist */
include source entryname='libref.catalog.cpddutl4.source' noerror ;
```

The CPDDUTL4 Catalog Entry

This SAS catalog entry updates the two tables. This entry is included by the CPDDUTL2 SOURCE entry.

```
/*-------------------------------------------------------------*
 * Update by variables and class variables for the tables      *
 *                                                             *
 *-------------------------------------------------------------*/

update table    /* set up by and class lists now that variables exist */
  name = ff2
    detail = (byvars= 'Datetime tvar3'
      )
    day = (classvars= 'Datetime tvar3'
      )
    month = (classvars= 'Datetime tvar3'
      )
    ;

update table    /* set up by and class lists now that variables exist */
  name = f42
    detail = (byvars= 'wvar4 Datetime'
      )
    day = (classvars= 'wvar4 Datetime'
      )
    ;
```

The CPDDUTL3 Catalog Entry

The CPDDUTL3 catalog entry prints the definitions for the two tables.

```
/*-------------------------------------------------------------*
* Print all the table definitions that were just created.      *
*--------------------------------------------------------------*/

print table name= ff2 ;

print table name= f42 ;
```

Viewing the SAS Log from the %CPDDUTL Example

The results of the %CPDDUTL job are shown in the SAS log. The sample SAS log for this job are shown in **SAS Log from the %CPDDUTL Job**.

Notes

You must use the %CPSTART macro with ACCESS=WRITE (Open Systems) or DISP=OLD (MVS) to initiate SAS/CPE before using many of the %CPDDUTL macro control statements. %CPDDUTL also requires an existing PDB.

Additional operating system statements are required to wrap around %CPDDUTL and other macros to form a complete batch job stream. For more information refer to the *SAS Companion* for your operating system environment or to your host specific documentation.

To execute %CPDDUTL catalog source entries, follow this path from the main window of the SAS/CPE interactive interface:

```
PDB ADMIN -> Configure Active PDB Dictionary -> Actions
-> Run Dictionary Utility
```

You cannot use the %CPDDUTL macro to change settings in a supplied table definition unless you first add that table definition from the master data dictionary to the data dictionary in your performance database (PDB), and modify the table definition in your PDB.

You can use the **%CPCAT** macro with %CPDDUTL to copy control statements to and from a SAS catalog.

Caution: *To update the data dictionary in batch mode you must use the %CPDDUTL macro. Updating the SAS/CPE data dictionary using any method other than the SAS/CPE Interactive Interface or the %CPDDUTL macro may result in a corrupted dictionary, which cannot be used by SAS/CPE.*

Sample SAS Log from the CPDDUTL Example

```
297    %cpddutl(entrynam=LIBREF.CATALOG.CPDDUTL.SOURCE);
NOTE: DDUTL Started at 03APR96:16:47:00 Active PDB is  /cpe/testpdb/
NOTE: Source LIBREF.CATALOG.CPDDUTL.SOURCE contains 14 records.
NOTE: Source LIBREF.CATALOG.CPDDUTL1.SOURCE contains 11 records.
WARNING: In LIBREF.CATALOG.CPDDUTL1.SOURCE line 000007 Table FF2 does not
exist.
WARNING: In LIBREF.CATALOG.CPDDUTL1.SOURCE line 000011 Table F42 does not
exist.
NOTE: Source LIBREF.CATALOG.CPDDUTL2.SOURCE contains 201 records.
NOTE: Table FF2 created (type INTERVAL).
NOTE: Variable TVAR1 created in table FF2
NOTE: Variable TVAR2 created in table FF2
NOTE: Variable TVAR3 created in table FF2
NOTE: Table F42 created (type EVENT).
NOTE: Variable WVAR1 created in table F42
NOTE: Variable WVAR2 created in table F42
NOTE: Variable WVAR3 created in table F42
NOTE: Variable WVAR4 created in table F42
NOTE: Active table is FF2 (type INTERVAL)
NOTE: Variable TVAR3 updated in table FF2
NOTE: Variable TVAR1 updated in table FF2
NOTE: Variable TVAR16 created in table FF2
NOTE: Active table is F42 (type EVENT)
NOTE: Variable WVAR3 deleted from table F42
NOTE: Source LIBREF.CATALOG.CPDDUTL4.SOURCE contains 22 records.
NOTE: Table FF2 updated (type INTERVAL).
NOTE: Table F42 updated (type EVENT).
NOTE: Source LIBREF.CATALOG.CPDDUTL3.SOURCE contains 7 records.
NOTE: Printed definitions for table FF2 follows:

TABLE NAME=FF2 COLLECTOR=SPECTRUM VERSION=CP1.0501
  CREATED=03APR96:16:47:02.18  UPDATED=03APR96:16:47:50.91
  EXTNAME=TYPEFF2
  LABEL='The FF2 test table'
  DESCRIPTION=' The FF2 test table description '
  IDNUM=0 TOOLNAME=. KEPT=YES
  DETAIL =( AGELIMIT=5
     BYVARS=' DATETIME TVAR3'
     )
  DAY =( AGELIMIT=90
     CLASSVARS=' DATETIME TVAR3'
     )
  WEEK =( AGELIMIT=0
     CLASSVARS=' DATETIME'
     )
  MONTH =( AGELIMIT=18
     CLASSVARS=' DATETIME TVAR3'
     )
  YEAR =( AGELIMIT=0
     CLASSVARS=' DATETIME'
     )

  VARIABLE NAME=DATETIME  IN-TABLE=FF2
    CREATED=03APR96:16:47:03.20  UPDATED=03APR96:16:47:46.87
    EXTNAME=.
    LABEL='Datetime_of sample/event'
    DESCRIPTION=' Datetime of sample/event '
```

```
    KEPT=YES FIXED=YES VALIDITY=. INTERPRET=DATETIME TYPE=NUMERIC
    LENGTH=8 FORMAT=DATETIME19.2 INFORMAT=. IDNUM=0
    OID=.
    SUBJECT='N/A'

  VARIABLE NAME=DURATION  IN-TABLE=FF2
    CREATED=03APR96:16:47:05.70  UPDATED=03APR96:16:47:05.70
    EXTNAME=.
    LABEL='Duration of interval'
    DESCRIPTION=' Duration of interval '
    KEPT=YES FIXED=YES VALIDITY=. INTERPRET=TIME TYPE=NUMERIC
    LENGTH=8 FORMAT=TIME12.2 INFORMAT=. IDNUM=0
    OID=.
    SUBJECT='N/A'
    DAY =(
      NOCOUNT NOSUM NOAVERAGE NOMAXIMUM NOMINIMUM NOUSS NOCV NORANGE
      NOVARIANCE NOSTD NONMISS
      )
    MONTH =(
      NOCOUNT NOSUM NOAVERAGE NOMAXIMUM NOMINIMUM NOUSS NOCV NORANGE
      NOVARIANCE NOSTD NONMISS
      )
    WEEK =(
      NOCOUNT NOSUM NOAVERAGE NOMAXIMUM NOMINIMUM NOUSS NOCV NORANGE
      NOVARIANCE NOSTD NONMISS
      )
    YEAR =(
      NOCOUNT NOSUM NOAVERAGE NOMAXIMUM NOMINIMUM NOUSS NOCV NORANGE
      NOVARIANCE NOSTD NONMISS
      )
    ISTATS =(
      NOCOUNT NOSUM NOAVERAGE NOMAXIMUM NOMINIMUM NOUSS NOCV NORANGE
      NOVARIANCE NOSTD NONMISS
      )

  VARIABLE NAME=LSTPDATE  IN-TABLE=FF2
    CREATED=03APR96:16:47:04.52  UPDATED=03APR96:16:47:04.52
    EXTNAME=.
    LABEL='Last process date'
    DESCRIPTION=' Last process date '
    KEPT=YES FIXED=YES VALIDITY=. INTERPRET=DATETIME TYPE=NUMERIC
    LENGTH=8 FORMAT=DATETIME19.2 INFORMAT=. IDNUM=0
    OID=.
    SUBJECT='N/A'
    DAY =(
      NOCOUNT NOSUM NOAVERAGE NOMAXIMUM NOMINIMUM NOUSS NOCV NORANGE
      NOVARIANCE NOSTD NONMISS
      )
    MONTH =(
      NOCOUNT NOSUM NOAVERAGE NOMAXIMUM NOMINIMUM NOUSS NOCV NORANGE
      NOVARIANCE NOSTD NONMISS
      )
    WEEK =(
      NOCOUNT NOSUM NOAVERAGE NOMAXIMUM NOMINIMUM NOUSS NOCV NORANGE
      NOVARIANCE NOSTD NONMISS
      )
    YEAR =(
      NOCOUNT NOSUM NOAVERAGE NOMAXIMUM NOMINIMUM NOUSS NOCV NORANGE
      NOVARIANCE NOSTD NONMISS
      )
```

```
    ISTATS =(
      NOCOUNT NOSUM NOAVERAGE NOMAXIMUM NOMINIMUM NOUSS NOCV NORANGE
      NOVARIANCE NOSTD NONMISS
      )

  VARIABLE NAME=TVAR1  IN-TABLE=FF2
    CREATED=03APR96:16:47:07.21  UPDATED=03APR96:16:47:24.24
    EXTNAME=tvar1longname
    LABEL='Test var one'
    DESCRIPTION=' Some other label '
    KEPT=YES FIXED=NO VALIDITY=. INTERPRET=COUNT TYPE=NUMERIC
    LENGTH=8 FORMAT=9.3 INFORMAT=. IDNUM=0
    OID=.
    SUBJECT='CPU DISK MEMORY'
    DAY =(
      COUNT NOSUM AVERAGE NOMAXIMUM NOMINIMUM NOUSS NOCV NORANGE
NOVARIANCE
      NOSTD NONMISS
      )
    MONTH =(
      COUNT NOSUM AVERAGE NOMAXIMUM NOMINIMUM NOUSS NOCV NORANGE
NOVARIANCE
      NOSTD NONMISS
      )
    WEEK =(
      NOCOUNT NOSUM NOAVERAGE NOMAXIMUM NOMINIMUM NOUSS NOCV NORANGE
      NOVARIANCE NOSTD NONMISS
      )
    YEAR =(
      NOCOUNT NOSUM NOAVERAGE NOMAXIMUM NOMINIMUM NOUSS NOCV NORANGE
      NOVARIANCE NOSTD NONMISS
      )
    ISTATS =(
      NOCOUNT NOSUM NOAVERAGE NOMAXIMUM NOMINIMUM NOUSS NOCV NORANGE
      NOVARIANCE NOSTD NONMISS
      )

  VARIABLE NAME=TVAR16  IN-TABLE=FF2
    CREATED=03APR96:16:47:26.54  UPDATED=03APR96:16:47:26.54
    EXTNAME=tvar16_long_name
    LABEL='A label for tvar16'
    DESCRIPTION=' description for tvar16 '
    KEPT=YES FIXED=NO VALIDITY=. INTERPRET=HEXFLAGS TYPE=CHARACTER
    LENGTH=8 FORMAT=$hex4. INFORMAT=. IDNUM=0
    OID=.
    SUBJECT='CPU'

  VARIABLE NAME=TVAR2  IN-TABLE=FF2
    CREATED=03APR96:16:47:08.77  UPDATED=03APR96:16:47:08.77
    EXTNAME=tvar2longname
    LABEL='Test var label'
    DESCRIPTION=' Test var description '
    KEPT=YES FIXED=NO VALIDITY=. INTERPRET=COUNT TYPE=NUMERIC
    LENGTH=8 FORMAT=9.3 INFORMAT=. IDNUM=0
    OID=.
    SUBJECT='CPU DISK'
    DAY =(
      COUNT NOSUM NOAVERAGE NOMAXIMUM NOMINIMUM NOUSS NOCV NORANGE
      NOVARIANCE NOSTD NONMISS
      )
```

```
    MONTH =(
      COUNT NOSUM NOAVERAGE NOMAXIMUM NOMINIMUM NOUSS NOCV NORANGE
      NOVARIANCE NOSTD NONMISS
      )
    WEEK =(
      NOCOUNT NOSUM NOAVERAGE NOMAXIMUM NOMINIMUM NOUSS NOCV NORANGE
      NOVARIANCE NOSTD NONMISS
      )
    YEAR =(
      NOCOUNT NOSUM NOAVERAGE NOMAXIMUM NOMINIMUM NOUSS NOCV NORANGE
      NOVARIANCE NOSTD NONMISS
      )
    ISTATS =(
      NOCOUNT NOSUM NOAVERAGE NOMAXIMUM NOMINIMUM NOUSS NOCV NORANGE
      NOVARIANCE NOSTD NONMISS
      )

  VARIABLE NAME=TVAR3  IN-TABLE=FF2
    CREATED=03APR96:16:47:10.33  UPDATED=03APR96:16:47:48.68
    EXTNAME=tvar3_longer_name_than_before
    LABEL='Test var 3 label'
    DESCRIPTION=' Test var 3 description '
    KEPT=YES FIXED=NO VALIDITY=. INTERPRET=NAME TYPE=CHARACTER
    LENGTH=20 FORMAT=$char15. INFORMAT=. IDNUM=0
    OID=.
    SUBJECT='CPU DISK'


NOTE: Printed definitions for table F42 follows:

TABLE NAME=F42 COLLECTOR=SPECTRUM VERSION=CP1.0501
  CREATED=03APR96:16:47:11.81  UPDATED=03APR96:16:48:05.36
  EXTNAME=TYPEF42
  LABEL='The test table F42'
  DESCRIPTION=' The test table F42 description '
  IDNUM=0 TOOLNAME=. KEPT=NO
  DETAIL =( AGELIMIT=7
     BYVARS=' WVAR4 DATETIME'
     )
  DAY =( AGELIMIT=120
     CLASSVARS=' WVAR4 DATETIME'
     )
  WEEK =( AGELIMIT=0
     CLASSVARS=' DATETIME'
     )
  MONTH =( AGELIMIT=0
     CLASSVARS=' DATETIME'
     )
  YEAR =( AGELIMIT=0
     CLASSVARS=' DATETIME'
     )

  VARIABLE NAME=DATETIME  IN-TABLE=F42
    CREATED=03APR96:16:47:12.44  UPDATED=03APR96:16:48:03.58
    EXTNAME=.
    LABEL='Datetime_of sample/event'
    DESCRIPTION=' Datetime of sample/event '
    KEPT=YES FIXED=YES VALIDITY=. INTERPRET=DATETIME TYPE=NUMERIC
    LENGTH=8 FORMAT=DATETIME19.2 INFORMAT=. IDNUM=0
    OID=.
```

```
    SUBJECT='N/A'

  VARIABLE NAME=LSTPDATE  IN-TABLE=F42
    CREATED=03APR96:16:47:13.47  UPDATED=03APR96:16:47:13.47
    EXTNAME=.
    LABEL='Last process date'
    DESCRIPTION=' Last process date '
    KEPT=YES FIXED=YES VALIDITY=. INTERPRET=DATETIME TYPE=NUMERIC
    LENGTH=8 FORMAT=DATETIME19.2 INFORMAT=. IDNUM=0
    OID=.
    SUBJECT='N/A'
    DAY =(
      NOCOUNT NOSUM NOAVERAGE NOMAXIMUM NOMINIMUM NOUSS NOCV NORANGE
      NOVARIANCE NOSTD NONMISS
      )
    MONTH =(
      NOCOUNT NOSUM NOAVERAGE NOMAXIMUM NOMINIMUM NOUSS NOCV NORANGE
      NOVARIANCE NOSTD NONMISS
      )
    WEEK =(
      NOCOUNT NOSUM NOAVERAGE NOMAXIMUM NOMINIMUM NOUSS NOCV NORANGE
      NOVARIANCE NOSTD NONMISS
      )
    YEAR =(
      NOCOUNT NOSUM NOAVERAGE NOMAXIMUM NOMINIMUM NOUSS NOCV NORANGE
      NOVARIANCE NOSTD NONMISS
      )
    ISTATS =(
      NOCOUNT NOSUM NOAVERAGE NOMAXIMUM NOMINIMUM NOUSS NOCV NORANGE
      NOVARIANCE NOSTD NONMISS
      )

  VARIABLE NAME=WVAR1  IN-TABLE=F42
    CREATED=03APR96:16:47:14.97  UPDATED=03APR96:16:47:14.97
    EXTNAME=wvar1longname
    LABEL='Wvar label'
    DESCRIPTION=' Wvar description '
    KEPT=YES FIXED=NO VALIDITY=. INTERPRET=COUNT TYPE=NUMERIC
    LENGTH=8 FORMAT=5. INFORMAT=. IDNUM=0
    OID=.
    SUBJECT='CPU IO'
    DAY =(
      COUNT NOSUM AVERAGE NOMAXIMUM NOMINIMUM NOUSS NOCV NORANGE
NOVARIANCE
      NOSTD NONMISS
      )
    MONTH =(
      NOCOUNT NOSUM NOAVERAGE NOMAXIMUM NOMINIMUM NOUSS NOCV NORANGE
      NOVARIANCE NOSTD NONMISS
      )
    WEEK =(
      NOCOUNT NOSUM NOAVERAGE NOMAXIMUM NOMINIMUM NOUSS NOCV NORANGE
      NOVARIANCE NOSTD NONMISS
      )
    YEAR =(
      NOCOUNT NOSUM NOAVERAGE NOMAXIMUM NOMINIMUM NOUSS NOCV NORANGE
      NOVARIANCE NOSTD NONMISS
      )
    ISTATS =(
      NOCOUNT NOSUM NOAVERAGE NOMAXIMUM NOMINIMUM NOUSS NOCV NORANGE
```

```
      NOVARIANCE NOSTD NONMISS
      )

  VARIABLE NAME=WVAR2  IN-TABLE=F42
    CREATED=03APR96:16:47:16.50  UPDATED=03APR96:16:47:16.50
    EXTNAME=wvar2longname
    LABEL='Wvar2 label'
    DESCRIPTION=' Wvar2 description '
    KEPT=YES FIXED=NO VALIDITY=. INTERPRET=COUNT TYPE=NUMERIC
    LENGTH=8 FORMAT=9.3 INFORMAT=. IDNUM=0
    OID=.
    SUBJECT='CPU DISK'
    DAY =(
      COUNT NOSUM NOAVERAGE NOMAXIMUM NOMINIMUM NOUSS NOCV NORANGE
      NOVARIANCE NOSTD NONMISS
      )
    MONTH =(
      COUNT NOSUM NOAVERAGE NOMAXIMUM NOMINIMUM NOUSS NOCV NORANGE
      NOVARIANCE NOSTD NONMISS
      )
    WEEK =(
      NOCOUNT NOSUM NOAVERAGE NOMAXIMUM NOMINIMUM NOUSS NOCV NORANGE
      NOVARIANCE NOSTD NONMISS
      )
    YEAR =(
      NOCOUNT NOSUM NOAVERAGE NOMAXIMUM NOMINIMUM NOUSS NOCV NORANGE
      NOVARIANCE NOSTD NONMISS
      )
    ISTATS =(
      NOCOUNT NOSUM NOAVERAGE NOMAXIMUM NOMINIMUM NOUSS NOCV NORANGE
      NOVARIANCE NOSTD NONMISS
      )

  VARIABLE NAME=WVAR4  IN-TABLE=F42
    CREATED=03APR96:16:47:19.75  UPDATED=03APR96:16:48:01.74
    EXTNAME=wvar4longname
    LABEL='Wvar4 label'
    DESCRIPTION=' Wvar4 description '
    KEPT=YES FIXED=NO VALIDITY=. INTERPRET=STRING TYPE=CHARACTER
    LENGTH=20 FORMAT=$char30. INFORMAT=. IDNUM=0
    OID=.
    SUBJECT='CPU DISK'

NOTE: Table views for F42 rebuilt successfully.

NOTE: Table views for FF2 rebuilt successfully.
NOTE: Processing of dictionary utility statements completed successfully.
NOTE: DDUTL Ended at 03APR96:16:48:55 Elapsed time   0:01:55.47
```

%CPDDUTL Macro Concepts

The %CPDDUTL macro allows you to manage the entire performance database (PDB). This is accomplished using %CPDDUTL control statements that act on the master data dictionary and the active performaance database. The active PDB is the PDB that has been specified in the most recent **%CPSTART** macro. The active PDB is also referred to as the current PDB, because it is the one currently affected by all %CPDDUTL statements. The current PDB can also be set through the interactive interface.

The master data dictionary contains a supplied data dictionary, table definitions, and variable definitions. A user-defined PDB contains a data dictionary and data that you have processed and reduced into one or more levels of the PDB, such as detail, day, week, month, and year.

A PDB can contain one or more tables. A table consists of the table's definition in the data dictionary and the data in the table at each level of the PDB. A table definition includes information such as the collector used to collect data, the table name and type, the levels into which data for this table should be processed, and definitions for variables and formula variables in the table.

Some %CPDDUTL control statements and parameters act on the table's data, for example **PURGE TABLE**, without changing or deleting the table's definition. This statement purges the data in the detail levels of the table, but does not prevent new data from being processed or reduced into the table and does not remove the table definition. Other %CPDDUTL control statements act on the table's data and the table's definition. For example, the **DELETE TABLE** statement deletes the data in the table as well as the definition of the table.

Within a table definition, variable and formula variable definitions include information for each variable and formula variable in the table, such as the variable name, description, interpretation type, the data type, the kind of statistics that are to be calculated for the variable at each of the non-detail levels in the PDB.

The data associated with a table are stored in one or more SAS data sets, depending on the level in which the data is stored in the PDB. For each table and level of the PDB, there is a SAS view that provides a logical picture of the data and the SAS data sets containing the data itself.

Control statements that act on the PDB's data dictionary, such as **VERIFY DICTIONARY**, affect all of the subordinate tables, variables, and formula variables in the data dictionary.

Control statements that act on one or more tables, such as **DELETE TABLE**, affect the specified tables and all of the variables and formula variables within the table.

Control statements that act on a variable or formula variable affect only the specified variable or formula variable in the Current Table in the active PDB. (See **Defining the Current Table**.) If you have not set the Current Table, an error results. Use the **SET TABLE** control statement to set any table in the active PDB to be the current table, as shown in the following example.

```
set table name=tab1;
update variable name=var1 description='survey';
update variable name=var2 format=5.3;
```

```
set table name=tab2;
update variable name=var2 label='automobile';
```

This example updates three variables within two different tables. Both tables contain a variable named VAR2. The first control statement that refers to variable VAR2 updates the VAR2 variable that is in table TAB1. The second control statement that refers to variable VAR2 updates the VAR2 variable that is in table TAB2.

Syntax Guidelines for %CPDDUTL

The control statements processed by %CPDDUTL have the following syntax:

```
FUNCTION OBJECT PARAMETERS;
```

where

- FUNCTION is always required and can be one of the following, as defined for each specific function: ADD, BUILD, COMPARE, CREATE, DELETE, END, GENERATE, INCLUDE, INSTALL, LIST, MAINTAIN, PRINT, PURGE, QUIT, SET, STATUS, SYNCHRONIZE, VERIFY, UPDATE, XREF
- OBJECT is always required and can be one of the following: DICTIONARY, DEFAULTS, FORMULA, FORMULAS, SOURCE, SYNTAX, TABLE, TABLES, VARIABLE, VARIABLES, or VIEWS, as applicable to the the specified function.
- PARAMETERS
  - may be required or may be optional, depending on the control statement
  - are separated by blanks
  - have one of these forms

    ```
    keyword

    keyword [=] value
    ```

    If the equal sign is missing in a keyword=*value* pair, the equal sign is assumed. The value for a keyword=*value* pair must not be omitted. However, you can omit the spaces around the = sign in a keyword=*value* pair.
  - a single parameter may contain other parameters and may be enclosed in parenthesis, depending on the control statement. For example,

    ```
    day = (agelimit=5 average count)
    ```
  - may contain strings in single quotes, depending on the control statement. The text of the string may be as long as 200 characters and must not contain embedded single or double quotation marks. If necessary, you can break a quoted string in the middle of a word and then continue the word in column 1 of the next line.
- at least one blank separates function, object, and each parameter
- each statement ends with a semicolon (;)
- comments can be listed anywhere that blanks are allowed. A comment can span multiple lines and can be used to comment out entire statements if required. A comment has this format:

```
/* text of comment */
```

Statements are processed in the order that they are read. If a statement has an error, none of the statements that follow are processed, but SAS/CPE continues to check the syntax of the remaining statements.

SAS/CPE Interpretation Types

An interpretation type (for example INT, C2RATE, STRING, DATE and so on) is assigned to a variable in SAS/CPE, based upon the characteristics of the data in that variable. The interpretation type describes the characteristics of the data in the variable and determines the default settings for a number of characteristics for the variable, such as maximum length, format, and so on.

In SAS/CPE supplied tables, the interpretation type is already assigned to each of the variables. However, if you add a variable to a supplied table or create a new table of variables, you need to assign interpretation types to your new variables.

Assigning the appropriate interpretation type to a variable is necessary not only for proper formatting for reports, but also for proper processing and reduction. Basically, a variable's interpretation type provides or implies the following:

- The default statistics to keep for the variable and how to calculate them. This is probably the most important implication of interpretation type.
- The default data type of the variable (character or numeric).
- The default maximum length of the variable.
- The default SAS format to use when displaying the data.

Note that SAS/CPE supports two types of tables: INTERVAL and EVENT. The statistics associated or calculated for an interpretation type depend on whether the variable is contained in an interval or event table.

An INTERVAL table records information collected over a (usually fixed) time interval. Thus, interval tables must have a DURATION variable. For example, an INTERVAL table that records paging subsystem data might include data such as the number of page faults over the life of the interval (duration) and the amount of paging space used over the life of the interval.

An EVENT table records information collected for an asynchronous event. For example, an EVENT table that records task termination events might include data such as the time of the task termination, the number of page faults over the life of the task, and the number of I/O operations performed by the task.

The datetime stamp included in an event table records when the event occurs, while interval metrics contain data sampled (typically) at regular intervals, and therefore the datetime stamp usually represents the start of the interval.

SAS/CPE interpretation types, and their default information, such as type, length, format, and interval and event statistics, are listed below. Definitions for the **statistics codes** are provided at the end of the interpretation types.

AVERAGE
    Arithmetic mean.

```
Type:                     Num
Max. Length:              8
Format:                   BEST12.2
Interval Statistics:      Aw
Event Statistics:         csA
```

C2RATE

Counter to rate. The interpretation type C2RATE is used by the process step in SAS/CPE on UNIX to convert a COUNTER to a RATE in an INTERVAL table when the data is processed into the PDB.

```
Type:                     Num
Max. Length:              8
Format:                   BEST12.2
Interval Statistics:      Aw
Event Statistics:         -
```

COUNT

Count of events. The COUNT interpretation is an accumulated count of the number of events, starting at 0, for the interval or event. An everyday example of a COUNT would be the number of page faults that occur for a job.

```
Default Type:                     Num
Max. Length:                      8
Default Format:                   BEST12.
Default Interval Statistics:      SA
Default Event Statistics:         cSA
```

Note: When an average is calculated on a COUNT in an interval table, the resulting value is always a RATE. This is because the only thing that can be used to normalize the interval observations is the DURATION. Hence, COUNT/DURATION= RATE, because there is no way to guarantee that the duration of all intervals will always be the same.

COUNTER

Incremental counter across interval boundaries. A COUNTER is an accumulated count of events, that does not get reset to 0 (i.e. it spans events or intervals). An everyday example of a COUNTER would be a regular odometer, which only gets reset to 0 when the available digits are used up. Interpretation type COUNTER has very limited usage.

```
Default Type:                     Num
Max. Length:                      8
Default Format:                   BEST12.
Default Interval Statistics:      -
Default Event Statistics:         -
```

DATE

SAS date value (number of days since 1Jan60).

```
Default Type:                     Num
Max. Length:                      8
Default Format:                   DATE8.
Default Interval Statistics:      -
Default Event Statistics:         -
```

DATETIME

SAS date time value (number of seconds since midnight 1Jan60).

```
Default Type:                      Num
Max. Length:                       8
Default Format:                    DATETIME19.2
Default Interval Statistics:       -
Default Event Statistics:          -
```

DECADDRESS

DECNet network device address.

```
Default Type:                      Char
Max. Length:                       200
Default Format:                    .
Default Interval Statistics:       -
Default Event Statistics:          -
```

 D2RATE

Delta to rate. The interpretation type D2RATE is used by the process step in SAS/CPE on UNIX, to convert a DELTA to a RATE in an INTERVAL table, when the data is processed into the PDB. A DELTA is a variable that represents the difference between two monotonically increasing or decreasing values.

```
Default Type:                      Num
Max. Length:                       8
Default Format:                    BEST12.2
Default Interval Statistics:       Aw
Default Event Statistics:          -
```

ENUM

Enumeration number (number of items within a set).

```
Default Type:                      Num
Max. Length:                       4
Default Format:                    5.
Default Interval Statistics:       -
Default Event Statistics:          -
```

FLOAT

Floating point number.

```
Default Type:                      Num
Max. Length:                       8
Default Format:                    BEST12.2
Default Interval Statistics:       -
Default Event Statistics:          -
```

GAUGE

A GAUGE is a number that represents an instantaneous reading. An example of a GAUGE would be the number of jobs currently in a given state. An everyday example of a GAUGE would be the reading on a car's speedometer.

```
Default Type:                      Num
Max. Length:                       6
```

```
Default Format:                   BEST12.2
Default Interval Statistics:      csA
Default Event Statistics:         csA
```

GAUGE differs from INT, in that statistics are gathered for a GAUGE. GAUGE differs from COUNT in how the average is calculated. In the case of a GAUGE, the average is a simple average (not divided by duration), because it is an instantaneous reading and does not represent an entire interval.

HEXFLAGS

Binary data flags.

```
Default Type:                     Char
Max. Length:                      200
Default Format:                   $HEX.
Default Interval Statistics:      -
Default Event Statistics:         -
```

INT

Integer number. An INT is a number that stands by itself and for which it makes no sense to perform statistical calculations. An example of an INT might be something like a hardware model number, the number of CPUs installed, or the version/release number of a piece of software.

```
Default Type:                     Num
Max. Length:                      6
Default Format:                   BEST12.
Default Interval Statistics:      -
Default Event Statistics:         -
```

IPADDRESS

Network device address.

```
Default Type:                     Char
Max. Length:                      15
Default Format:                   .
Default Interval Statistics:      -
Default Event Statistics:         -
```

LABEL

SAS label for a table or variable.

```
Default Type:                     Char
Max. Length:                      40
Default Format:                   .
Default Interval Statistics:      -
Default Event Statistics:         -
```

MAXIMUM

Numeric maximum.

```
Default Type:                     Num
Max. Length:                      8
Default Format:                   BEST12.2
Default Interval Statistics:      X
Default Event Statistics:         X
```

MINIMUM

Numeric minimum.

```
Default Type:                    Num
Max. Length:                     8
Default Format:                  BEST12.2
Default Interval Statistics:     N
Default Event Statistics:        N
```

NAME

String containing one word.

```
Default Type:                    Char
Max. Length:                     64
Default Format:                  .
Default Interval Statistics:     -
Default Event Statistics:        -
```

NETADDRESS

TCP/IP network device address.

```
Default Type:                    Char
Max. Length:                     11
Default Format:                  .
Default Interval Statistics:     -
Default Event Statistics:        -
```

PCTGAUGE

Gauge that shows a percentage. It is a number between 0 and 1 and it represents a proportion.

```
Default Type:                    Num
Max. Length:                     6
Default Format:                  PERCENT7.2
Default Interval Statistics:     csA
Default Event Statistics:        csA
```

Note that the PERCENT, PCTGAUGE, and PCTGAUGE100 are displayed using the PERCENT7.2 SAS output format. That output format multiplies a number by 100 before displaying it. For example, a PERCENT variable with a value of .2345 would be displayed as 23.4%.

PCTGAUGE100

Percentage gauge that needs to be divided by 100. It is a number between 0 and 1 and it represents a proportion. This interpretation type is used with SAS/CPE process task on UNIX.

Note that the PERCENT, PCTGAUGE, and PCTGAUGE100 are displayed using the PERCENT7.2 SAS output format. That output format multiplies a number by 100 before displaying it. For example, a PERCENT variable with a value of .2345 would be displayed as 23.4%.

```
Default Type:                    Num
Max. Length:                     6
Default Format:                  PERCENT7.2
Default Interval Statistics:     csA
```

```
Default Event Statistics:      csA
```

PERCENT

Numeric value between zero and one. A PERCENT is a number between 0 and 1 and it represents a proportion. An example of PERCENT would be %CPU busy. An everyday example of a PERCENT could be a fuel gauge.

```
Default Type:                  Num
Max. Length:                   6
Default Format:                PERCENT7.2
Default Interval Statistics:   Aw
Default Event Statistics:      csA
```

When choosing between PERCENT and PERCENT100, the distinction simply involves whether the data coming into the PDB is between 0 and 1 (PERCENT) or between 0 and 100 (PERCENT100).

Note that the PERCENT, PCTGAUGE, and PCTGAUGE100 are displayed using the PERCENT7.2 SAS output format. That output format multiplies a number by 100 before displaying it. For example, a PERCENT variable with a value of .2345 would be displayed as 23.4%.

PERCENT100

A PERCENT100 is a number between 0 and 100 and it represents the actual mathematical percentage of a proportion. An example of PERCENT100 would be %CPU busy.

```
Default Type:                  Num
Max. Length:                   6
Default Format:                5.2
Default Interval Statistics:   Aw
Default Event Statistics:      csA
```

When choosing between PERCENT and PERCENT100, the distinction simply involves whether the data coming into the PDB is between 0 and 1 (PERCENT) or between 0 and 100 (PERCENT100).

RATE

Events per second.

```
Default Type:                  Num
Max. Length:                   8
Default Format:                BEST12.2
Default Interval Statistics:   Aw
Default Event Statistics:      csA
```

STRING

Group of printable characters.

```
Default Type:                  Char
Max. Length:                   200
Default Format:                .
Default Interval Statistics:   -
Default Event Statistics:      -
```

SUM

Numeric sum of the values.

```
Default Type:                  Num
Max. Length:                   8
Default Format:                BEST12.2
Default Interval Statistics:   S
Default Event Statistics:      S
```

TIME

SAS time value (number of seconds since midnight). TIME is treated the same as COUNT, because TIME represents an elapsed time, which is simply a count of seconds.

```
Default Type:                  Num
Max. Length:                   8
Default Format:                TIME12.2
Default Interval Statistics:   SA
Default Event Statistics:      cSA
```

TIMETICKS

Count of timeticks in hundredths of a second.

```
Default Type:                  Num
Max. Length:                   8
Default Format:                BEST12.
Default Interval Statistics:   SA
Default Event Statistics:      cSA
```

UNIXTIME

Number of seconds since 1Jan70.

```
Default Type:                  Num
Max. Length:                   8
Default Format:                DATETIME19.2
Default Interval Statistics:   -
Default Event Statistics:      -
```

YNFLAG

A single character, either Y or N.

```
Default Type:                  Char
Max. Length:                   1
Default Format:                $CHAR1.
Default Interval Statistics:   -
Default Event Statistics:      -
```

Statistic Codes

The meanings of the statistics codes are as follows:

```
-        No default
A        Average
C,c      Count
D        Standard Deviation
h        Sum(DURATION*rate**2)
K        Variance
M        Number missing
```

```
N,n      Minimum
p        Sum(count**2/DURATION)
Q,q      Uncorrected Sum of Squares
S,s      Sum
w        Weighted Sum
X,x      Maximum
Y        Range
```

Lowercase characters indicate that the statistic is hidden. Hidden statistics may be required in order to calculate other requested statistics. For example, if you request the average, SAS/CPE must also keep the sum and the count to calculate the average.

Note: The names of variables in the reduction levels are created by adding these same codes as the final character of the variable name. For example, if you requested sum and minimum for variable LU62IOC, those statistics would be named LU62IOCS and LU62IOCN, respectively. Variable names that are shorter than seven characters are padded with underscores, such that the sum for variable SMFQIO would be SUMFQIO_S. Blank is used for Average instead of A, such that variable BATCPU would be BATCPU instead of BATCPU_A. The names are not case sensitive.

Statistical Notes

- In an interval table, statistical calculations for variables with interpretation type COUNT, TIME, or TIMETICKS are normalized with respect to the DURATION of the interval. This is because an Average is calculated based on an implied "per what." For EVENT data this would be per job, per transaction, etc. For INTERVAL data, the obvious choice of per interval may not be appropriate, since the interval in the data can vary dynamically for some collectors. Other collectors may record data in fixed intervals, but the user can change the interval. In these cases the intervals are not the same, therefore it would be misleading to compare or analyze them as if they were the same.

  By normalizing COUNT, TIME, and TIMETICKS values by the duration of the interval, we arrive at "per second" values. This results in rates for COUNT values (for example, page faults per second), and utilizations for TIME and TIMETICKS data (for example, CPU seconds per second).

- If a weighted average is requested for variables with an interpretation type other than COUNT, TIME, or TIMETICKS in an INTERVAL type table, the statistical calculations are weighted by the duration of the interval.

- If neither of the previous items apply, such as for variables in an EVENT table, the statistical calculations are not weighted.

SAS/CPE Interpretation Defaults - Summary Table

Interpretation	Type	Max Length	Interval Stats	Event Stats	Format
AVERAGE	Num	8	Aw	csA	best12.2
C2RATE	Num	8	Aw		best12.2
COUNT	Num	8	SA	cSA	best12.
COUNTER	Num	8			best12.
DATE	Num	8			date8.
DATETIME	Num	8			datetime19.2
DECADDRESS	Char	6			.
D2RATE	Num	8	Aw		best12.2
ENUM	Num	4			5.
FLOAT	Num	8			best12.2
GAUGE	Num	6	csA	csA	best12.2
HEXFLAGS	Char	200			$hex.
INT	Num	6			best12.
IPADDRESS	Char	15			.
LABEL	Char	40			.
MAXIMUM	Num	8	X	X	best12.2
MINIMUM	Num	8	N	N	best12.2
NAME	Char	64			.
NETADDRESS	Char	11			.
PCTGAUGE	Num	6	csA	csA	percent7.2
PCTGAUGE100	NUM	6	csA	csA	percent7.2
PERCENT	Num	6	Aw	csA	percent7.2
PERCENT100	Num	6	Aw	csA	5.2
RATE	Num	8	Aw	csA	best12.2
STRING	Char	200			.
SUM	Num	8	S	S	best12.2
TIME	Num	8	SA	cSA	time12.2
TIMETICKS	NUM	8	SA	cSA	best12.

```
|-------------|-----|----------|--------------|-----------|--------------|
| UNIXTIME    |Num  |    8     |              |           | datetime19.2 |
|-------------|-----|----------|--------------|-----------|--------------|
| YNFLAG      |Char |    1     |              |           | $char1.      |
+-------------+-----+----------+--------------+-----------+--------------+
```

Defining the Current Table

Current Table is the name of the table to which control statements for variables and formula variables apply.

Use the following statement at any time to set the name of the Current Table.

```
SET TABLE NAME=current-tablename ;
```

However, it is not usually necessary for you to set the current table name because most of the %CPDDUTL control statments, for example, SET TABLE, ADD TABLE, CREATE TABLE, UPDATE TABLE, set the Current Table name based on a specific table reference.

For example, after the %CPDDUTL control statement successfully completes this statement,

```
ADD TABLE NAME=UCST  ... ;
```

the Current Table is set to the table named UCST.

Notes

When a control statement refers to _ALL_ tables, %CPDDUTL treats that as multiple control statements, one for each table which has a KEPT status of Yes. Because you do not know the order of the tables in the expanded statement and thus you do not know the final value that will be provided for the Current Table, you can insert a SET TABLE statement between a statement that refers to _ALL_ tables and a statement that depends on the value of Current Table.

Similarly, if the most recent control statement references a table, it may set the Current Table to a different table than the one on which you want to work next (or if there was no previous table reference). You should insert a SET TABLE statement in front of the next control statement to make sure the Current Table is set to the table that you want.

Control Statements for the %CPDDUTL Macro

To run the %CPDDUTL macro, you write control statements and store them in either a SAS catalog source entry or in an external file. The control statements tell the **%CPDDUTL** macro what actions to perform on the data dictionary. The control statements allow you to:

- create new tables or add supplied tables
- update, delete, or print existing tables
- create, update, delete, or print variables in a table
- perform other miscellaneous tasks on the data dictionary.

The control statements on which the %CPDDUTL macro runs are free-format. They can appear at any position on the line and can span multiple lines. Select any of the control statements listed below to receive additional information on that item.

Additional information about %CPDDUTL is also available in the following documents:

- **Syntax Guidelines for %CPDDUTL Statements**
- **%CPDDUTL Macro Concepts**
- **The %CPDDUTL Macro**

Control Statements for %CPDDUTL

Statements for Table Definitions

The control statements for table definitions enable you to manage tables in the PDB's data dictionary by performing tasks such as copying a table definition from the supplied table definitions in the master data dictionary, creating your own table definitions, and printing and maintaining table definitions. Many of the control statements for table definitions set or read the name of the Current Table.

- **ADD TABLE**
- **COMPARE TABLES**
- **CREATE TABLE**
- **DELETE TABLE**
- **INSTALL TABLE**
- **LIST TABLES**
- **MAINTAIN TABLE**
- **PRINT TABLE**
- **PURGE TABLE**
- **SET TABLE**
- **STATUS TABLE**
- **UPDATE TABLE**
- **XREF TABLE**

Statements for Variable Definitions

The control statements for variable definitions allow you to create, delete, list, and update variable definitions for a table. Many of the control statements for variables apply to the table specified as the Current Table.

- ☐ **CREATE VARIABLE**
- ☐ **DELETE VARIABLE**
- ☐ **LIST VARIABLES**
- ☐ **UPDATE VARIABLE**

Statements for Formula Variable Definitions

The following statements allow you to create, delete, list, and update formula variable definitions in a table. Many of the statements for formula variable definitions apply to the table specified as the Current Table.

- ☐ **CREATE FORMULA**
- ☐ **DELETE FORMULA**
- ☐ **LIST FORMULAS**
- ☐ **UPDATE FORMULA**

Additional Statements

The following statements enable you to perform miscellaneous tasks such as building views, including additional control statements, and setting default values to be used when creating new table, variable, and formula variable definitions. These statements also allow you to verify the contents of a data dictionary or the syntax of control statements.

- ☐ **BUILD VIEWS**
- ☐ **END**
- ☐ **GENERATE SOURCE**
- ☐ **INCLUDE SOURCE**
- ☐ **PRINT SOURCE**
- ☐ **QUIT**
- ☐ **SAVE SOURCE**
- ☐ **SET DEFAULTS**
- ☐ **STOP**
- ☐ **SYNCHRONIZE DICTIONARY**
- ☐ **VERIFY DICTIONARY**
- ☐ **VERIFY SYNTAX**

ADD TABLE

Adds a supplied table definition to the active PDB's data dictionary

Purpose

The ADD TABLE statement copies a table definition from the master data dictionary to the data dictionary in the active PDB. To display a list of supplied table definitions, follow this path from the main menu in the interactive interface:

Explore CPE -> All Supplied Tables

The ADD TABLE statement performs the following:

- migrates all of the table definition information for the table, including all of the definition information for its variables, to the active PDB data dictionary.
- copies the list of BY variables (for the detail level) into the lists of class variables for the day, week, month, and year levels.
- adds values for any parameters that you set using the SET DEFAULTS statement.
- completes the table by creating, at each level of the PDB, one or more empty SAS data sets for storing the table's data at that level.

Syntax

```
ADD TABLE
        NAME= table-name ;
```

ADD TABLE Parameters

NAME=*table-name*

names the table definition to be migrated from the master data dictionary to the active PDB's data dictionary, and names the table to be generated in the PDB. This *table name* must exist in the master data dictionary, and it must not already exist in the dictionary of the active PDB.

Notes

When this statement successfully completes, the Current Tablename is set to the table named in this statement.

The ADD TABLE statement differs from the CREATE TABLE statement, which creates an entirely new table definition. The ADD TABLE statement copies an existing table definition from the master data dictionary and adds default values.

COMPARE TABLES

Compares the data dictionary information for two tables

Purpose

The COMPARE TABLES statement compares the data dictionary information for two tables and lists the differences in the SAS log. You can use this statement to compare two different tables in the active PDB or you can use it to compare a table in the active PDB to a table in the master data dictionary.

For example, when you install a new version of SAS/CPE the master tables are often updated and using this statement, you can compare and identify differences between the master table definition and the table definition in the active PDB. You can then use the **MAINTAIN TABLE** to update the table definition in the active PDB.

Syntax

```
COMPARE TABLES
          NAME=table_name
         <AGES | NOAGES >
         <DATES | NODATES >
         <FROM= PDB | SUPPLIED>
         <FROM2= PDB | SUPPLIED>
         <NAME2=table_name2>
         <TRUNCATE | NOTRUNCATE>
         <VARS | NOVARS>
         <VER | NOVER>
         <VOLATILE | NOVOLATILE>;
```

COMPARE TABLES Parameters

NAME= *table_name*

Names the first SAS/CPE table in the comparison. This parameter is required. The table name must be specified and must exist in the location specified by the FROM= parameter.

Optional Keyword Parameters

AGES I NOAGES

Specifies whether or not to compare the age limit information for the specified tables. AGES compares the information and NOAGES ignores the age limit information. **The default is NOAGES.**

DATES I NODATES

Specifies whether or not to compare the creation date, last update, and last processing date information in the dictionary. DATES compare this information and NODATES does not compare this information. **The default is NODATES.**

FROM= PDB I SUPPLIED

Specifies where to look for the dictionary information for the specified *table-name*. PDB indicates that the information is located in the active PDB, and SUPPLIED indicates that the information is located in the master data dictionary. **The default is PDB**. (See the notes for this macro.)

FROM2= PDB | SUPPLIED
: Specifies where to look for the dictionary information for the specified *table-name2*. PDB indicates that the information is located in the active PDB, and SUPPLIED indicates that the information is located in the master data dictionary. **The default is SUPPLIED.** (See the notes for this macro.)

NAME2= *table_name2*
: Names the second SAS/CPE table for this comparison. **The default is the name specified for the NAME= parameter**. (See also the notes for this macro statement.)

TRUNCATE | NOTRUNCATE
: Specifies whether the comparison data written to the SAS log should be truncated. When TRUNCATE is specified, the LINESIZE= SAS option should be set to greater than 82 for best results. If NOTRUNCATE is specified more of the attributes being compared are shown on the SAS log. The SAS LINESIZE= option can be set to a large value to avoid lines wrapping when displayed in the SAS log. **The default is TRUNCATE.**

VARS | NOVARS
: Specifies whether the variable definitions in the tables should be compared. VARS compares the variable definitions in the specified tables and NOVARS does not. **The default is VARS.**

VER | NOVER
: Specifies whether the version of the variables will be compared. VER means to compare the variables and NOVER indicates that the version should not be compared. **The default is NOVER.**

VOLATILE | NOVOLATILE
: Specifies whether or not volatile dictionary information will be compared. This type of dictionary information includes things such as the current total observations and the table's view status flag that indicates whether views need to be rebuilt. VOLATILE indicates to compare this information and NOVOLATILE indicates that this information will not be compared. **The default is NOVOLATILE.**

Examples: COMPARE TABLES

Example 1

This example compares a table in the active PDB with a supplied table in the master data dictionary. Both tables have the same name. As specified, the versions of the variables in the table and the reduction level age limit information in the dictionary are compared. Because a value for the NAME2= parameter is not specified, the NAME2= parameter defaults to the value of the NAME= parameter and compares two tables with the same name.

```
compare table
              name=TABXYZ ver ages ;
```

Example 2

This example compares the dictionary information for two different tables in the active PDB.

```
compare table
            name=TABXYZ from=PDB
            name2=TAB123 from2=PDB
            novars ;
```

Notes

This statement does not change either of the tables being compared and the table set as the **Current Table** is not changed.

The NAME= and NAME2= parameters can have the same name only if the values of the FROM= and FROM2= parameters are different.

Tables in two different PDBs cannot be compared.

CREATE TABLE

Creates a new table definition in the PDB's data dictionary

Purpose

The CREATE TABLE statement creates a new user-defined table definition in the active PDB's data dictionary, and in doing so it also automatically creates the required variable definitions for DATETIME, LSTPDATE, and DURATION. (DURATION is created for TYPE=INTERVAL tables only.) This statement completes the table by initializing, at each level of the PDB, one or more empty SAS data sets for storing the table's data.

Following the CREATE TABLE statement you can add additional variables and formula variables with the CREATE VARIABLE and CREATE FORMULA statements. You should also use the UPDATE TABLE statement to create BY and CLASS variable lists. If you later adjust these lists using the UPDATE TABLE statement, the new lists replace the existing lists.

Refer to the SET DEFAULTS statement for more information on the default values that apply if you do not specify all of the parameters.

Syntax

```
CREATE TABLE
   NAME= table-name
   TYPE= INTERVAL | EVENT
  <COLLECTOR= collector | GENERIC>
  <DESCRIPTION= 'string'>
  <DETAIL= (AGELIMIT=number)>
  <DAY= (AGELIMIT=number)>
  <WEEK= (AGELIMIT=number)>
  <MONTH= (AGELIMIT=number)>
  <YEAR= (AGELIMIT=number)>
  <EXTNAME= name>
  <IDNUM= number>
  <KEPT= YES | NO>
  <LABEL= 'string'>
  <TOOLNAME= name>;
```

CREATE TABLE Parameters

NAME=*table-name*

is the name of the table definition and table to be created. The rules for *table-name* are as follows:

- It must be a valid SAS name, except that it must not be longer than seven characters and it must begin with U (for a user defined table). The name can contain letters and digits, but cannot contain blank spaces or special characters except the underscore (_) character. This convention prevents conflict with current and future supplied table definitions. For more information about SAS names, refer to "SAS Names" in Chapter 4 of *SAS Language: Reference, Version 6, First Edition*.
- The name is not case sensitive; thus, NAME=utable1 and NAME=UTABLE1 are equivalent.

TYPE= INTERVAL | EVENT

is the type of data in the table. Reduction statistics are calculated differently based on the table type. For more information about the calculations, refer to the **CREATE VARIABLE** statement. You cannot change the table type once it has been created, unless you delete the table definition and then create it again. However, when you delete the table definition you will also delete any data in the table.

Valid values for TYPE are:

INTERVAL

indicates that the data in this table are collected in specific timed intervals, i.e. synchronously. The interval may be regular or irregular. SAS/CPE creates the DURATION variable for tables of this type. The DURATION variable contains the amount of time in seconds, for which the data are collected, starting at the time in the DATETIME variable.

EVENT

indicates that the data in this table are collected in response to specific events instead of at regular intervals, i.e. asynchronously.

The DURATION variable cannot exist in this type of data. Reduction will fail if the DURATION variable exists in an event table. The time of the specific event is recorded in the DATETIME variable and the LSTPDATE variable definition is automatically created for every table.

In any given table the data must be either interval data or event data, but not both. If you have both types of data, you should use a separate table for each type. You might use TYPE=INTERVAL to record network traffic in intervals of every 15 minutes and you might use TYPE=EVENT to record events such as the completion of a task.

Optional Keyword Parameters

COLLECTOR=*collector* | GENERIC

specifies the name of the SAS/CPE supported collector that created the log file data. If you are using a user-defined collector or a third-party collector instead of a SAS/CPE supported collector, use the value GENERIC. If you are using a SAS/CPE supported collector, specify the name of the collector.

UNIX Current valid values for UNIX are:

- ACCTON - UNIX Accounting
- GENERIC - SAS/CPE Generic Data Format
- HP-OV - NetView/6000 or HP Network Node Manager
- HP-PCS - Performance Collection Software by HP
- PROBEX - Probe/X by Landmark Systems in SunNet Manager Format
- SPECTRUM - Spectrum by Cabletron Inc.
- SUNETMGR - SunNet Manager by Sun/Connect
- TRAKKER - TRAKKER by Concord Communications

MVS Current valid values for MVS are:

- ☐ SMF - IBM MVS System Management Facilities
- ☐ GENERIC - SAS/CPE Generic Data Format

If the name of the collector contains special characters, enclose the name in single quotation marks. For example, if you are using HP-PCS:

```
collector='hp-pcs'
```

DESCRIPTION='*string*'

is a 200-character string that you can use to describe the data in the table. This description provides information about the table when you list the tables in the PDB, through the SAS/CPE interactive interface. The string must be enclosed in single quotation marks. If the string spans multiple lines, break it in the middle of a word and continue in the first column of the next line.

DETAIL=(AGELIMIT=*number*)
DAY=(AGELIMIT=*number*)
WEEK=(AGELIMIT=*number*)
MONTH=(AGELIMIT=*number*)
YEAR=(AGELIMIT=*number*)

defines the age range for data to be retained at each reduction level. Existing data in each level of the PDB are "aged out" or removed when the range of DATETIME reaches the value specified in the AGELIMIT parameter. The default value and representation of the number value at each level are:
DETAIL - *number* represents days and the default is 10 days.
DAY - *number* represents days and the default is 45 days.
WEEK - *number* represents weeks and the default is 15 weeks.
MONTH - *number* represents months and the default is 18 months.
YEAR - *number* represents years and the default is 5 years.

The *number* must be an integer, but cannot contain a decimal point.

Note: If AGELIMIT=0 at the DETAIL level, your data is stored in DETAIL until the next reduce or process step runs. Therefore, if reduce runs immediately after the process step the data are processed, reduced into the non-levels, and then removed from DETAIL. However, if the process step runs again before the data have been reduced, the existing data in DETAIL are removed before the non-detail levels are updated.

Using AGELIMIT=0 at the DETAIL level is useful if you are collecting and processing large amounts of data on a daily basis, but, to avoid losing data at non-detail levels, you should always reduce the data immediately after you process the data. Furthermore, AGELIMIT=0 at any level other than DETAIL indicates that data will not be stored at that level.

EXTNAME=*table-name*

is the name of the external data source from which data are processed into the detail level of the PDB. The data source could be a SAS data set or an external file, depending on the collector that you used to collect the data.

If COLLECTOR=GENERIC for this table, EXTNAME= must be the name of the SAS data set or View as it exists in the library specified in the GENLIB= parameter on the <u>**%CSPROCES**</u> (UNIX) or <u>**%CMPROCES**</u> (MVS) macro. The name must be a valid SAS name. It can be a maximum of seven characters long, must begin with a letter or underscore (_), can contain letters and digits, and cannot contain blanks or special characters except the underscore character. The name is not case sensitive.

If you do not specify this parameter a blank value is stored in the data dictionary. The *blank* external name will default to the value specified in the NAME= parameter when the next process task runs.

For more information on SAS names, see Chapter 4 of *SAS Language: Reference, Version 6, First Edition.*

IDNUM=*number*

specifies a numeric identifier that represents different uses for each collector. Refer to the information on a specific collector through the online help in the SAS/CPE interactive interface.

This parameter is used only with SAS/CPE on UNIX.

KEPT= YES | NO

indicates to the process task whether data for this table are to be kept in the detail level of the PDB. If you specify NO, the table definition and existing data at any level of the PDB are retained in the data dictionary, but new data for this table are not processed into the detail level of the PDB and any existing data in the detail are not processed to the non-detail levels of the PDB. **The default value is NO.**

The KEPT= parameter is ignored when you specify a list of tables to process on the **%CSPROCES** (UNIX) or **%CMPROCES** (MVS) macro.

LABEL=*'string'*

is a 40-character string describing the data in the table. The string must be enclosed in single quotation marks. This label is used in the views created for this table.

TOOLNAME=*name*

is the name of the software that transforms the logged data and places it into SAS data sets, from which the process task processes them into the detail level of the PDB. This name cannot exceed 32 characters.

Valid options for MVS are:

- MXG - if the data is staged using MXG software
- SASDS - if the data is staged using a generic collector

UNIX The only valid option for UNIX is SASDS, however, this parameter should be used only if the table you are creating is processed by a generic collector.

Notes

When this statement successfully completes, the **Current Table** is set to the table named in this statement.

If you want to copy an existing table definition from the master data dictionary use the **ADD TABLE** statement.

To create a table "like" another table, use the **GENERATE SOURCE** statement.

To create a table from MIB (Management Information Base) definitions (for Open Systems) refer to the Appendix section in *SAS/CPE Software for Open System: Getting Started*.

DELETE TABLE

Deletes a table definition from the active PDB's data dictionary and the table's data from the PDB's reduction levels

Purpose

The DELETE TABLE statement deletes from the active PDB's data dictionary, the table definitions and the definitions of variables and formula variables in the table. It also deletes the data in the table from the PDB's reduction levels.

Syntax

```
DELETE TABLE
        NAME=table-name | _ALL_
       <NOERROR> ;
```

DELETE TABLE Parameters

NAME=*table-name* | _ALL_

is the name of the table to be deleted. The table name must already exist in the data dictionary. Specify _ALL_ to delete all tables.

Caution: *If you specify _ALL_, you will not be prompted to confirm this request.*

Optional Keyword Parameters

NOERROR

specifies whether error conditions are to be treated as warnings for the current %CPDDUTL job. This is useful if you specify statements that delete and redefine a table in the dictionary table because it allows the job to include the DELETE TABLE statement the first time the job is run, before the table exists. The job issues a warning that the table was not found, but continues to run. **By default, NOERROR is not specified and if an error occurs %CPDDUTL ends.** If you specify the NOERROR parameter and an error occurs you will receive a warning message, but your job will not end.

Notes

The previous setting of the **Current Table** is not changed after you run the DELETE TABLE statement, regardless of the success or failure of the DELETE TABLE statement. However, if the table you delete is the Current Table, the Current Table will be undefined when the DELETE TABLE statement completes. The Current Table must be re-defined using a SET TABLE statement. For more information see **Defining the Current Table**.

If you want to stop using the table, but do not want to delete the definitions and data, use the **UPDATE TABLE** statement with KEPT=NO. No more data will be processed or reduced for the table, but the current table definition and data will still exist in the PDB.

If you want to delete the data in the table, but keep the table definition, use the **PURGE TABLE** statement.

INSTALL TABLE

Copies the dictionary information for a PDB table into the master data dictionary

Purpose

This statement copies the dictionary information for a PDB table into the master data dictionary, replacing any information in the master data dictionary for the specified table. By installing your own tables in the master data dictionary the table can be used just like a SAS/CPE supplied table and can be used by other users at your site. The PDB is not changed by the INSTALL TABLE statement. If you choose the REPLACE option, the supplied table is created or replaces an existing table definition with the same name.

Syntax

```
INSTALL TABLE
          NAME= table_name
         <REPLACE | NOREPLACE>
         <RETAIN | NORETAIN> ;
```

INSTALL TABLE Parameters

NAME= *table-name*

name of table definition to be installed. This paramenter is required and the specified table definition must exist in the active PDB. If this table definition name already exists in the master data dictionary you must specify the REPLACE parameter to install the new table definition.

Optional Keyword Parameters

REPLACE | NOREPLACE

specifies whether or not to replace an existing table definition in the master data dictionary, when the existing table definition and the new table definition have the same table name. REPLACE means that an existing table definition in the master data dictionary will be replaced with the table definition named in this statement. NOREPLACE means that an existing table definition in the master data dictionary will not be replaced. **The default is NOREPLACE.**

RETAIN | NORETAIN

specifies whether or not this table definition should be installed in the SITELIB library. RETAIN means that you want this table definition to be installed. NORETAIN means that you do not want this table definition installed. **The default is NORETAIN.**

When you specify RETAIN, you are updating the SITELIB library and therefore, must have write access to SITELIB. To obtain write access to SITELIB, specify SITACC=WRITE (UNIX) or SITACC=OLD (MVS) on the %CPSTART macro before using the %CPDDUTL macro and the INSTALL TABLE control statement.

Example: INSTALL TABLE

This example installs a table definition (TABXYZ) and if a table definition with this name already exists in the master data dictionary, it replaces the existing table definition with the new table definition. Also, because the RETAIN option is used, the table definition will be maintained when future updates to SAS/CPE are installed.

```
install table
     name=TABXYZ replace retain;
```

Notes

When this statement completes, the **Current Table** is set to the table named in this statement.

To run INSTALL TABLE, you must have a PGMLIBW libref. The libref must have write access to the same library that the PGMLIB libref points to. To see where PGMLIB points, from a SAS command line in SAS/CPE, issue the LIBNAME command. You can then issue the libname statement to provide write access, as shown in the following examples.

MVS On MVS, if PGMLIB points to 'SAS.CPE.PGMLIB' you should issue the following command:

```
libname pgmlibw 'sas.cpe.pgmlib' disp=old;
```

UNIX On UNIX, if PGMLIB points to /usr/local/sas/saspgm/cpe/pgmlib you should issue the following command:

```
libname pgmlibw '/usr/local/sas/saspgm/cpe/pgmlib';
```

This gives the INSTALL TABLE command update access to the master data dictionary, which is stored in PGMLIB. The INSTALL TABLE statement will fail if any other user is using SAS/CPE and has the PGMLIB library allocated.

When you install a maintenance tape to update SAS/CPE, the table definitions that are installed into the supplied dictionary will be overwritten and therefore, user-defined table definitions will be lost. To avoid problems, you should have a master PDB that contains the user-defined definitions for all previously installed tables and perform the INSTALL TABLE again after SAS/CPE maintenance has been applied. Some PDB table information is not installed into the master data dictionary. In particular, CLASS variable lists will be the same as the detail-level BY variables list and variable statistics will default to the values specified for the ISTATS= parameter when the variable was created.

Update access to the root location where SAS/CPE is installed must be available and allowed by your security system. If update access is not available, an error message is issued and the table is not installed.

LIST TABLES

Prints a list of tables in the active PDB

Purpose

The LIST TABLES statement prints a list of all of the tables and their labels for the active PDB. The list is printed in the SAS log. The list can be useful at the end of a job that creates many tables because the list confirms what tables are in the PDB.

Syntax

```
LIST TABLES;
```

Example: LIST TABLE

Below is an example of what you might see in the SAS Log after running the LIST TABLE statement.

```
2      %cpddutl(entrynam=sasuser.cpddutl.list.source,list=y);
NOTE: Search path replaced, now includes CPE libname.
NOTE: Search path replaced, now includes CPE libname.
NOTE: DDUTL Started at 26FEB96:17:00:18 Active PDB is /u/username/newpdb/
NOTE: Source SASUSER.CPDDUTL.LIST.SOURCE contains 1 records.
00001  list tables;
NOTE: List of tables in PDB /u/username/newpdb/ follows:

Table    Label
-------------------------------------------------
F42      The test table TABXYZ
FF2      Default label 1
XDCCAPT  DCOLLECT tape capacity
XDCVOLS  DCOLLECT active volume information
XTY70    RMF CPU Activity and Address Space Stati
XTY72    RMF Workload Activity

NOTE: Processing of dictionary utility statements completed successfully.
NOTE: DDUTL Ended at 26FEB96:17:00:20 Elapsed time   0:00:01.99
```

MAINTAIN TABLE

Updates or replaces dictionary information in the active PDB with information from the master data dictionary

Purpose

This statement updates the table and variable definitions for supplied tables defined in a performance database (PDB). The active PDB's data dictionary is updated with the information in the master data dictionary for this table definition. This statement is useful for applying changes to a table when you install a maintenance release for SAS/CPE.

Syntax

```
MAINTAIN TABLE
         NAME= table_name | _ALL_
         <REPORT | NOREPORT>,
         <SCOPE= ALL | NEWVARS>,
         <UPDATE | NOUPDATE> ;
```

MAINTAIN TABLE Parameters

NAME= *table_name* | _ALL_
: Names the SAS/CPE table to be maintained. The table must exist in the active PDB and in the master data dictionary. Specify _ALL_ to maintain all tables in the active PDB.

Optional Keyword Parameters

REPORT | NOREPORT
: Specifies whether or not a report is generated in the SAS log. REPORT generates the report and NOREPORT does not. The statement will be faster if NOREPORT is used. **The default is REPORT**.

SCOPE= ALL | NEWVARS
: specifies what parts of the PDB's table definition are replaced. If ALL is specified, then all dictionary attributes for the table and all of its variables will be replaced. If NEWVARS is specified, then only new variables will be added to the table. New variables are variables that exist in the master data dictionary's table definition, but do not currently exist in the PDB table definition. **The default is SCOPE=NEWVARS.**

UPDATE | NOUPDATE
: allows the effects of the MAINTAIN statement to be investigated and reviewed before committing any changes to the PDB. UPDATE commits the changes and NOUPDATE allows you to review the affects of this statement before committing the changes. **The default is NOUPDATE.**

Example: MAINTAIN TABLE

Example 1

This example adds new variables from the master data dictionary to the table definition of the TABXYZ table. A report is not printed in the SAS log.

```
maintain table
     name=TABXYZ update noreport ;
```

Example 2

This example maintains all tables in the PDB. The attributes of the table definition are maintained and existing variables are changed. A report is not printed in the SAS log.

```
maintain table
      name=_ALL_ scope=all
      update noreport ;
```

Example 3

This example uses the NOUPDATE parameter to report on changes that would occur if the UPDATE parameter was used. NOUPDATE allows you to review the affects of the statement before committing the changes.

```
maintain table
    name= _ALL_ scope=all
    noupdate report  ;
```

Notes

The PDB should be backed up before applying maintenance with this statement. This statement may cause the data in the table to change if any of the following conditions occur.

- A variable is no longer available from the collector. Future observations will have missing values for these variables.
- The default interpretation statistics change, thus the type and method for calculating statistics will change the data. Statistics that you selected prior to running this statement may be redefined (for SCOPE=ALL).
- A variable's length is shortened. This may cause some strings to be truncated.
- SAS output formats are changed. This format change may alter the way the data display.

This statement may take a long time to run, depending on the size of the table (number of observations). If NOUPDATE is specified with NOREPORT, only the syntax and validity of the operands are tested and appropriate messages are written in the SAS log. However, this method may still take some time.

Variables or formulas that you have added will not be removed. However, if there is a newly-supplied variable with the same name as a current variable, the attributes of the new variable will replace the attributes of the current variable. Variable name conflicts of this type may be detected by using the REPORT and NOUPDATE parameters. The only way to resolve this type of conflict is to delete or rename the user-defined variable or formula before applying the maintenance.

The data for variables that are replaced will be passed to the new variables.

PRINT TABLE

Prints a table definition from the active PDB

Purpose

The PRINT TABLE statement prints a table definition from the active PDB. This includes all of the table's variable and formula variable definitions and the source statements for the formula variables. The output is printed in the SAS log.

Syntax

```
PRINT TABLE
      NAME= table-name | _ALL_ ;
```

PRINT TABLE Parameters

NAME=*table-name* | _ALL_
: is the name of the table definition to be printed. The name must already exist in the active PDBs data dictionary. Specify _ALL_ to print all table definitions in the active PDB.

Notes

When this statement successfully completes, the **Current Table** is set to the table named in this statement (if a single table is printed) or to the last table printed (if all tables are printed). If NAME=_ALL_ and you depend on the value of the Current Table for following statements, use a **SET TABLE** statement after this statement to explicitly set the value of the Current Table.

The output from this statement is formatted like the control statements used for input, so that you can make changes and resubmit the table definition.

Caution: *Use the PRINT TABLE statement with caution because it produces a large amount of output.*

PURGE TABLE

Deletes the data in a table in the active PDB without deleting the table's definition

Purpose

The PURGE TABLE statement purges data from a table in the active PDB, leaving the data dictionary definition of the table, its variables, and its formula variables unchanged. The result is an empty table.

Syntax

```
PURGE TABLE
     NAME= table-name | _ALL_ ;
```

PURGE TABLE Parameters

NAME=*table-name* | _ALL_
: is the name of the table to be purged. The name must already exist in the active PDB's data dictionary. Specify a specific table name or specify _ALL_ to purge all tables.

Notes

When this statement successfully completes, the **Current Table** is set to the table named in this statement (if a single table is purged) or to the last table purged (if all tables are purged). If you specify NAME=_ALL_ and you depend on the value of the Current Table for statements that follow this statement, use a **SET TABLE** statement after this statement to explicitly set the value of the Current Table.

To delete the data in a table as well as the table's definition, use the **DELETE TABLE** statement.

SET TABLE

Sets the Current Table name

Purpose

The SET TABLE statement specifies the **Current Table**. All subsequent control statements are applied to the new active table named in this statement.

Syntax

```
SET TABLE
   NAME= table-name ;
```

SET TABLE Parameters

NAME=*table-name*

is the name of the table to be set as the **Current Table**. The name must already exist in the data dictionary in the active PDB.

STATUS TABLE

Prints the status of a table

Purpose

Prints, in the SAS log, the status of a table in the active PDB. Status information includes the date range and number of observations at each of the five reduction levels, the age of data to be kept for each of the five reduction levels, and more.

Syntax

```
STATUS TABLE
   NAME= table-name | _ALL_ ;
```

STATUS TABLE Parameters

NAME=*table-name*

is the name of an existing table in the active PDB. Specify a specific table name or speficy _ALL_ to provide the status for all tables in the active PDB.

Notes

When this statement successfully completes, the **Current Table** is set to the table named in this statement (if the status for a single table is printed) or to the last table (if the status is printed for all tables). If you specify NAME=_ALL_ and you depend on the value of the Current Table for statements that follow this statement, use a **SET TABLE** statement after this statement to explicitly set the value of the Current Table.

UPDATE TABLE

Updates a table definition in a PDB's data dictionary

Purpose

The UPDATE TABLE statement updates the data dictionary definition for an existing table in the active PDB. All of the parameters except NAME= are optional. If you specify any optional parameters, the specified values replace the existing values for those parameters. If parameters are omitted, the existing values for those parameters are retained.

Syntax

```
UPDATE TABLE
   NAME= table-name
  <COLLECTOR= collector | GENERIC>
  <DESCRIPTION= 'string'>
  <DETAIL=(<AGELIMIT= number>
          <BYVARS= 'name-list'>)>
  <DAY=(<AGELIMIT= number>
       <CLASSVARS= 'name-list'>)>
  <WEEK=(<AGELIMIT= number>
       <CLASSVARS= 'name-list'>)>
  <MONTH=(<AGELIMIT= number>
       <CLASSVARS= 'name-list'>)>
  <YEAR=(<AGELIMIT= number>
       <CLASSVARS= 'name-list'>)>
  <EXTNAME= name>
  <IDNUM= number>
  <KEPT= YES | NO >
  <LABEL= 'string'>
  <TOOLNAME= name> ;
```

UPDATE TABLE Parameters

NAME=*table-name*
: is the name of the table definition to be updated. The name must already exist in the active PDB's data dictionary.

Optional Keyword Parameters

COLLECTOR=*collector* | GENERIC
: specifies the name of the SAS/CPE supported collector that created the log file data. If you are using a user-defined collector or a third-party collector instead of a SAS/CPE supported collector, use the value GENERIC. If you are using a SAS/CPE supported collector, specify the name of the collector.

Current valid values for UNIX are:

- ☐ ACCTON - UNIX Accounting
- ☐ GENERIC - SAS/CPE Generic Data Format
- ☐ HP-OV - NetView/6000 or HP Network Node Manager

- ☐ HP-PCS - Performance Collection Software by HP
- ☐ PROBEX - Probe/X by Landmark Systems in SunNet Manager Format
- ☐ SPECTRUM - Spectrum by Cabletron Inc.
- ☐ SUNETMGR - SunNet Manager by Sun/Connect
- ☐ TRAKKER - TRAKKER by Concord Communications

MVS Current valid values for MVS are:

- ☐ SMF - IBM MVS System Management Facilities
- ☐ GENERIC - SAS/CPE Generic Data Format

If the name of the collector contains special characters, enclose the name in single quotation marks. For example, if you are using HP-PCS:

```
collector='hp-pcs'
```

DESCRIPTION='*string*'

is a 200-character string that you can use to describe the data in the table. This description provides information about the table when you list the tables in the PDB, through the SAS/CPE interactive interface. The string must be enclosed in single quotation marks. If the string spans multiple lines, break it in the middle of a word and continue in the first column of the next line.

DETAIL=(AGELIMIT=*number*)
DAY=(AGELIMIT=*number*)
WEEK=(AGELIMIT=*number*)
MONTH=(AGELIMIT=*number*)
YEAR=(AGELIMIT=*number*)

defines the age range that the data can have at each reduction level. Existing data in each level of the PDB are "aged out" or removed when the range of DATETIME reaches the value specified in the AGELIMIT parameter. The default value and representation of the number value at each level are:
DETAIL - *number* represents days and the default is 10 days.
DAY - *number* represents days and the default is 45 days.
WEEK - *number* represents weeks and the default is 15 weeks.
MONTH - *number* represents months and the default is 18 months.
YEAR - *number* represents years and the default is 5 years.

The *number* must be an integer, but cannot contain a decimal point.

Note: If AGELIMIT=0 at the DETAIL level, your data is stored in DETAIL until the next reduce or process task runs. Therefore, if the reduce task runs immediately after the process step, the data is processed, reduced into the non-detail levels, and then removed from DETAIL. However, if the process step runs again before the data have been reduced, the existing data in DETAIL are overwritten.

Using AGELIMIT=0 is useful if you are collecting and processing large amounts of data on a daily basis, but, to avoid losing data, you should always reduce the data immediately after processing the data. However, AGELIMIT=0 at any other level means that no data is kept at that level.

DETAIL=(BYVARS='*name-list*')

is a list of variables by which the SAS/CPE process task merges data into the PDB. The order of the variables determines the sort order of the table's existing data at the detail level and the table's incoming data. Items in the list must be separated by blanks. The list must be enclosed in single quotation marks and cannot exceed 200 characters in length.

Only variables that are already defined in this table at the time this statement is encountered can be used in the list. The DATETIME variable must be in the list. The data sorts in the new order when the next process task runs. This is the only time the data is sorted. Formula variables are not allowed in the BY variables list.

Notes: If you change the BY variables list for a table and you have any reports that use this table, you must also change the BY variables list in the report definition.

During the process step SAS/CPE does not delete data with duplicate BY variable values. When duplicate BY variables are located, information about the number of observations with duplicate BY variables is printed in the summary report that is produced each time the process task runs.

DAY=(CLASSVARS='*name-list*')
WEEK=(CLASSVARS='*name-list*')
MONTH=(CLASSVARS='*name-list*')
YEAR=(CLASSVARS='*name-list*')

is a list of variables used to classify or group the data for each reduction level except the detail level. Each level can contain different variables. The order of the variables determines the sort order of the table's data at the specified level and affects the sort order for reports based on the data.

The lists must be enclosed in single quotation marks and cannot exceed 200 characters in length. Use blanks to separate the variables in the list and name the variables as they are named in the detail level. Only variables that are already defined in this table at the time this statement is encountered can be used in the list. Formula variables are not allowed in the list. The DATETIME variable must be in the list. The data sorts in the new order when the next process step runs. This is the ONLY time the data is sorted.

In this statement, do not list statistics based on the variables. For more information, see the statistics keyword list in the **CREATE VARIABLE**, **UPDATE VARIABLE**, **CREATE FORMULA**, and **UPDATE FORMULA** statements.

EXTNAME=*table-name*

is the name of the external data source from which data are processed into the detail level of the PDB. The data source could be a SAS data set or an external file, depending on the collector that you used to collect the data.

If COLLECTOR=GENERIC for this table, EXTNAME= must be the name of the SAS data set or View as it exists in the library specified in the GENLIB= parameter on the **%CSPROCES** (UNIX) or **%CMPROCES** (MVS) macro. The name must be a valid SAS name. It can be a maximum of seven characters long, must begin with a letter or underscore (_), can contain letters and digits, and cannot contain blanks or special characters except the underscore character. The name is not case sensitive.

If you do not specify this parameter a blank value is stored in the data dictionary. The *blank* external name will default to the value specified in the NAME= parameter when the next process task runs.

For more information on SAS names, see Chapter 4 of *SAS Language: Reference, Version 6, First Edition.*

 IDNUM=*number*

specifies a numeric identifier that represents different uses for each collector. Refer to the information on a specific collector through the online help in the SAS/CPE interactive interface.

This parameter is used only with SAS/CPE on UNIX.

KEPT= YES | NO

indicates to the process task whether data for this table are to be kept in the detail level of the PDB. If you specify NO, the table definition and existing data at any level of the PDB are retained in the data dictionary, but new data for this table are not processed into the detail level of the PDB and any existing data in the detail are not processed to the non-detail levels of the PDB. **The default value is NO.**

The KEPT= parameter is ignored when you specify a list of tables to process on the %CSPROCES (UNIX) or %CMPROCES (MVS) macro.

LABEL='*string*'

is a 40-character string describing the data in the table. The string must be enclosed in single quotation marks. This label is used in the views created for this table.

TOOLNAME=*name*

is the name of the software that transforms the logged data and places it into SAS data sets, from which the process task processes them into the detail level of the PDB. This name cannot exceed 32 characters.

 Valid options for MVS are:

- MXG - if the data is staged using MXG software
- SASDS - if the data is staged using a generic collector

UNIX The only valid option for UNIX is SASDS, however, this parameter should be used only if the table you are creating is processed by a generic collector.

Notes

After you create a table definition using the CREATE TABLE statement, the UPDATE TABLE statement provides the only way to modify a list of BY variables or CLASS variables.

When this statement successfully completes, the current table name is set to the table named in this statement.

You cannot change the table type (Internal/Event), but you can create a table definition like an existing table definition using **GENERATE SOURCE**. You must then edit the new table definition name and type and run %CPDDUTL to create the table definition.

XREF TABLE

Prints a formula listing for a table

Purpose

The XREF TABLE statement prints a list of formula variables for the specified table in the active PDB. For each formula variable, it prints a list of the variables that are used to construct the formula. The list is printed in the SAS log.

Syntax

```
XREF TABLE
     NAME= table-name | _ALL_ ;
```

XREF TABLE Parameters

NAME=*table-name* | _ALL_
: is the name of an existing table in the active PDB. Specify a specific table name or specify _ALL_ to provide a listing for all tables in the active PDB.

Notes

When this statement successfully completes, the **Current Table** is set to the table named in this statement (if a cross reference is run for a single table) or to the last table referenced (if a cross reference is run for all tables). If you specify NAME=_ALL_ and you depend on the value of the Current Table for statements that follow this statement, use a **SET TABLE** statement after this statement to explicitly set the value of the Current Table.

To print the source statements that are used to calculate the values of the formula variables, use the **PRINT TABLE** statement.

CREATE VARIABLE

Creates a new variable definition in a table

Purpose

The CREATE VARIABLE statement creates the definition for a new variable in the current table in the active PDB.

You can also use this statement to create a new variable that is similiar to an existing variable in the same table or another table in the active PDB.

Syntax

```
CREATE VARIABLE
    INTERPRET= interpretation
    NAME= variable-name
    TYPE= NUMERIC | CHARACTER
  <DAY= (statistic-keywords-list)>
  <MONTH= (statistic-keywords-list)>
  <WEEK= (statistic-keywords-list)>
  <YEAR= (statistic-keywords-list)>
  <DESCRIPTION= 'string'>
  <EXTNAME= name>
  <FORMAT= SAS-format>
  <IDNUM= number>
  <INFORMAT=>
  <ISTATS=(statistic-keywords-list)>
  <KEPT= YES | NO>
  <LABEL= 'string'>
  <LENGTH= number>
  <LIKE= '<< SUPPLIED | PDB .> table-name .> like-var-name'>
  <OID= oid-specification>
  <SUBJECT= 'subject-keyword-list'>
  <VALIDITY=> ;
```

CREATE VARIABLE Parameters

INTERPRET=*interpretation*

indicates the type of information that the variable represents. This parameter is required. You can specify one of the following values:

AVERAGE
C2RATE
COUNT
COUNTER
DATE
DATETIME
DECADDRESS
D2RATE
ENUM
FLOAT
GAUGE
HEXFLAGS
MAXIMUM
MINIMUM
NAME
NETADDRESS
PCTGAUGE
PCTGAUGE100
PERCENT
PERCENT100
RATE
STRING
SUM
TIME

INT	**TIMETICKS**
IPADDRESS	**UNIXTIME**
LABEL	**YNFLAG**

The value can be uppercase or lowercase. For additional information and default values for the interpretation values listed above, refer to **SAS/CPE Interpretation Type Definitions** or **SAS/CPE Interpretation Summary Table**.

Note that default values do not apply for formula variables.

NAME=*variable-name*
names the variable to be created. The name must not already exist in the table. The name cannot be longer than seven characters. It can contain letters, numbers and the underscore (_) character, but cannot contain blank spaces or any other special characters.

TYPE=NUMERIC | CHARACTER
is the type of the variable. The type can be either NUMERIC or CHARACTER. You cannot change the type of the variable once you have created it unless you delete the variable and create it again.

Optional Keyword Parameters

DAY=(*statistic-keywords-list*)
WEEK=(*statistic-keywords-list*)
MONTH=(*statistic-keywords-list*)
YEAR=(*statistic-keywords-list*)
is the list of statistic calculations required for this variable at the specified reduction levels for the current table. Use blanks to separate the keywords in the list.

You specify a class variable list for each level of a table in the PDB. For example, you might specify machine and shift as class variables for a specifc level in a table. SAS/CPE groups the data based upon the values of the class variables. The statistics requested are calculated for each class variable group in each reduction level of each table in the PDB.

When creating a new variable specify all statistics that you want kept at each reduction level, using the CREATE VARIABLE statement. If you do not specify statistics for a level, no statistics are kept at that level.

When updating a variable, you do not need to respecify statistics that are already being kept. For example, if you are already keeping the statistics COUNT and SUM and you want to also keep AVERAGE, you need only specify AVERAGE in the UPDATE VARIABLE statement.

The statistic list can contain one or more of these values at each level:

AVERAGE | NOAVERAGE
is the arithmetic mean.

COUNT | NOCOUNT
is an accumulated count of the number of observations that have nonmissing values for the variable, starting at 0.

CV | NOCV
is the coefficient of variation.

MAXIMUM | NOMAXIMUM
is the maximum value.

MINIMUM | NOMINIMUM
is the minimum value.

NMISS | NONMISS
the number of observations with missing variable values.

RANGE | NORANGE
is the range or difference between the maximum and minimum of the values for all observations.

STD | NOSTD
is the standard deviation or square root of variance. Like the variance, it is a measure of the dispersion about the mean but in the same unit of measure as the data.

SUM | NOSUM
is the sum of values.

USS | NOUSS
is the uncorrected sum of squares.

VARIANCE | NOVARIANCE
is a measure of the dispersion or variability of the data about the mean. When values are close to the mean, the variance is small. When values are scattered widely about the mean, the variance is large.

DESCRIPTION='*string*'
is a 200-character string that describes the variable. This description provides information about the variable when you list the variables in a table in the PDB through the SAS/CPE interactive interface. The string must be enclosed in single quotation marks. If the string spans multiple lines, break it in the middle of a word and continue in the first column of the next line.

EXTNAME=*name*
is the name of the variable as it appears in the external data source from which data are processed into the detail level of the PDB. The data source could be a SAS data set or an external file, depending on the collector that you used to collect the data.

If COLLECTOR=GENERIC for this table, EXTNAME= must be the name of the variable as it exists in the SAS data set or View. The variable name must be a valid SAS name. It can be a maximum of seven characters long, must begin with a letter or underscore (_), can contain letters and digits, and cannot contain blanks or special characters except the underscore character. The name is not case sensitive.

If you do not specify this parameter a blank value is stored in the data dictionary. The *blank* external name will default to the value specified in the NAME= parameter when the next process task runs.

For more information on SAS names, see SAS names in Chapter 4 of *SAS Language: Reference, Version 6, First Edition*.

FORMAT=*SAS-format*
: is a SAS format to be used with this variable or formula variable. Variables and formula variables will require character formats when their values contain characters. Variables and formula variables whose values contain numbers require numeric formats. These formats are used for all presentation of the data for this variable or formula variable.

For more information on default formats related to the formula or variable's interpretation type, see the INTERPRET= parameter on the **CREATE VARIABLE** or **CREATE FORMULA** statement. Refer to *SAS Language: Reference, Version 6, First Edition* for more information on SAS formats.

IDNUM=*number*
: specifies a numeric identifier that represents different uses for each collector. Refer to the information on a specific collector through the online help in the SAS/CPE interactive interface.

This parameter is used only with SAS/CPE on UNIX.

INFORMAT=
: is not currently used.

ISTATS=(*statistic-selector-keywords*)
: lists the default statistics for a variable. The statistics are saved with the variable definition, but they are not calculated within the current table. These statistics are used when you run **INSTALL TABLE** or **ADD TABLE**, because the master data dictionary doesn't keep reduction level statistics information.

You specify a class variable list for each level of a table in the PDB. For example, you might specify machine and shift as class variables for a specifc level in a table. SAS/CPE groups the data based upon the values of the class variables. The statistics requested are calculated for each class variable group in each reduction level of each table in the PDB.

The statistics that are calculated for the current table are those specified by the DAY=, WEEK=, MONTH=, and YEAR= parameters. Therefore, when you install a table in the master data dictionary, it stores the ISTATS with the table definition. When you later add that table to another PDB, the ADD TABLE statement populates the DAY=, WEEK=, MONTH=, and YEAR= statistics based on the ISTATS= list of statistics. You can then customize the added table using the interactive interface or an UPDATE VARIABLE statement with the DAY=, WEEK, MONTH=, and YEAR= parameters.

AVERAGE | NOAVERAGE
: is the arithmetic mean for all observations.

COUNT | NOCOUNT

is an accumulated count of the number of observations that have non-missing values, starting at 0.

CV I NOCV
is the coefficient of variation. It is calculated as the standard deviation divided by the mean and multiplied by 100.

MAXIMUM I NOMAXIMUM
is the maximum value for all observations.

MINIMUM I NOMINIMUM
is the minimum value for all observations.

NMISS I NONMISS
the number of observations with missing variable values.

RANGE I NORANGE
is the maximum of the difference between the maximum and minimum values for the variable MAXIMUM I MINIMUM.

STD I NOSTD
is the standard deviation or square root of variance. Like the variance, it is a measure of the dispersion about the mean, but in the same unit of measure as the data.

SUM I NOSUM
is the sum of values for all observations

USS I NOUSS
is the uncorrected sum of squares.

VARIANCE I NOVARIANCE
is a measure of the dispersion or variability of the data about the mean. When values are close to the mean, the variance is small. When values are scattered widely about the mean, the variance is large.

Notes: ISTATS= can be specified on the **SET DEFAULTS**, **CREATE VARIABLE**, and **UPDATE VARIABLE** statements. If you install or add a table for which ISTATS have not been specified, the table is given the default statistic values for ISTATS= , which have been specified in SET DEFAULTS for the current set of %CPDDUTL statements. If default values have not been set via SET DEFAULTS, the variable is treated as if all of statistics in the ISTATS= list were set to NO. If the table is installed and then added, the added table does not keep any statistics at the DAY, WEEK, MONTH, or YEAR level unless you set them using UPDATE VARIABLE.

If you are using a SET DEFAULTS statement that will apply to a single variable, a useful default setting is one based on the variable's interpretation. (For more about the relation between interpretation and initial statistics, see **GENERATE SOURCE**.) If the SET DEFAULTS statement will apply to a number of variables, a useful default setting is ISTATS=(AVERAGE).

KEPT= YES I NO

indicates to the process step or reduce step whether data for this variable are to be kept in the PDB. If you specify NO, the variable's definition and the existing data (only for an existing variable) are retained in the dictionary, but no new data for this variable are processed or reduced into the PDB. **The default value is NO.**

LABEL='*string*'
: is a 40-character string describing the data in the variable at the DETAIL level. The string must be enclosed in single quotation marks. In the DAY, WEEK, MONTH, and YEAR levels, the labels are formed automatically by concatenating the statistic name, a period, and the string.

LENGTH=*number*
: is the maximum length of the variable as stored in the PDB. **The default value is 0.** Character variables can be as long as 200 characters; numeric variables can have a length of between 2 and 8 bytes.

LIKE='<< SUPPLIED | PDB .> *table-name .> like-var-name*'
: specifies the location of the existing variable from which you want to create the new variable. This parameter has three parts.

The first is the location of the data dictionary. The value is SUPPLIED (for the master data dictionary) or PDB (for the current PDB). This first part is optional. If it is specified, it must be followed by a period (.). **If it is omitted, PDB is used.**

The second part is a valid table name within the location specified in the first part. The second part is optional, but must be specified if the first part is specified. If the second part is specified, a period (.) must follow the name. **If it is not specified, the current table from the active PDB is used.**

The third part of the parameter is a variable name which must exist in the table specified by the first and second parts of the parameter. **The third part is not optional.**

The new variable is created with exactly the same attributes as the variable named in the *like-var-name*.

OID=*oid-specification*
: is an SNMP OID of the form *n.n.n.n.n.n* which must be unique for the variable if you specify it. Use OID=. to specify none.

This parameter is used only with SAS/CPE on UNIX.

SUBJECT='*subject-keyword-list*'
: specifies a list of keywords that can be used to categorize this variable. The maximum length of the list is 200 characters. Use SUBJECT=' ' to leave the list blank. You must use blanks to separate keywords in the list and the list must be enclosed in single quotation marks.

When updating the SUBJECT= parameter list, you must specify all keywords that you want to use at the time that you update the list because this parameter does not use pre-existing values.

VALIDITY=
is not currently used.

Examples: CREATE VARIABLE

Example 1

This example creates a variable that is like a variable in a different table in the active PDB and then changes the description and external name for the new variable.

```
set table name=TABXYZ ;               /* set current table */
create variable                       /* create new variable */
  name=CPUBUSY
  like='PDB.TABLEABC.PCTCPUBY' ;      /* like this variable */
update variable                       /* update new variable */
  name=CPUBUSY
  description='Total CPU percent busy'        /* override */
  extname=newextname ;          /*changes external name of new variable*/
```

Example 2

This example creates a variable that is like a variable in the master data dictionary.

```
set table name=TABABC ;
create variable
  name=NIORATE
  like='SUPPLIED._HPOV.NETIO' ;
```

Example 3

This example adds a supplied table definition to the active PDB and then creates a new variable in the table definition in the active PDB.

```
/*                                                      */
/*    NB:- Needs update access to the active PDB.       */
/*       - A list of initial statistics is provided by  */
/*         the CREATE VARIABLE statement.  Because no   */
/*         SET DEFAULT statement exists earlier in the  */
/*         statement stream, any initial statistic not  */
/*         mentioned in the ISTATS= list on the CREATE  */
/*         VARIABLE statement is set to its built-in    */
/*         default, which is the NO state.              */
delete table      /*deletes table & data from PDB in case job is re-run*/
  name=tabxyz noerror ;
add table         /*adds table from master data dictionary*/
  name=tabxyz ;
create variable /*creates new table in table in active PDB*/
  name=uuxx length=8 type=numeric format=5.
  interpret=count label='Special variable'
  description='Site-specific special variable'
  istats=(RANGE AVERAGE)
  ;
```

Notes

The DATETIME, LISTPDATE, and DURATION variables are automatically created for you by SAS/CPE. If you create SHIFT and HOUR variables SAS/CPE will calculate these for you based on the DATETIME variable for the observations and the shift matrix that you defined for the PDB using the **%CSPROCES** or **%CMPROCES** macro.

You can create a variable with attributes similiar to those of another variable by specifying the LIKE= and NAME= parameters on the CREATE VARIABLE statement. **When you specify the LIKE= parameter you must specify the NAME= parameter, but you cannot specify any other required or optional parameters or you will receive error messages.** All other parameters that are currently set for the variable specified in the LIKE= parameter are applied to the variable specified in the NAME= parameter.

After you create the new variable, you can use the **UPDATE VARIABLE** statement to update the new variable in the data dictionary. Specifically, you should change the value of the EXTNAME= parameter for the new variable to avoid conflicts with existing variables that have the same external name.

DELETE VARIABLE

Deletes a variable definition and the variable's data from a table

Purpose

The DELETE VARIABLE statement deletes a variable definition from the current table in the active PDB. It also deletes the variable's data from the PDB and rebuilds the Views when %CPDDUTL macro completes.

Syntax

```
DELETE VARIABLE
        NAME=variable-name
       <NOERROR> ;
```

DELETE VARIABLE Parameters

NAME=*variable-name*
: is the name of the variable to be deleted. The name must already exist in the dictionary.

Optional Keyword Parameters

NOERROR
: specifies whether or not to treat error conditions as warnings for the current %CPDDUTL job. This is useful if you have statements that need to delete and then later redefine a variable, because the variable can be missing and subsequent statements are still processed. **By default, NOERROR is not specified and if an error occurs %CPDDUTL ends**. If you specify the NOERROR parameter and an error occurs you will receive a warning message, but your job will not end.

Notes

The Current Table must be set before you can run this statement.

If you want to stop using the variable, but do not want to delete the definition and the data, use the UPDATE VARIABLE statement with KEPT=NO. Data will no longer be processed or reduced for the variable, but the definition and the current data will still exist.

LIST VARIABLES

Prints a list of nonformula variables for the current table

Purpose

The LIST VARIABLES statement prints, in the SAS log, a list of all of nonformula variables and their labels in the current table in the active PDB. This is a good way to verify the variables that exist in the table.

Syntax

```
LIST VARIABLES;
```

Notes

The **Current Table** must be set before you can run this statement.

Formula variables are not printed by this statement. Use the LIST FORMULAS statement to print formula variables.

UPDATE VARIABLE

Updates the definition of a variable in a table

Purpose

The UPDATE VARIABLE statement updates the data dictionary definition for a nonformula variable in the current table in the active PDB. *If a parameter is omitted, the existing value is retained.* For example, if you specify only the DESCRIPTION= parameter, only the value of the description changes; the values for other parameters do not change.

Syntax

```
UPDATE VARIABLE
    NAME= variable-name
   <DAY= (<statistic-keyword-list>)
    <MONTH= (<statistic-keyword-list>)
    <WEEK= (<statistic-keyword-list>)
    <YEAR= (<statistic-keyword-list>)
   <DESCRIPTION= 'string'>
   <EXTNAME= name>
   <FORMAT= SAS-format>
   <IDNUM= number>
   <INFORMAT=>
   <INTERPRET= interpretation>
   <ISTATS=(statistic-selector-keywords)>
   <KEPT=  YES | NO>
   <LABEL= 'string'>
   <OID= oid-specification>
   <SUBJECT= 'subject-keyword-list'>
   <VALIDITY= > ;
```

UPDATE VARIABLE Parameters

NAME=*variable-name*
: is the name of the variable to bc updated. The name must already exist in the table or the CREATE VARIABLE statement for the variable must be included earlier in the stream of control statements.

Optional Keyword Parameters

DAY=(*statistic-keywords-list*)
WEEK=(*statistic-keywords-list*)
MONTH=(*statistic-keywords-list*)
YEAR=(*statistic-keywords-list*)
: is the list of statistic calculations required for this variable at the specified reduction levels for the current table. Use blanks to separate the keywords in the list.

You specify a class variable list for each level of a table in the PDB. For example, you might specify machine and shift as class variables for a specifc level in a table. SAS/CPE groups the data based upon the values of the class variables. The statistics requested are calculated for each class variable group in each reduction level of each table in the PDB.

When creating a new variable specify all statistics that you want kept at each reduction level, using the CREATE VARIABLE statement. If you do not specify statistics for a level, no statistics are kept at that level.

When updating a variable, you do not need to respecify statistics that are already being kept. For example, if you are already keeping the statistics COUNT and SUM and you want to also keep AVERAGE, you need only specify AVERAGE in the UPDATE VARIABLE statement.

The statistic list can contain one or more of these values at each level:

AVERAGE | NOAVERAGE
: is the arithmetic mean.

COUNT | NOCOUNT
: is an accumulated count of the number of observations that have nonmissing values for the variable, starting at 0.

CV | NOCV
: is the coefficient of variation.

MAXIMUM | NOMAXIMUM
: is the maximum value.

MINIMUM | NOMINIMUM
: is the minimum value.

NMISS | NONMISS
: the number of observations with missing variable values.

RANGE | NORANGE
: is the range or difference between the maximum and minimum of the values for all observations.

STD | NOSTD
: is the standard deviation or square root of variance. Like the variance, it is a measure of the dispersion about the mean but in the same unit of measure as the data.

SUM | NOSUM
: is the sum of values.

USS | NOUSS
: is the uncorrected sum of squares.

VARIANCE | NOVARIANCE
: is a measure of the dispersion or variability of the data about the mean. When values are close to the mean, the variance is small. When values are scattered widely about the mean, the variance is large.

DESCRIPTION='*string*'
: is a 200-character string that describes the variable. This description provides information

about the variable when you list the variables in a table in the PDB through the SAS/CPE interactive interface. The string must be enclosed in single quotation marks. If the string spans multiple lines, break it in the middle of a word and continue in the first column of the next line.

EXTNAME=*name*

is the name of the variable as it appears in the external data source from which data are processed into the detail level of the PDB. The data source could be a SAS data set or an external file, depending on the collector that you used to collect the data.

If COLLECTOR=GENERIC for this table, EXTNAME= must be the name of the variable as it exists in the SAS data set or View. The variable name must be a valid SAS name. It can be a maximum of seven characters long, must begin with a letter or underscore (_), can contain letters and digits, and cannot contain blanks or special characters except the underscore character. The name is not case sensitive.

If you do not specify this parameter a blank value is stored in the data dictionary. The *blank* external name will default to the value specified in the NAME= parameter when the next process task runs.

For more information on SAS names, see SAS names in Chapter 4 of *SAS Language: Reference, Version 6, First Edition.*

FORMAT=*SAS-format*

is a SAS format to be used with this variable or formula variable. Variables and formula variables will require character formats when their values contain characters. Variables and formula variables whose values contain numbers require numeric formats. These formats are used for all presentation of the data for this variable or formula variable.

For more information on default formats related to the formula or variable's interpretation type, see the INTERPRET= parameter on the **CREATE VARIABLE** or **CREATE FORMULA** statement. Refer to *SAS Language: Reference, Version 6, First Edition* for more information on SAS formats.

IDNUM=*number*

specifies a numeric identifier that represents different uses for each collector. Refer to the information on a specific collector through the online help in the SAS/CPE interactive interface.

This parameter is used only with SAS/CPE on UNIX.

INFORMAT=

is not currently used.

INTERPRET=*interpretation*

indicates the type of information that the variable represents. This parameter is required. You can specify one of the following values:

AVERAGE	**MAXIMUM**
C2RATE	**MINIMUM**

COUNT	**NAME**
COUNTER	**NETADDRESS**
DATE	**PCTGAUGE**
DATETIME	**PCTGAUGE100**
DECADDRESS	**PERCENT**
D2RATE	**PERCENT100**
ENUM	**RATE**
FLOAT	**STRING**
GAUGE	**SUM**
HEXFLAGS	**TIME**
INT	**TIMETICKS**
IPADDRESS	**UNIXTIME**
LABEL	**YNFLAG**

The value can be uppercase or lowercase. For additional information and default values for the interpretation values listed above, refer to **SAS/CPE Interpretation Type Definitions** or **SAS/CPE Interpretation Summary Table**.

Note that default values do not apply for formula variables.

ISTATS=(*statistic-selector-keywords*)

Applies changes to the default statistics that are stored with the variable definition. These statistics are not calculated within the current table, but are used when you run **INSTALL TABLE** or **ADD TABLE** statements, because the master data dictionary doesn't keep reduction level statistics information. If an initial statistic is not set using the UPDATE VARIABLE statement mentioned, the existing setting for that statistic is not changed.

For more information about the ISTATS= parameter, see the descriptions of the ISTATS= parameter in the **CREATE VARIABLE** statement and in the **SET DEFAULTS** statements.

Notes: ISTATS= can be specified on the SET DEFAULTS, CREATE VARIABLE, and UPDATE VARIABLE statements. If you install or add a table for which ISTATS have not been specified, the table is given the default statistic values that have been specified in SET DEFAULTS for the current set of %CPDDUTL statements. If default values have not been set via SET DEFAULTS, the variable is treated as if all of statistics in the ISTATS= list were set to NO. If the table is installed and then added, the added table does not keep any statistics at the DAY, WEEK, MONTH, or YEAR level unless you set them using UPDATE VARIABLE.

If you are using a SET DEFAULTS statement that will apply to a single variable, a useful default setting is one based on the variable's interpretation. (For more about the relationship between interpretation and initial statistics, see **GENERATE SOURCE**.) If the SET DEFAULTS statement will apply to a number of variables, a useful default setting is ISTATS=(AVERAGE).

KEPT= YES | NO

indicates to the process step or reduce step whether data for this variable are to be kept in the PDB. If you specify NO, the variable's definition and the existing data (only for an existing variable) are retained in the dictionary, but no new data for this variable are processed or reduced into the PDB. **The default value is NO.**

LABEL=*'string'*

is a 40-character string describing the data in the variable at the DETAIL level. The string must be enclosed in single quotation marks. In the DAY, WEEK, MONTH, and YEAR levels, the labels are formed automatically by concatenating the statistic name, a period, and the string.

OID=*oid-specification*

is an SNMP OID of the form *n.n.n.n.n.n* which must be unique for the variable if you specify it. Use OID=. to specify none.

This parameter is used only with SAS/CPE on UNIX.

SUBJECT=*'subject-keyword-list'*

specifies a list of keywords that can be used to categorize this variable. The maximum length of the list is 200 characters. Use SUBJECT=' ' to leave the list blank. You must use blanks to separate keywords in the list and the list must be enclosed in single quotation marks.

When updating the SUBJECT= parameter list, you must specify all keywords that you want to use at the time that you update the list because this parameter does not use pre-existing values.

VALIDITY=

is not currently used.

Example: UPDATE VARIABLE

This example modifies a variable in a table that has been installed in the master data dictionary.

```
/*  NB: - Needs update access to the active PDB            */
/*      - This statement stream                             */
/*           sets the current table name                    */
/*           modifies a variable in the table.              */
/*      - The UPDATE VARIABLE statement changes the         */
/*        setting of three initial statistics.  The         */
/*        other initial statistics retain the settings      */
/*        they had.                                         */

set table name=TABXYZ
update variable
  name=uuxx
  description='Site-specific special variable - ver 2'
  istats=(MAXIMUM NORANGE AVERAGE)
  ;
```

Notes

The **Current Table** must be set before you can run this statement.

You can use the **PRINT TABLE** statement before and after the update, to see the current settings and to verify your changes.

To update the definition for a formula variable, use the **UPDATE FORMULA** statement.

CREATE FORMULA

Creates a definition for a new formula variable in a table

Purpose

The CREATE FORMULA statement creates the definition for a new formula variable in the current table in the active PDB. Data values for the forumla variable are not stored in the PDB, but they are calculated when they are requested, such as when a report is generated.

Syntax

```
CREATE FORMULA
    NAME= formula-var-name
   <DESCRIPTION= 'string'>
   <FORMAT= SAS-format>
   <INTERPRET= interpretation>
   <KEPT= YES | NO>
   <LABEL= 'string'>
   <LENGTH= number>
   <LEVELS= '<DETAIL> <DAY> <WEEK> <MONTH> <YEAR>'>
   <SOURCE= {source-statements}>
   <SUBJECT= 'subject-keyword-list'>
   <TYPE= NUMERIC | CHARACTER> ;
```

CREATE FORMULA Parameters

NAME=*formula-var-name*
: is the name of the formula variable to be created. The name must not already exist in the table. It cannot be longer than seven characters. The name can contain letters and digits, but cannot contain blank spaces or special characters, except for the underscore (_) character.

Optional Keyword Parameters

DESCRIPTION='*string*'
: is a 200-character string that provides information about the formula variable when you list the formula variables in a table in the PDB, through the SAS/CPE interactive interface. The string must be enclosed in single quotation marks. If the string spans multiple lines, break it in the middle of a word and continue in the first column of the next line.

FORMAT=*SAS-format*
: is a SAS format to be used with this variable or formula variable. Variables and formula variables will require character formats when their values contain characters. Variables and formula variables whose values contain numbers require numeric formats. These formats are used for all presentation of the data for this variable or formula variable.

For more information on default formats related to the formula or variable's interpretation type, see the INTERPRET= parameter on the **CREATE VARIABLE** or **CREATE FORMULA** statement. Refer to *SAS Language: Reference, Version 6, First Edition* for more information on SAS formats.

INTERPRET=*interpretation*

indicates the type of information that the variable represents. This parameter is required. You can specify one of the following values:

AVERAGE	**MAXIMUM**
C2RATE	**MINIMUM**
COUNT	**NAME**
COUNTER	**NETADDRESS**
DATE	**PCTGAUGE**
DATETIME	**PCTGAUGE100**
DECADDRESS	**PERCENT**
D2RATE	**PERCENT100**
ENUM	**RATE**
FLOAT	**STRING**
GAUGE	**SUM**
HEXFLAGS	**TIME**
INT	**TIMETICKS**
IPADDRESS	**UNIXTIME**
LABEL	**YNFLAG**

The value can be uppercase or lowercase. For additional information and default values for the interpretation values listed above, refer to **SAS/CPE Interpretation Type Definitions** or **SAS/CPE Interpretation Summary Table**.

Note that default values do not apply for formula variables.

KEPT= YES | NO

indicates whether the value for this formula variable is calculated in the View. If you specify NO, the variable's definition is retained in the dictionary, but values are not calculated for this formula variable.

LABEL='*string*'

is a 40-character string describing the values calculated by the formula variable. The string must be enclosed in single quotation marks. This label is used in the views that contain this formula variable.

LENGTH=*number*

is the maximum length of the variable as stored in the PDB. **The default value is 0**. Character variables can be as long as 200 characters; numeric variables can have a length of between 2 and 8 bytes.

LEVELS='*levels*'

is a list of levels at which the formula variable is to be available. If the formula variable relies on other variables or formula variables, these variables and formula variables must exist at all of the levels specified. The levels must be enclosed in single quotation marks, for example, LEVELS='DETAIL DAY'.

Note: The formula variable, not a statistic based on the formula variable, is available at the specified levels.

SOURCE={*source-statements*}

specifies the code for the formula, for example, SOURCE={ x1=a + b; x2=c/d;

x3=max(x1,x2); }. *source-statements* can be any SAS DATA step formula statements that create the variable named in the NAME= parameter. Note that when using this parameter, intermediate values are not required to be in alphabetical order.

Caution: *Do not omit the curly brackets.* If you omit the curly brackets you will get various errors. Also, do not make a change in the source code that would cause the variable type to change, such as from numeric to charcter. See the **CREATE FORMULA** statement.

SUBJECT='*subject-keyword-list*'

specifies a list of keywords that can be used to categorize this variable. The maximum length of the list is 200 characters. Use SUBJECT=' ' to leave the list blank. You must use blanks to separate keywords in the list and the list must be enclosed in single quotation marks.

When updating the SUBJECT= parameter list, you must specify all keywords that you want to use at the time that you update the list because this parameter does not use pre-existing values.

TYPE=NUMERIC | CHARACTER

is the type of the formula variable. The type can be either NUMERIC or CHARACTER. You cannot change the type of the formula variable after you create it, unless you delete the formula variable and create it again.

Notes

The **Current Table** must be set before you can run this statement.

Formula variables cannot have default statistics at the DAY, WEEK, MONTH, or YEAR level, because formula variables are created by means of a View and there is no data kept at the levels. If you want statistics at the non-detail levels, you must create additional formula variables at each level for which you want statistics.

In addition to being calculated as needed, formula variables are created in alphabetical order in the view after all other variables have been defined. Therefore, the definition of a formula variable can refer to another formula variable in the same table, as long as the variable you refer to is listed alphabetically before the variable in which it is used. For example, a variable named A could be used within the calculations of the value for a variable named B, because A occurs before B alphabetically. However, you can define one formula variable and in its SOURCE= parameter, define intermediate variables in any order, i.e. they do not have to be in alphabetical order. For example, you might use the following:

```
SOURCE={c=var1 + var2;
        b= var3;
        a=c/b;
       }
```

DELETE FORMULA

Deletes a formula variable definition from a table

Purpose

The DELETE FORMULA statement deletes a formula variable definition from the current table in the active PDB.

Syntax

```
DELETE FORMULA
       NAME= formula-var-name
      <NOERROR> ;
```

DELETE FORMULA Parameters

NAME=*formula-var-name*
: is the name of the formula variable to be deleted. The name must already exist in the active PDB's data dictionary.

Optional Keyword Parameters

NOERROR
: specifies whether or not to treat error conditions as warnings for the current %CPDDUTL job. This is useful if you have statements that need to delete and then later redefine a formula variable, because the formula variable can be missing and subsequent statements are still processed. **By default, NOERROR is not specified and if an error occurs %CPDDUTL ends**. If you specify the NOERROR parameter and an error occurs you will receive a warning message, but your job will not end.

Notes

The **Current Table** must be set before you can run this statement.

If you want to stop calculating the formula variable, but retain its definition in the table, use the **UPDATE FORMULA** statement with KEPT=NO.

LIST FORMULAS

Prints a list of formula variables

Purpose

The LIST FORMULAS statement prints in the SAS log a list of all of the formula variables and their labels from the current table in the active PDB.

Syntax

```
LIST FORMULAS;
```

Notes

The **Current Table** must be set before you can run this statement.

To list the source statements that describe the calculations used for the formula variable, see the **PRINT TABLE** statement.

UPDATE FORMULA

Updates the definition of a formula variable in a table

Purpose

The UPDATE FORMULA statement updates the data dictionary definition for a formula variable in the current table. If a parameter is omitted, the existing value for that parameter is retained. For example, if you specify only the DESCRIPTION= parameter, only the value of the description changes; the values for the other parameters remain the same.

Syntax

```
UPDATE FORMULA
        NAME=formula-var-name
        <DESCRIPTION= 'string'>
        <FORMAT= SAS-format>
        <INTERPRET= interpretation
        <KEPT= YES | NO>
        <LABEL= 'string'>
        <LEVELS='<DETAIL> <DAY> <WEEK> <MONTH> <YEAR>'>
        <SOURCE= {source-statements}>
        <SUBJECT= 'subject-keyword-list'> ;
```

UPDATE FORMULA Parameters

NAME=*formula-var-name*
: is the name of the formula variable to be updated. The name must already exist in the table or the CREATE FORMULA statement for the formula variable must be included earlier in the stream of control statements.

Optional Keyword Parameters

DESCRIPTION='*string*'
: is a 200-character string that provides information about the formula variable when you list the formula variables in a table in the PDB, through the SAS/CPE interactive interface. The string must be enclosed in single quotation marks. If the string spans multiple lines, break it in the middle of a word and continue in the first column of the next line.

FORMAT=*SAS-format*
: is a SAS format to be used with this variable or formula variable. Variables and formula variables will require character formats when their values contain characters. Variables and formula variables whose values contain numbers require numeric formats. These formats are used for all presentation of the data for this variable or formula variable.

: For more information on default formats related to the formula or variable's interpretation type, see the INTERPRET= parameter on the **CREATE VARIABLE** or **CREATE FORMULA** statement. Refer to *SAS Language: Reference, Version 6, First Edition* for more information on SAS formats.

INTERPRET=*interpretation*

indicates the type of information that the variable represents. This parameter is required. You can specify one of the following values:

AVERAGE	MAXIMUM
C2RATE	MINIMUM
COUNT	NAME
COUNTER	NETADDRESS
DATE	PCTGAUGE
DATETIME	PCTGAUGE100
DECADDRESS	PERCENT
D2RATE	PERCENT100
ENUM	RATE
FLOAT	STRING
GAUGE	SUM
HEXFLAGS	TIME
INT	TIMETICKS
IPADDRESS	UNIXTIME
LABEL	YNFLAG

The value can be uppercase or lowercase. For additional information and default values for the interpretation values listed above, refer to **SAS/CPE Interpretation Type Definitions** or **SAS/CPE Interpretation Summary Table**.

Note that default values do not apply for formula variables.

KEPT= YES | NO

indicates whether the value for this formula variable is calculated in the View. If you specify NO, the variable's definition is retained in the dictionary, but values are not calculated for this formula variable.

LABEL='*string*'

is a 40-character string describing the values calculated by the formula variable. The string must be enclosed in single quotation marks. This label is used in the views that contain this formula variable.

LEVELS='*levels*'

is a list of levels at which the formula variable is to be available. If the formula variable relies on other variables or formula variables, these variables and formula variables must exist at all of the levels specified. The levels must be enclosed in single quotation marks, for example, LEVELS='DETAIL DAY'.

Note: The formula variable, not a statistic based on the formula variable, is available at the specified levels.

SOURCE={*source-statements*}

specifies the code for the formula, for example, SOURCE={ x1=a + b; x2=c/d; x3=max(x1,x2); }. *source-statements* can be any SAS DATA step formula statements that create the variable named in the NAME= parameter. Note that when using this parameter, intermediate values are not required to be in alphabetical order.

Caution: *Do not omit the curly brackets.* If you omit the curly brackets you will get various errors. Also, do not make a change in the source code that would cause the variable type to change, such as from numeric to charcter. See the **CREATE FORMULA** statement.

SUBJECT='*subject-keyword-list*'

specifies a list of keywords that can be used to categorize this variable. The maximum length of the list is 200 characters. Use SUBJECT=' ' to leave the list blank. You must use blanks to separate keywords in the list and the list must be enclosed in single quotation marks.

When updating the SUBJECT= parameter list, you must specify all keywords that you want to use at the time that you update the list because this parameter does not use pre-existing values.

Notes

The **Current Table** must be set before you can run this statement.

Formula variables cannot have default statistics at the DAY, WEEK, MONTH, or YEAR level, because formula variables are created as needed and there is no data kept at the levels. If you want statistics at the non-detail levels, you must create additional formula variables at each level for which you want statistics.

BUILD VIEWS

Builds views for a table

Purpose

The BUILD VIEWS statement builds views associated with a table in the active PDB. All table definitions in the master data dictionary have views associated with them. Also, on MVS, you can optionally have an additional set of views for compatibility with MXG.

When you create or update a table definition, variable definition, or formula variable definition through the interactive interface, you can specify whether or not you want the views created at that time. If you do not choose to create the views you can create the views later using this statement.

Views are automatically rebuilt as needed when the %CPDDUTL macro completes, even if you do not specify the BUILD VIEWS statement. The exception to this rule is that views are not rebuilt when you end %CPDDUTL with a STOP or QUIT statement instead of an END statement. In those cases, you need to execute this statement to rebuild views. Additionally, if views are inadvertently removed, you can use the BUILD VIEWS control statement to re-create them.

The contents of the view are automatically determined by the variables and formula variables that exist in the table as defined in the data dictionary.

Syntax

```
BUILD VIEWS
      NAME=table-name | _ALL_ ;
```

BUILD VIEWS Parameters

NAME=*table-name* | _ALL_
: is the name of the table for which you want to build views. The table must exist in the active PDB's data dictionary by the time this statement is encountered. If you specify _ALL_, views are built for all tables in the PDB.

Notes

The process of building views for tables with many variables can be lengthy.

The BUILD VIEWS statement has no effect on the table set or named as the **Current Table** and the Current Table is not set to the table named in this statement.

MVS On MVS, if you would like to have view names that match your MXG data set names, set the CPXPDBNM macro variable to PDB before the BUILD VIEWS statement in the %CPDDUTL job. MXG views allow you to use the data with the names used by the MXG collector. Thus, each table will exist with its MXG name and each variable in the table will exist with its MXG name within the table. You can set this macro variable by following this path through the SAS/CPE interactive interface:

PDB Admin -> Set Active PDB Options

END

Ends the dictionary utility

Purpose

This statement causes dictionary utility processing to terminate as soon as the END statement is encountered. No following statements are processed. Views are built for any tables modified by previous statements, even if the BUILD VIEWS statement is not specified within the %CPDDUTL statements.

If you do not code an END, STOP, or QUIT statement at the end of the %CPDDUTL control statement stream, an END statement is implied.

Syntax

`END;`

Examples: END

The following example ends the dictionary utility. Views are rebuilt when the end statement is encountered.

```
delete table name=TABXYZ noerror ;
add table name=TABXYZ ;
update variable name= ...
   .. other statements ..
end ;           /* end now and build views */
   .. other statements never executed ..
```

GENERATE SOURCE

Generates initial %CPDDUTL control statements for creating tables

Purpose

To generate dictionary utility control statements, such as CREATE TABLE, CREATE VARIABLE, CREATE FORMULA, which can be used to create or re-create a SAS/CPE table. Control statements can be generated for an existing table or for a SAS data set. The generated statements can be stored in an output file or a SAS source catalog entry.

This statement is useful if you want to create the control statements that you can later use to re-create your PDB or that another SAS/CPE user can use to create a PDB table like yours. The statement can also save you time if you intend to use the GENERIC collector to load information from a SAS data set into your PDB.

When using a SAS data set or view (DATASET=) as input for GENERATE SOURCE, you should review and verify the accuracy of the generated statement. Specifically, you should review the DATETIME and DURATION variables and the interpretation type in the CREATE VARIABLE statement. GENERATE SOURCE will attempt to assign attributes such as interpretation type using information such as keywords from the variable labels or format types in the SAS data set. However, these attributes may not always be accurate. You should verify the generated statement and use UPDATE VARIABLE to update the paramenters as needed. You should also specify BY and CLASS variables on the UPDATE TABLE statement, because these cannot be read from the input data set.

Syntax

```
GENERATE SOURCE
        DATASET='input-SAS-data-set' | TABLE=<input-table-name | _ALL_>
        ENTRYNAME='SAS-catalog-entry' | FILENAME='physical-filename'
       <NAME=new-table-name>
       <NOERROR>
       <REPLACE | NOREPLACE>
       <TYPE=INTERVAL | EVENT> ;
```

GENERATE SOURCE Parameters

DATASET=*'input-SAS-data-set'*

names the SAS data set, DATA step view, PROC SQL view, or SAS/ACCESS view for which you want to create dictionary control statements. Use the format of *libref.membername* for the data set name. This data set must be defined in a SAS library and the data set name must be enclosed in quotes. You must specify this parameter or the TABLE= parameter, but not both.

TABLE=< *input-table-name* | _ALL_ >

is the name of the SAS/CPE table for which the dictionary control statements should be created. This table must already exist in the active PDB. Specify _ALL_ to create dictionary control statements for all tables in the active PDB. You must specify this parameter or the DATASET= parameter, but not both.

ENTRYNAME=*'SAS-catalog-entry'*
is the name of a SAS catalog entry. The value of this parameter specifies one of the following:

- ☐ the location of the SAS catalog entry in which to save %CPDDUTL control statements for the SAVE or GENERATE SOURCE statements.
- ☐ the location of the SAS catalog entry from which to include %CPDDUTL control statements for the INCLUDE SOURCE statement.

The name must be a four-level entry name with a type of SOURCE and must be enclosed in single quotes. You must specify either this parameter or the FILENAME= parameter, but not both.

FILENAME=*'physical-filename'*
is the physical location and name of a file or external data set. The value of this parameter specifies one of the following:

- ☐ the location in which to save the %CPDDUTL control statements for the SAVE or GENERATE SOURCE statements.
- ☐ the location from which to include the %CPDDUTL control statements for the INCLUDE SOURCE statement.

The specified location includes the complete directory path or high-level-qualifiers plus the name of the file or external data set. The name must be enclosed in single quotation marks. You must specify either this parameter or the ENTRYNAME= parameter, but not both.

Optional Keyword Parameters

NAME=*new-table-name*
names the SAS/CPE table to use in the NAME= parameter of the CREATE TABLE statement that is generated. When TABLE= is specified and NAME= is not specified, the input-table-name on the TABLE= parameter is used. When DATASET= is specified and NAME= is not specified, the name is formed by concatenating 'U' to the first six characters of the input SAS-data-set member name.

NOERROR
causes error conditions to be treated as warnings for the current %CPDDUTL job. This is useful if some included statements refer to elements that do not exist, and you still require subsequent statements to be processed. **By default, NOERROR is not specified and if an error occurs %CPDDUTL ends.** If you specify the NOERROR parameter and an error occurs you will receive a warning message, but your job will not end.

REPLACE | NOREPLACE
REPLACE indicates that any existing source in either a catalog or a file will be replaced; NOREPLACE indicates that the existing source is not replaced. **The default is NOREPLACE.**

TYPE=INTERVAL | EVENT
Sets the type of the table whose source is being generated. TYPE= is only valid when DATASET= is also specified. **If TYPE= is not specified and DATASET= is specified, the default for TYPE= will be EVENT.**

Examples: GENERATE SOURCE

Example 1

The following example generates %CPDDUTL source statements that define a table called TABXYZ, based on an existing table in the active PDB. The generated statements are written to a catalog entry and any previous output in the catalog entry is replaced.

```
generate source
   table=TABXYZ                          /* existing table as input */
   entryname='SASUSER.DICT.TABXYZ.SOURCE'    /* output */
   replace ;
```

Example 2

The following example generates %CPDDUTL source statements for all tables in the active PDB. The generated statements are written to an external file and any previous output in the catalog entry is replaced.

```
generate source
   table=_ALL_        /* all existing tables in PDB as input */
   filename='physical-filename-source'    /* output */
   replace ;
```

Example 3

The following example generates %CPDDUTL source statements that can be used to define the SAS data set SASUSER.TABABC as a table called TABLE1.

```
generate source
   name=TABABC                           /* new name to use */
   dataset='SASUSER.TABLE1'              /* SAS data set as input */
   entryname='SASUSER.DICT.TABLE1.SOURCE'    /* output */
   replace ;
```

Notes

After you edit the output from GENERATE SOURCE it can be used as input for the %CPUDDUTL macro.

Consider the following items before using the DATASET= parameter.

- ☐ Variable names longer than seven characters in the SAS data set or view are translated to seven character names by truncating the original names and appending a number if there is a conflict.
- ☐ DATETIME and LSTPDATE variables are automatically created.
- ☐ The type of the table will default to EVENT if you do not specify the TYPE= parameter. If you specify the table type as INTERVAL, the DURATION variable is automatically create.

- ☐ Default statistics correlate with the interpretation type. Therefore, if you change the interpretation type you may also need to change the statistics.

- ☐ For each variable, SAS/CPE looks up the approximate interpretation in a table and returns with the set of initial statistics that is assigned to that interpretation. For the initial statistics used for a variable, for a specific interpretation type, see the uppercase letters in the Default Statistics column of the **SAS/CPE Interpretation Summary Table** or review the statistic definitions in the **SAS/CPE Interpretation Types** document.

INCLUDE SOURCE

Includes additional control statements

Purpose

The INCLUDE SOURCE statement allows you to include additional %CPDDUTL control statements into a stream of %CPDDUTL statements. You can manage groups of statements that perform a specific function (for example, delete and redefine a particular table) and then include and process them with the %CPDDUTL statements, in order to process larger tasks in one execution of the %CPDDUTL macro.

A group of statements may be stored in an external data set or file, or as a SAS catalog entry. The same group of external statements can be included in the %CPDDUTL statement stream in as many places as is required.

Refer to the %CPDDUTL macro example for a sample of this type of job.

Caution: *Do not include a group into itself. This recursion is not detected or prevented.*

Syntax

```
INCLUDE SOURCE
        ENTRYNAME= 'SAS-catalog-entry' | FILENAME= 'physical-file-name'
       <NOERROR> ;
```

INCLUDE SOURCE Parameters

ENTRYNAME=*'SAS-catalog-entry'*

is the name of a SAS catalog entry. The value of this parameter specifies one of the following:

- □ the location of the SAS catalog entry in which to save %CPDDUTL control statements for the SAVE or GENERATE SOURCE statements.
- □ the location of the SAS catalog entry from which to include %CPDDUTL control statements for the INCLUDE SOURCE statement.

The name must be a four-level entry name with a type of SOURCE and must be enclosed in single quotes. You must specify either this parameter or the FILENAME= parameter, but not both.

FILENAME=*'physical-filename'*

is the physical location and name of a file or external data set. The value of this parameter specifies one of the following:

- □ the location in which to save the %CPDDUTL control statements for the SAVE or GENERATE SOURCE statements.
- □ the location from which to include the %CPDDUTL control statements for the INCLUDE SOURCE statement.

The specified location includes the complete directory path or high-level-qualifiers plus the name of the file or external data set. The name must be enclosed in single quotation marks. You must specify either this parameter or the ENTRYNAME= parameter, but not both.

Optional Keyword Parameters

NOERROR

causes error conditions to be treated as warnings for the current %CPDDUTL job. This is useful if some included statements refer to elements that do not exist, and you still require subsequent statements to be processed. **By default, NOERROR is not specified and if an error occurs %CPDDUTL ends**. If you specify the NOERROR parameter and an error occurs you will receive a warning message, but your job will not end.

PRINT SOURCE

Prints messages during execution of %CPDDUTL

Purpose

The PRINT SOURCE statement prints messages in the SAS log at specific points while running a stream of %CPDDUTL statements. You specify the text of the message.

Syntax

```
PRINT SOURCE
      SOURCE={
                source to be printed
                } ;
```

Parameters

SOURCE = {*multiple source lines*}

is the text that you want to display. Place the text within the curly brackets and make sure to place the brackets on separate lines as shown in the example. If you place the brackets in other locations, such as putting them on the same line as the text, your output may display incorrectly.

For example:

```
print source
      source={
              +--------+
              |        |
              |  TEST  |
              |        |
              +--------+
             };
```

%CPDDUTL then displays the following output in the SAS LOG:

```
+--------+
|        |
|  TEST  |
|        |
+--------+
```

Caution: *The curly brackets must not be omitted and should be placed in the locations shown above or as shown in the definition of the SOURCE= parameter. If you omit one or both of the curly brackets, you will get unpredictable results. If you place them in locations other than those shown in the above example, the format of your output may change.*

QUIT

Stops the dictionary utility

Purpose

To stop the %CPDDUTL dictionary utility upon reaching this statement. This statement is an alias of the **STOP** statement. Like the STOP statement, no views are rebuilt.

If you do not code an END, STOP, or QUIT statement at the end of the %CPDDUTL control statement stream, an **END** statement is implied.

Syntax

```
QUIT;
```

SAVE SOURCE

Saves source in an external file or SAS catalog

Purpose

To save source in an external file or in a SAS catalog entry.

Syntax

```
SAVE SOURCE
    SOURCE= { any single or multiple lines of text }
    ENTRYNAME='SAS-catalog-entry' | FILENAME='physical-filename' ;
```

SAVE SOURCE Parameters

SOURCE = {*multiple source lines*}
: is the text that you want to save. Place the text within the curly brackets and make sure to place the brackets on separate lines as shown in the example. If you place the brackets in other locations, such as putting them on the same line as the text, your output may not appear in the same format as what you typed.

For example:

```
save source
     source={
               +--------+
               |        |
               |  TEST  |
               |        |
               +--------+
             }
             entryname='sasuser.save.mysource' ;
```

ENTRYNAME=*'SAS-catalog-entry'*
: is the name of a SAS catalog entry. The value of this parameter specifies one of the following:

- the location of the SAS catalog entry in which to save %CPDDUTL control statements for the SAVE or GENERATE SOURCE statements.
- the location of the SAS catalog entry from which to include %CPDDUTL control statements for the INCLUDE SOURCE statement.

The name must be a four-level entry name with a type of SOURCE and must be enclosed in single quotes. You must specify either this parameter or the FILENAME= parameter, but not both.

FILENAME=*'physical-filename'*
: is the physical location and name of a file or external data set. The value of this parameter specifies one of the following:

- the location in which to save the %CPDDUTL control statements for the SAVE or

GENERATE SOURCE statements.

- the location from which to include the %CPDDUTL control statements for the INCLUDE SOURCE statement.

The specified location includes the complete directory path or high-level-qualifiers plus the name of the file or external data set. The name must be enclosed in single quotation marks. You must specify either this parameter or the ENTRYNAME= parameter, but not both.

Note

You can use the **%CPCAT** macro as an alternate of copying statements into a source catalog entry.

SET DEFAULTS

Sets defaults for creating table, variable, and formula variable definitions

Purpose

The SET DEFAULTS statement sets default values for parameters on the CREATE TABLE, CREATE VARIABLE, and CREATE FORMULA statements, except the NAME= parameter and BY and CLASS variable lists.

Default values are used with CREATE statements as follows. If you create a variable, table, or formula variable, the parameter values specified on the associated CREATE statement are in effect. If you do not specify values for some parameters on a create statement, those parameter values are given the values specified in the most recent SET DEFAULTS statment in the current %CPDDUTL stream. If you do not specify a parameter on a create statement and have not specified a value for that parameter on the SET DEFAULTS statement, the values specified in the **Built-In Defaults Table** for this statement are used.

The parameters and values specified on a SET DEFAULTS statement affect %CPDDUTL jobs and control statements during the current %CPDDUTL statement stream. If you issue a second SET DEFAULTS statement during the current %CPDDUTL statement stream, the first set of defaults are updated by the second set of defaults. For example, if you specify

```
SET DEFAULTS COLLECTOR=GENERIC LABEL='LABEL1'
```

and then specify

```
SET DEFAULTS COLLECTOR=SPECTRUM
```

the original value for label and the new value for collector become the defaults.

Syntax

```
SET DEFAULTS
   <COLLECTOR= collector | GENERIC>
   <DESCRIPTION= 'string'>
   <DETAIL=(<AGELIMIT= number>)>
   <DAY=(<AGELIMIT= number><statistic-keywords-list>)>
   <WEEK=(<AGELIMIT= number><statistic-keywords-list>)>
   <MONTH=(<AGELIMIT= number><statistic-keywords-list>)>
   <YEAR=(<AGELIMIT= number><statistic-keywords-list>)>
   <EXTNAME= name>
   <FORMAT= SAS-format>
   <IDNUM=number>
   <INFORMAT= >
   <INTERPRET= interpretation
   <ISTATS=(statistic-keywords-list)>
   <KEPT= YES | NO>
   <LABEL= 'string'>
   <LENGTH= number>
   <LEVELS= '<DETAIL> <DAY> <WEEK> <MONTH> <YEAR>'>
   <OID= oid-specification>
   <SUBJECT='subject-keyword-list'>
```

```
<TOOLNAME=name>
<VALIDITY=> ;
```

SET DEFAULTS Parameters

COLLECTOR=*collector* | GENERIC

specifies the name of the SAS/CPE supported collector that created the log file data. If you are using a user-defined collector or a third-party collector instead of a SAS/CPE supported collector, use the value GENERIC. If you are using a SAS/CPE supported collector, specify the name of the collector.

UNIX Current valid values for UNIX are:

- ACCTON - UNIX Accounting
- GENERIC - SAS/CPE Generic Data Format
- HP-OV - NetView/6000 or HP Network Node Manager
- HP-PCS - Performance Collection Software by HP
- PROBEX - Probe/X by Landmark Systems in SunNet Manager Format
- SPECTRUM - Spectrum by Cabletron Inc.
- SUNETMGR - SunNet Manager by Sun/Connect
- TRAKKER - TRAKKER by Concord Communications

MVS Current valid values for MVS are:

- SMF - IBM MVS System Management Facilities
- GENERIC - SAS/CPE Generic Data Format

If the name of the collector contains special characters, enclose the name in single quotation marks. For example, if you are using HP-PCS:

```
collector='hp-pcs'
```

DESCRIPTION='*string*'

specifies a default description string for tables, variables, and formula variables. See the **CREATE TABLE**, **CREATE VARIABLE**, and **CREATE FORMULA** statements for more information.

DETAIL=(AGELIMIT=*number*)
DAY=(<AGELIMIT=*number*><*statistic-keyword-list*>)
WEEK=(<AGELIMIT=*number*><*statistic-keyword-list*>)
MONTH=(<AGELIMIT=*number*><*statistic-keyword-list*>)
YEAR=(<AGELIMIT=*number*><*statistic-keyword-list*>)

AGELIMIT= defines the time span for data to be retained at each level. For DETAIL and DAY, the number represents days. For WEEK, the number represents weeks; for MONTH, it represents months; and for YEAR, it represents years. The *number* must be an integer, but cannot contain a decimal point.

Note: If AGELIMIT=0 at the DETAIL level, your data is stored in DETAIL until the next reduce or process step runs. Therefore, if reduce runs immediately after the process step the data are processed, reduced into the non-levels, and then removed from DETAIL. However, if the process step runs again before the data have been reduced, the existing data in DETAIL are removed before the non-detail levels are updated.

Using AGELIMIT=0 at the DETAIL level is useful if you are collecting and processing large amounts of data on a daily basis, but, to avoid losing data at non-detail levels, you should always reduce the data immediately after you process the data. Furthermore, AGELIMIT=0 at any level other than DETAIL indicates that data will not be stored at that level.

statistic-keyword-list is the list of statistics required for this variable at a specific reduction level. The list can contain one or more of the following statistics.

```
AVERAGE | NOAVERAGE            NMISS | NONMISS
COUNT | NOCOUNT                RANGE | NORANGE
CV | NOCV                      STD | NOSTD
MAXIMUM | NOMAXIMUM            SUM | NOSUM
MINIMUM | NOMINIMUM            USS | NOUSS
VARIANCE | NOVARIANCE
```

This parameter sets a default for the **CREATE TABLE** and **CREATE VARIABLE** statements.

EXTNAME= *name*
specifies a default external name for tables and variables. See the **CREATE TABLE** and **CREATE VARIABLE**, statements for more information.

FORMAT=*SAS-format*
specifies the default SAS format to use. See the **CREATE VARIABLE** and **CREATE FORMULA** statements for more information.

IDNUM=*number*
specifies a numeric identifier that represents different uses for each collector. Refer to the information on a specific collector through the online help in the SAS/CPE interactive interface.

This parameter is used only with SAS/CPE on UNIX.

INFORMAT=
is not currently used.

INTERPRET=*interpretation*
indicates how SAS/CPE software should calculate statistics and use the variable in the reduce task and build views task. See the **CREATE VARIABLE** and **CREATE FORMULA** statements for more information.

ISTATS=(*statistic-selector-keywords*)
sets the default statistics for a variable, if you do not set the default statistics when you create the variable. For more information see the **CREATE VARIABLE** statement.

KEPT= YES | NO

specifies a default keep status. See the **CREATE TABLE**, **CREATE VARIABLE**, and **CREATE FORMULA** statements for more information.

LABEL='*string*'
: specifies a default label for tables, variables, and formula variables. See the **CREATE TABLE**, **CREATE VARIABLE**, and **CREATE FORMULA** statements for more information.

LENGTH=*number*
: specifies the default length to use. See the **CREATE VARIABLE** and **CREATE FORMULA** statements for more information.

LEVELS='*level-list*'
: specifies the levels at which a formula variable is to be available. If the formula variable relies on other variables, these variables must exist at all of the reduction levels specified. This parameter sets a default for the **CREATE FORMULA** statement.

OID=*oid-specification*
: is an SNMP OID of the form n.n.n.n.n.n, which must be unique for the variable if you specify it. Use OID=. to specify none. This parameter sets a default for the **CREATE VARIABLE** statement.

This parameter is used only with SAS/CPE on UNIX.

SUBJECT='*subject-keyword-list*'
: specifies the default subject list to use. See the **CREATE VARIABLE** and **CREATE FORMULA** statements for more information.

TOOLNAME=*name*
: is the name of the software that transforms the logged data and places it into SAS data sets, from which the process task processes them into the detail level of the PDB. This name cannot exceed 32 characters. This sets a default for the **CREATE TABLE** statement.

Valid options for MVS are:

- MXG - if the data is staged using MXG software
- SASDS - if the data is staged using a generic collector

The only valid option for UNIX is SASDS and this parameter is valid only if you the table you are creating is processed by a generic collector.

VALIDITY=
: is not currently used.

Example: SET DEFAULTS

This example adds a new variable to a table.

```
/*     - Needs update access to the active PDB.           */
```

```
/*     - This statement stream                              */
/*         sets the default initial statistics to ON        */
/*           for RANGE and AVERAGE; the other               */
/*           default initial statistics remain OFF          */
/*         creates a new variable in the table in the       */
/*            active PDB                                    */
/*     - The CREATE VARIABLE statement does not provide     */
/*       its own settings of initial statistics, so the     */
/*       defaults from SET DEFAULTS and built-in            */
/*       defaults are used.                                 */

set table name=utab;

set defaults
  istats= ( RANGE AVERAGE )
  ;
create variable
  name=uuxx length=8 type=numeric format=5.
  interpret=count label='Special variable'
  description='Site-specific special variable' ;
```

Notes

If the value for a parameter is not specified in a CREATE TABLE, CREATE VARIABLE, or CREATE FORMULA statement and the value for that paramenter is not specified in the SET DEFAULTS statement, the built-in defaults listed in the Built-In Defaults Table are used.

Parameter defaults are not used on UPDATE statements.

Built-In Defaults for the SET DEFAULT Statement

Built-in Default	In SAS/CPE %CPDDUTL Macro	In SAS/CPE Interactive Interface
COLLECTOR= *collector*	blank	blank
DAY=(AGELIMIT= *number*)	45	45
DAY=(CLASSVARS=' *name-list* ')	none	none
DAY=(*statistic-keywords -list*)	none	none
DESCRIPTION=' *string* '	blank	blank
DETAIL=(AGELIMIT= *number*)	10	10
DETAIL=(BYVARS=' *name-list* ')	none	none
EXTNAME= *name*	blank	blank
FORMAT= *SAS-format*	blank	blank
INTERPRET= *interpretation*	blank	blank
ISTATS=	blank	blank
KEPT=YES|NO	NO	NO (Variables) YES (Formula Vars)
LABEL='*string*'	blank	blank
LENGTH=*number*	0	0
LEVELS='*reduction-level-list*'	none	none
MONTH=(AGELIMIT=*number*)	18	18
MONTH=(CLASSVARS='*name-list*')	none	none
MONTH=(*statistic-keywords-list*)	none	none
NAME=*name*	blank	blank
SUBJECT='*subject-keyword-list*'	none	none
TOOLNAME=*name*	blank	blank

WEEK=(AGELIMIT=number)	15	15
WEEK=(CLASSVARS='name-list')	none	none
WEEK=(statistic-keywords-list)	none	none
YEAR=(CLASSVARS='name-list')	none	none
YEAR=(AGELIMIT=number)	5	5
YEAR=(statistic-keywords-list)	none	none

STOP

Stops the dictionary utility

Purpose

This statement causes dictionary utility processing to terminate as soon as the STOP statement is encountered. No following statements are processed and no views are built for any modified tables.

This statement is useful if you are testing your control statements or if you do not want to rebuild views when this statement is run, because it does not rebuild views for the modified tables. However, you must remember to use the BUILD VIEWS statement later to build the views or to rerun your statements without the STOP statement.

If you do not code an END, STOP, or QUIT statement at the end of the %CPDDUTL control statement stream, an **END** statement is implied.

Syntax

```
STOP;
```

Note

The **VERIFY SYNTAX** statement also stops views from being built, but unlike the STOP statement, VERIFY SYNTAX checks the remaining statements instead of ignoring them.

This is an alias for the QUIT statement.

SYNCHRONIZE DICTIONARY

Corrects structure errors in the data dictionary

Purpose

The SYNCHRONIZE DICTIONARY statement corrects structure errors in the data dictionary for the active PDB.

Syntax

```
SYNCHRONIZE DICTIONARY;
```

Notes

This statement attempts to rebuild the data dictionary for the current PDB. After you run the SYNCHRONIZE DICTIONARY statement, run the **VERIFY DICTIONARY** statement to ensure that the data dictionary is usable.

Caution: *Do not attempt to edit the SAS data sets that contain the performance database without using the SAS/CPE interface or the %CPDDUTL macro. That is, do not use any other SAS tools or external tools to edit the contents of these data sets. If you do so, SAS/CPE software may determine that the dictionary is unaccessable, and will refuse to use the dictionary.*

If, despite cautions, you modified the PDB's DICTLIB library, the SYNCHRONIZE DICTIONARY control statement attempts to undo the modifications. If you added extra variables to the data dictionary, they are deleted. If you removed any variables, they are restored. If you changed the characteristics of any variables, the undo may fail and you may need to recover a workable version of the data dictionary from backups.

VERIFY DICTIONARY

Checks the format of the data dictionary

Purpose

The VERIFY DICTIONARY statement checks the structure and integrity of the SAS/CPE data dictionary in the active PDB, and reports any errors. Error messages are printed in the output window or the SAS log.

Syntax

```
VERIFY DICTIONARY;
```

Notes

The VERIFY DICTIONARY statement examines the data dictionary more extensively than the %CPSTART macro. SAS/CPE software automatically verifies that the dictionary is usable each time you start the %CPSTART macro and, in the interactive interface, each time you start SAS/CPE software or switch the active PDB.

Caution: *Do not attempt to edit the SAS data sets that contain the performance database without using the SAS/CPE interface or the %CPDDUTL macro.* That is, do not use any other SAS tools or external tools to edit the contents of these data sets. If you do so, SAS/CPE software may determine that the dictionary is unaccessable, and will refuse to use the dictionary. For more information, refer to the **SYNCHRONIZE DICTIONARY** statement.

VERIFY SYNTAX

Runs job to check %CPDDUTL syntax

Purpose

The VERIFY SYNTAX statement turns syntax check mode on and execution off. This statement applies to your current statement stream of %CPDDUTL.

Syntax

```
VERIFY SYNTAX;
```

Notes

This control statement checks whether the syntax in the %CPDDUTL statements that follow the VERIFY SYNTAX statement is correct. The VERIFY SYNTAX statement does not update the data dictionary in the active PDB nor does it perform any error checking, because the data dictionary is not accessed during syntax-check mode.